MOVIE STARS

DO THE DUMBEST THINGS™

MOVIE STARS

DO THE DUMBEST THINGS™

Margaret Moser, Michael Bertin, and Bill Crawford

RENAISSANCE BOOKS

Los Angeles

Copyright © 1999 by Margaret Moser and Bill Crawford

All rights reserved. This book may not be reproduced, in whole or in part, in any form, without written permission. Inquiries should be addressed to: Permissions Department, Renaissance Books, 5858 Wilshire Boulevard, Suite 200, Los Angeles, California 90036.

Library of Congress Cataloging-in-Publication Data

Moser, Margaret.
    Movie stars do the dumbest things / Margaret Moser, Michael Bertin, and Bill Crawford.
       p.   cm.
    Includes bibliographical references, filmographies, and index.
    ISBN 1-58063-107-X (pbk. : alk. paper)
    1. Motion picture actors and actresses—Anecdotes. 2. Motion picture actors and actresses Biography Dictionaries. I. Bertin, Michael. II. Crawford, Bill, 1955– . III. Title.
    PN1994.9.M67 1999
    791.43'028'0922—dc21
    [B]   99-36450
                                                 CIP

10 9 8 7 6 5 4 3 2 1

Design by Lee Fukui

Published by Renaissance Books

Manufactured in the United States of America

Distributed by St. Martin's Press

First Edition

Dedicated to the
film crews,
maids,
waiters,
janitors,
fans,
lovers,
and others
who clean up
the mess.

Acknowledgments

Thanks to our agent Jim Hornfischer, and our editor James Robert Parish, who generously shared with us his vast knowledge of Hollywood lore, as well as his unpublished movie star marriage/divorce database. Also, special thanks to Frank Smejkal for creating the "dumbest" Internet site on the Web (www.dumbest.com) and to Stephen Moser for research on Hollywood stars.

Margaret Moser would like to thank beloved cohorts Nick Barbaro, Louis Black, Marjorie Baumgarte, Chris Gray, and Raoul Hernandes at the *Austin Chronicle*; and best friend E. A. Srere and brother Stephen because "if we'd been born in Beverly Hills, we'd be home by now . . ." Bye-bye Belton!

Michael Bertin would like to thank Mom and Dad.

Bill Crawford would like to thank Amelia, Diana, Joe, and his brother Jon, whose passion for movies goes way beyond the dumb. Greetings Olivia! Also, special thanks to James Robert Parish for his incredible eye for clippings and his amazing patience and good humor.

CONTENTS

PART 1: THE MOVIE STARS

PART 2: WACKY, WAY-OUT BONUS CHAPTERS

INTRODUCTION

Movie Stars Do the Dumbest Things is the dumbest book ever written about Hollywood—the *Plan 9 from Outer Space* of film literature.

Let's face it. Being a movie star ain't rocket science. Pioneer film studio boss Lewis J. Selznick once claimed that the movie business "took less brains than anything else in the world." According to screen legend Spencer Tracy, the job of acting didn't "require much brainwork." Maybe that's the reason that movie stars have been prone to incredible stupidity ever since the first knucklehead jumped around in front of a camera over a century ago. After all, movie stars have huge egos, huge salaries, and huge amounts of free time—the perfect recipe for doing the dumbest things.

We are not the first to notice all the stupid things going on in Hollywood. In the roaring twenties, things got so dumb and "immoral" in the movie capital that federal regulators threatened to step in. Film producers even forced movie stars to sign contracts agreeing "to maintain a standard of conduct with due respect to public conventions and morals."

Fat chance! Like prohibition, the morals crackdown had the opposite effect. It inspired movie stars to flaunt conventions even more. And when the power of the studios faded in the 1950s, the lunatics really took over the asylum. Movie stars began to make so much money and wield so much power that they could indulge their dumbest fantasies, and sue anyone who dared to criticize them.

Some people love to grumble about film stars. "Hollywood is where they shoot too many movies and not enough actors," famed gossip columnist Walter Winchell once groused. But we don't grump about dumb stuff. We love it! It takes us out of our tawdry, normal, decent, everyday lives and throws us into a world where our dogs can and will fly first class, and even our personal assistants have assistants of their own. According to one observer, "Hollywood is a trip through a sewer in a glass-bottomed boat." Man, what a view!

These dumbest incidents, my friends, we cannot keep secret any longer. Can your heart stand the shocking facts? *Movie Stars Do the Dumbest Things.*

KEY TO ENTRIES

Except for the two bonus sections in part 1—Hit List of the Dumbest of Dumb Things Movie Stars Have Done and (Other) Young Movie Stars Do the Dumbest Things—and three chapters in part 2, the movie star chapters are listed in alphabetical order according to the last name of the featured movie star and include the following sections:

DUMBEST QUOTE

Lists the dumbest quote(s) spoken by the movie star in question.

FACTS OF LIFE (and Death)

ORIGIN: Lists the full name, date of birth, place of birth, and (where appropriate) the date and place of death.

FORMATIVE YEARS: Lists formal and/or informal educational experiences.

FAMILY PLANNING: Lists spouses, dates of marriages and divorces, and, occasionally, other related factoids. We do not list legitimate or illegitimate children in this section, but we do wish them good luck. Hey, it's not their fault they were born to crazy movie stars!

ROMANTIC INTERESTS: Lists girlfriends and/or boyfriends and/or other objects of desire.

SELECTED HITS (and Misses)

Lists the subject's major films (with the year of release) and key TV series (with years on the air).

WARNING: THIS IS NOT A COMPLETE LISTING. READERS WHO TREAT IT AS SUCH WILL QUICKLY LOSE THEIR MINDS IN AN ORGY OF STATISTICAL FRUSTRATION.

QUICKIE BIO

A brief biography of the movie star.

———— DOES THE DUMBEST THINGS

Lists the dumbest incidents in the career of the movie star. We have marked the dumbest of the dumb items with an honorary icon. The icons correspond to the following categories:

 Movie Stars Do the Dumbest Things with Animals

 Movie Stars Do the Dumbest Things on Drugs

 Movie Stars Do the Dumbest Things with Food

 Movie Stars Do the Dumbest Things with Words

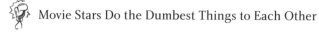 Movie Stars Do the Dumbest Things to Each Other

 Movie Stars Do the Dumbest Things to Themselves

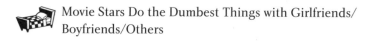 Movie Stars Do the Dumbest Things with Girlfriends/
Boyfriends/Others

 Movie Stars Do the Dumbest Things with Money

 Movie Stars Do the Dumbest Things with Politics

 The Dumbest Movie Stars of All Time

All the information included in this book has appeared somewhere else in print, usually in several places. But we are only human, and movie stars have done an awful lot of dumb things. So help us out. If you notice any errors, or know of any dumb stuff we have overlooked, please notify us immediately. Write to us care of Renaissance Books, 5858 Wilshire Boulevard, Suite 200, Los Angeles, California 90036. Or contact us via our Web site: www.dumbest.com.

MOVIE STARS

DO THE DUMBEST THINGS™

PART 1

THE
MOVIE
STARS

EXTRA SPECIAL SUPERDELUXE BONUS SECTION: HIT LIST OF THE DUMBEST OF DUMB THINGS MOVIE STARS HAVE DONE

We have chosen the dumbest of the dumb items from the book and listed them below. Look for the full details of the dumbest incidents—marked with a dumbest icon—in the appropriate chapters of this book. Think you know something dumber? Contact us at www.dumbest.com.

 Movie Stars Do the Dumbest Things with Animals

1. Johnny Depp and his love for animals

2. Jim Carrey and his doggy massage

3. Errol Flynn and his pooch

4. Brigitte Bardot and her mynah defense

5. Drew Barrymore's kitty ashes

6. Burt Reynolds and deer hunting

7. Marilyn Monroe and pooch poo

8. Marlon Brando's electric eels

9. Joan Collins and the fur-loving tiger

10. Bruce Willis and the smashed chickens

 Movie Stars Do the Dumbest Things with Drugs

1. Robert Downey Jr. and the Goldilocks incident

2. Liza Minnelli and Skylab

3. Oliver Stone and "smart drugs"

4. Dennis Hopper and the Mexican film set

5. Sharon Stone and the spoon

6. Marlene Dietrich's Las Vegas act

7. Peter Lawford at the Betty Ford Clinic

8. Bette Midler's New Year's party favors

9. Jack Nicholson and the campfire scene

10. Elizabeth Taylor's doctor's orders

 ## Movie Stars Do the Dumbest Things with Food

1. Marlon Brando's pants

2. Divine's doo doo

3. Mae West's cleansing diet

4. Jane Fonda's first diet

5. Keanu Reeves's Buddha diet

6. Leonardo DiCaprio's food fight

7. Bette Midler's food fight

8. Marilyn Monroe's spaghetti bra

9. River Phoenix's crab consciousness

10. Arnold Schwarzenegger's muscle builder

 ## Movie Stars Do the Dumbest Things with Words

1. Jim Carrey and his butt talk

2. Burt Reynolds on morality

3. Mia Farrow in the courtroom

4. Joan Crawford's privates

5. Errol Flynn and dot dot dot

6. Elvis and the yoga ballad

7. Brigitte Bardot and the Russians

8. Charlie Chaplin and his member

9. Marlon Brando and his shoe cues

10. Liza Minnelli and the sound of silence

 ## Movie Stars Do the Dumbest Things to Each Other

1. Pamela Anderson Lee and Tommy's home videos

2. Mia Farrow and Woody Allen's Polaroids

3. Cher and Gregg Allman's last meal

4. Richard Burton and Elizabeth Taylor and Eddie Fisher and . . .

5. Ted Danson roasting Whoopi Goldberg

6. Sean Penn and Madonna, his prisoner of love

7. Dean Martin awarding Sammy Davis Jr. to Old Blue Eyes

8. Oliver Stone partying with Cameron Diaz

9. Don Johnson's young romance with Melanie Griffith

10. Bruce Willis and Demi Moore sharing a family meal

 ## Movie Stars Do the Dumbest Things to Themselves

1. Charlie Chaplin and the liquid prophylactic

2. Bette Davis and cigarettes

3. Sammy Davis Jr. and his cologne

4. Clint Eastwood's hair

5. Jean Harlow's drowning husband

6. James Dean, the ashtray

7. Marlene Dietrich's dental design

8. Errol Flynn and his cocaine application

9. Jack Nicholson and the full stinger

10. Burt Reynolds and the dummy

Movie Stars Do the Dumbest Things with Girlfriends/Boyfriends/Others

1. Marlon Brando's abortion party
2. Warren Beatty and Jack Nicholson share the goods
3. Joan Crawford and her maid
4. Richard Burton and his socks
5. Peter Lawford and his Acujack
6. Eddie Murphy and the cross-dresser
7. Hugh Grant and Divine Brown
8. Producer Robert Evans and the barfing prostitute
9. Pamela Anderson Lee and her boy toys
10. Jean Harlow and her pick-up date

Movie Stars Do the Dumbest Things with Money

1. Charlie Sheen and Heidi's girls
2. Kim Basinger and Kimwood
3. Bruce Willis and his screwball ideas
4. Demi Moore's doll house
5. Judy Garland and her bag of money
6. Mickey Rooney's Weenie Whirl
7. Jayne Mansfield's pink palace
8. Dean Martin's percentages
9. Frank Sinatra's eighty-eight martinis
10. Burt Reynolds and his fire retardant hair

Move Stars Do the Dumbest Things with Politics

1. Jane Fonda smiling in North Vietnam

2. Warren Beatty on communism and boredom

3. Sammy Davis Jr. and his love for Nixon

4. Peter Lawford on board Air Force One

5. Frank Sinatra and the speaker of the house

6. Frank Sinatra and JFK

7. Marilyn Monroe and JFK

8. Brigitte Bardot in Greece

9. Barbra Streisand at President Clinton's inauguration

10. Spike Lee's spiky observations

 ## The Dumbest Movie Stars of All Time

1. Marlon Brando

2. Elizabeth Taylor

3. Dennis Hopper

4. Frank Sinatra

5. Cher

6. Marilyn Monroe

7. Elvis Presley

8. Errol Flynn

9. Barbra Streisand

10. Burt Reynolds

Woody Allen

FACTS OF LIFE

ORIGIN: Born Allen Stewart Konigsberg, December 1, 1935, Brooklyn, New York.

FORMATIVE YEARS: Suspended from New York University.

FAMILY PLANNING: Married Harlene Rosen (high school friend), March 15, 1956; divorced 1962; married Louise Lasser (actress), February 2, 1966; divorced 1969; married Soon-Yi Previn (adopted daughter of girlfriend Mia Farrow), December 23, 1997.

ROMANTIC INTERESTS: Diane Keaton (actress), and her sister Robin; Mariel Hemingway (actress), and her sister Hannah; Mia Farrow (actress), and her sister Steffi.

SELECTED HITS (and Misses)

FILMS: *What's New, Pussycat?* (1965),* *Casino Royale* (1965),* *Take the Money and Run* (1969), *Bananas* (1971), *Annie Hall* (Oscars for Best Director, Best Original Screenplay—1977), *Interiors* (1978), *Manhattan* (1979), *Broadway Danny Rose* (1984), *The Purple Rose of Cairo* (1985), *Hannah and Her Sisters* (Oscar for Best Original Screenplay—1986), *Crimes and Misdemeanors* (1989), *Scenes from a Mall* (1991),* *Husbands and Wives* (1992), *Manhattan Murder Mystery* (1993), *Zelig* (1993), *Bullets Over Broadway* (1994), *Everyone Says I Love You* (1996), *Celebrity* (1998), *The Imposters* (1998),* *Antz* (voice only, 1998).*

*Not directed by Woody Allen.

QUICKIE BIO

Diminutive Woody Allen broke into show biz in New York City as a bungling and horny stand-up schlemiel, and has thrived as one ever since. Though he managed to build a career writing, directing, producing, and starring in comedies, dramas, and romances, Woody was a little too woody when it came to the adopted daughter of his long-time squeeze actress Mia Farrow. After his romance with Soon-Yi Previn became all too public, Allen cut back on his production activities and starred in an animated film (*Antz*, 1998) about talking insects. Observed Woody, New York's favorite neurotic, "Why am I so popular in countries where they torture people?"

WOODY ALLEN DOES
THE DUMBEST THINGS

✪ Before Allen married his first wife (Harlene Rosen), his pals were worried about his lack of sexual experience. When they asked Woody if he was a virgin, he nervously said, "No." The buddies almost believed him, but still insisted that Allen spend time training with a hooker. When they told Allen the cost, he said, "Do you think she'll take a traveler's check?"

✪ One of Woody's buddies wanted to see just how little he really did know about sex. "You understand that a woman's two breasts are like a man's testicles, right?" the friend explained to Allen in mock seriousness. "That a woman's left breast hangs lower than her right, just like a man's testicles?" Woody replied, "Oh yeah, I know that." The jokester told Allen that there were four separate compartments to a woman's private parts. "Don't worry," said Allen, soaking up the fictional biology lesson. "I know. I know."

✪ For the title of his first screenplay, Allen borrowed one of Warren Beatty's favorite pick-up lines, *What's New, Pussycat?* (1965). Woody later confessed, "I want to be reincarnated as Warren Beatty's fingertips."

✪ While working on *What's New, Pussycat?* the comedian ate fillet of sole at the same restaurant every night for six months. The rest of the time he stayed in his room alone, playing the clarinet and eating "literally hundreds" of Hershey candy bars. Later the filmmaker explained, "I'm not really a recluse."

✪ Allen always has refused to eat anything he thought anyone else had put their hands on.

✪ When once called for jury duty in New York City, Woody showed up wearing a large hat which he refused to take off. He then demanded to be put in a separate room with his secretary.

✪ The star took dozens of cases of canned tuna with him on a trip to Europe and, generally, takes tuna everywhere he goes. He even takes his cans out to restaurants.

✪ Allen was paranoid about the germs in actress/girlfriend Mia Farrow's Manhattan apartment. Whenever he visited, he ate only from paper plates and drank from paper cups. He tried to take part in raising Mia's several children, but his germ phobia often got in the way. Woody admitted, "I don't have to be there when the diapers are changed or anything really awful happens."

✪ Woody refused to stay over at Farrow's place because she didn't have a shower. So Farrow built one for him. Allen looked at it and said he couldn't use it. Why not? The drain was in the middle of the shower floor, not on the side. Allen was afraid that if he stepped on the drain, he'd touch some germs.

✪ Gal pal Mia Farrow once asked Allen to change his bedsheets from polyester to cotton. This was a radical move for Woody. He discussed the matter many times with his psychiatrist before he felt ready to make the switch.

✪ Toward the end of their relationship, Allen, the perpetual hypochondriac, refused to have sex with Farrow. He didn't just complain of a headache. He told her he was afraid that he had Lyme disease, chronic fatigue syndrome, and even AIDS.

In January 1992, fifty-six-year-old Allen left six Polaroid snapshots on the mantelpiece in his apartment. The photos featured twenty-one-year-old Soon-Yi Previn posed in very provocative positions. Mia Farrow found the pictures and recognized her adopted daughter. Farrow knew that Woody was fond of Soon-Yi, but she didn't know he was *that* fond of her. Farrow went ballistic over this realization and, additionally, accused Allen of allegedly sexually molesting the child they had together. Allen raised a series of accusations on his own, and the couple split up with recriminations flying freely.

✪ Later on that year (1992), Soon-Yi was dismissed from a summer camp counselor job in Maine, largely because she was spending all her time on the pay phone. Others reported that she talked between six and

WOODY ALLEN 11

eight times a day to a caller who identified himself as Mr. Simon. Guess what? It turns out that Simon was Woody.

★ Woody and Soon-Yi once had sex in a hearse.

★ Allen was very confused about the inspirations for his movies, which dealt with subjects such as neurotic men who sleep with much younger women. "The plots of my movies don't have any relationship to my life," the comic genius once explained. Later he clarified, "Almost all of my work is autobiographical."

★ After marrying the adopted daughter of the mother of his children, Woody and Soon-Yi acquired a baby girl, by a means they would not divulge, and named her Bechet after a famed jazz clarinet player. Upon hearing the "good" news, Mia Farrow reportedly called Woody "an old pedophile." She went on to fume, "The notion that he has now made his natural son Satchel the uncle of this child. . . . There's this incredibly twisted, sordid relationship."

Brigitte Bardot

FACTS OF LIFE

ORIGIN: Born Camille Javal, September 28, 1934, Paris, France.

FORMATIVE YEARS: Attended the National Conservatory of Music and Dancing, Paris, France.

FAMILY PLANNING: Married Roger Vadim (director), December 12, 1952; divorced 1957; married Jacques Charrier (actor), 1959; divorced 1962; married Gunter Sachs (playboy), July 14, 1966; divorced October 1969; married Bernard d'Ormale (politician), August 1992.

ROMANTIC INTERESTS: Mick Jagger (musician), Raf Vallone (actor), Sean Connery (actor), Jean-Paul Belmondo (actor), Louis Malle (director).

SELECTED HITS (and Misses)

FILMS: *Act of Love* (1954), *Doctor at Sea* (1955), *Helen of Troy* (1955), *And God Created Woman* (1956), *Mam'zelle Pigally* (1958), *The Night Heaven Fell* (1958), *Babette Goes to War* (1959), *The Truth* (1961), *Love on a Pillow* (1962), *Contempt* (1963), *Viva Maria* (1965), *Dear Brigitte* (1965), *Les Femmes* (1969), *The Novices* (1970), *Don Juan '73* (1973).

QUICKIE BIO

Brigitte Bardot . . . the just-rolled-out-of-bed look, the pout, the figure inspired a generation of, well, inspiration. Bardot began her career as a teenage cover girl, identified only by the initials BB. Her protective mother tried (but failed) to keep BB from the hands of French film director Roger

Vadim. Vadim met Bardot when she was fifteen, married her when she was eighteen, and displayed her bare essentials to the world when she was twenty-one in *And God Created Woman* (1956). As she grew older, the sex kitten grew less interested in sex and more interested in kittens. She retired from film in 1974 to devote her life to animals and right-wing politicians. As the founder of *La Fondation Brigitte Bardot*, the aging sex symbol kept her clothes on and her mouth wide open.

BRIGITTE BARDOT DOES THE DUMBEST THINGS

- Brigitte Bardot went to see a soccer game and got confused. "They ought to give them several [balls]," she suggested. "Then they would stop fighting."

- On a family holiday, director Roger Vadim snuck into teenage Brigitte's room. When her father started banging on the door, Vadim and BB jumped naked into the snow from the second story to avoid being caught.

- Whenever her menstrual period started, teenage Bardot called Vadim to let him know that she wasn't pregnant. The code phrase she used to describe the event was "the Russians have come."

- When teenage Brigitte Bardot gave up her virginity to aspiring director Roger Vadim, she asked if she was a woman yet. "Twenty-five percent," he told her. The second time they did it, she asked again. "About fifty-five percent," he said. The third time they made love she asked again. "One hundred percent," he said. So she ran to the window stark naked and announced to the world, "I'm a real woman!"

- Brigitte and a female friend were in the kitchen when a grease fire started. As the pal was trying to extinguish the fire, BB ran out of the kitchen and slammed the door shut, trapping the other woman in the kitchen. When Vadim intervened, Brigitte cried out, "If I open the door, all my furniture will go up in flames."

- When Brigitte and Roger had a fight, she locked him out of her room. He kicked the door open, chased her down, pulled a mattress off a bed, covered her with it, and jumped up and down on her butt.

- A Vatican exhibit in 1959 at the Brussels World Fair portrayed BB as the symbol of evil. The display was removed after seven days because it was so popular the crowds were getting out of control.

⭐ After he divorced Bardot, Roger Vadim hired hunky Irish movie actor Stephen Boyd to star with his ex-wife in *The Night Heaven Fell* (1958). When Vadim brought Boyd to her apartment, Brigitte greeted him—completely nude. Nonetheless, Boyd was not impressed with BB's acting technique. "When I'm trying to play serious love scenes, she's positioning her bottom for the best angle shots."

⭐ Like Judy Garland, Bardot made a number of unsuccessful suicide attempts. After taking an overdose of pills twice and cutting her wrists once, all of which failed to end her misery, she tried to walk into the ocean and drown herself.

⭐ Years later, Brigitte threatened to kill herself when her then husband, Bernard d'Ormale, tried to bar her from going to Bosnia during the Serbian conflict to save starving cats and dogs.

🐶 When Bardot saw a man feed his pet mynah bird a hamburger and fries, she started beating him with her umbrella. Then she stole his bird. The police eventually had to rescue the junk-food loving pet from Bardot's home.

⭐ When she heard that they were using live snakes on stage, Bardot threatened to picket a London stage production of William Shakespeare's *Antony and Cleopatra*. BB claimed that the stage lights and the applause hurt the reptiles.

✪ After her dogs started getting death threats, the movie siren hired bodyguards to protect her pooches ... at a cost of $10,000 a month.

✪ When the city officials of Paris began fining dog owners who failed to clean up their pets' poop, Bardot staged a protest and accused the city officials of "aggression."

Brigitte arrived at the Greek Parliament in Athens, Greece, with flowers in her hair and blew kisses to the crowd before accepting a United Nations award for her animal rights activities. "I don't speak Greek and I do not speak English, I speak only French," she said in perfect English. Then she added, "I know that Greek people are not very nice to animals but do not fear, because neither are the French. Luckily they have me to look after all their animals but who will look after yours?" Bardot left the Parliament building barefoot, explaining, "I want to feel the history with my toes."

✪ Bardot conferred with Pope John Paul II in 1993 and offered to help send money to Africa to rescue starving animals. When Vatican officials suggested that it might be more valuable to use the funds to feed starving people in Africa, BB lost interest.

✪ In her autobiography, Bardot referred to her ex-husband Jacques Charrier as "a vulgar, dictatorial, and uncontrolled macho, a gigolo, alcoholic and despicable." She described her son as a "tumor feeding off me." Charrier sued Brigitte and won. Then Charrier wrote a book dissing BB. BB sued him and won.

✪ In 1998 Bardot condemned the Islamic ritual of lamb sacrifice saying, "My homeland, my earth, is again invaded ... by an overpopulation of foreigners, notably Muslims." She went on to say, "They'll slit our throats one day and we'll deserve it." The sex kitten was fined by the French government for "inciting racial hatred."

✪ Bardot had more success with her letter-writing campaign to stop a ritual in Transylvania. Inhabitants of a certain town celebrated each year by blindfolding several men and letting them behead roosters with sticks. After Brigitte's concerted effort, the men agreed to substitute clay roosters for the real cocks.

Kim Basinger

FACTS OF LIFE

ORIGIN: Born December 8, 1953, Athens, Georgia.

FORMATIVE YEARS: Dropped out of the University of Georgia, Athens, Georgia.

FAMILY PLANNING: Married Ron Britton (Hollywood makeup artist) 1980; divorced 1988; married Alec Baldwin (actor), August 19, 1993.

ROMANTIC INTERESTS: Dale Robinette (model), Jon Peters (producer), Robert Redford (actor), Phil Walsh (personal fitness trainer), Prince (musician).

SELECTED HITS (and Misses)

FILMS: *Hard Country* (1981), *Never Say Never Again* (1983), *The Man Who Loved Women* (1983), *The Natural* (1984), *Nine 1/2 Weeks* (1986), *No Mercy* (1986), *Blind Date* (1987), *My Stepmother Is an Alien* (1989), *Batman* (1989), *The Marrying Man* (1991), *Cool World* (1992), *Wayne's World 2* (1993), *The Getaway* (1993), *L.A. Confidential* (Oscar for Best Actress—1997), *Celebrity* (1998).

QUICKIE BIO

K im Basinger has been described as "the most self-indulgent, dumb, most irritating person I have ever met." The writer added, "She's as dumb as a shoe." Dubbed "rubberlips" by her school chums, Kim Basinger so underwhelmed her teachers in Athens, Georgia, that they thought she was autistic.

17

Her pushy parents claimed she was shy, not autistic, and entered their daughter in local beauty pageants. Teenage Basinger moved to New York and, in a short time, became a top model and a shampoo spokesperson as the "Breck girl." Not satisfied with wearing fancy clothes and making huge amounts of money in New York, Kim sang under the stage name Chelsea, and moved to Los Angeles in 1976 to make it as an actress. She hit it big in *Batman* (1989) before appearing in seven straight misfires, including the role of Honey Horne (accent on the "e") in *Wayne's World 2* (1993). *People* magazine declared that "her lips may be the poutiest and most provocative in screen history." The collagen injections helped. At least Kim knew her artistic limitations. "All I know about acting is, you just do it," she confessed. "God bless Stanislavsky, but I can't even pronounce his name."

KIM BASINGER
DOES THE DUMBEST THINGS

✪ When she married makeup artist Ron Britton in 1980, statuesque Kim announced, "Toys R Us, we are it!" Blushing bride Kim demanded that Ron change his last name from Snyder to Britton so that his initials would match the "K. B." on her luggage.

✪ Britton claimed that kinky Kim allegedly asked him to set up a threesome with a friend of his named Sandy. As the two men passed Kim back and forth, hubby Ron recalled hearing Kim squeal, "This is great!" Kim later insisted, "It's lies, all lies." After their divorce in 1988, Britton said of his ex-spouse, "It was either her or Lassie, and she was housebroken."

✪ In 1982, Basinger suffered an attack of agoraphobia (the fear of crowds) and did not leave her home for four months. Finally, she underwent therapy. Then she did an eight-page nude layout for *Playboy* in 1983. The retiring Basinger explained, "I considered the spread almost a silent film for myself."

✪ Basinger fell for petite, outré rock star Prince on the set of *Batman* (1989). Prince reportedly turned her into his personal love slave. Kim appeared with the diminutive funkmeister in a rock video entitled "Scandalous Sex Suite," and moaned and groaned along with her boyfriend on the song "Steamy Lover's Dialogue," which was included on the *Batman* soundtrack.

✪ Kim became enamored with actor Alec Baldwin (b. 1958) on the set of *The Marrying Man* (1991). At an Earth Day concert in New York City's Central Park, Kim and Alec tried to remain incognito by wearing sunglasses as they made out passionately. "Actors are all having sex with each other all the time," Baldwin later explained, "and they're all spending all their money, and they're all oversleeping, and they're all pretty indulgent. Beautiful pigs."

★ Alec Baldwin became so infatuated with Basinger that he joined Co-Dependents Anonymous to get over her. "There's an enormous amount of electricity between us, but sometimes the current gets overloaded and there's a short."

★ Kim and Alec had similar interests. "I like to be naked in movies. I have a reputation to uphold," Alec Baldwin confessed. In turn, Kim declared, "Sometimes I have this dream that I'd like to walk naked down the street and leave all my fame behind."

★ When Baldwin and Basinger brought their newborn baby home from the hospital in 1995, a photographer videotaped them from inside a pickup truck. Alec sprayed the truck with shaving cream, then fought the picture taker, giving him a broken nose. A judge ruled that the photographer was 25 percent responsible for the assault and that Baldwin bore 75 percent of the responsibility.

★ In 1989, Basinger became intrigued with Braselton, Georgia, located about ten miles from her home town of Athens. She was stuck in traffic one day when an idea formed in her brain. "I had on this see-thru skirt, and no panties," she later recalled. "I kept my left arm on the stick shift a lot and suddenly it hit me: 'I want to go public with Braselton.' See, I want it to be like Dollywood. What do you think of the name Kimwood?"

★ Kim bought Braselton for $20 million and declared, "I'm Barbara Stanwyck in *The Big Valley*." She sold the town four years later.

★ The reason Kim sold Braselton was that she went bankrupt after a judge ordered her to pay $8.1 million in damages for backing out of the feature film *Boxing Helena*. At the time of her financial debacle, the actresses's personal expenses were $43,100 per month, including $6,100 for clothes and $7,000 for "pet care and other personal expenses."

★ Basinger liked pets so much that she was horrified when she learned that thirty-six beagles were being used for drug research. She decided to save the canines, but when she demanded to be given the dogs, she learned that they were bred for research and couldn't survive outside a lab. She left, beagle-less.

★ "I have many friends—humans as well as horses—that I'd like to put in movies," Kim once bragged. Her husband Alec Baldwin was such a fanatic about horses that he accused the horse-drawn carriage drivers in New York City's Central Park of practicing "animal cruelty." When the "cabbies" objected to his accusations, Alec invited them to step outside and fight. "Come on," the equestrian-loving thespian beckoned. "Come on out."

★ Alec Baldwin became very involved with politics. During the impeachment proceedings against President Bill Clinton, Alec observed on the *Late Night with Conan O'Brien* TV talk show, "If we were in other countries . . . all of us together would go down to Washington and we would stone Henry Hyde [the Republican House of Representatives Chairman of the Impeachment Committee] to death." Later, the actor said of Republicans in general, "We would go to their homes, and we'd kill their wives and children. We'd kill their families."

★ Baldwin and Basinger threw a fundraiser for President Clinton, then threw a fit when they found that goose liver was on the President's menu. The animal-loving Baldwin called a high-ranking official in the Democratic National Committee and complained, "Can you imagine what it feels like to have a pipe shoved down your throat?" The item was pulled from the menu.

Warren Beatty

FACTS OF LIFE

ORIGIN: Born Henry "Little Henry" Warren Beaty, March 30, 1937, Richmond, Virginia. Added an extra "t" to his last name.

FORMATIVE YEARS: Dropped out of Chicago's Northwestern University in 1956, saying, "It was a pain in the a**."

FAMILY PLANNING: Married Annette Bening (actress), March 1992.

ROMANTIC INTERESTS: Natalie Wood (actress), Lana Wood (Natalie Wood's sister), Joan Collins (actress), Leslie Caron (actress), Julie Christie (actress), Mary Tyler Moore (actress), Cher (actress), Michelle Phillips (actress, ex-wife of Dennis Hopper), Brooke Hayward (actress, ex-wife of Dennis Hopper), Carly Simon (singer), Britt Ekland (actress), Diane Keaton (actress), Madonna (actress), Jessica Savitch (reporter). According to a French magazine, Warren Beatty has had sex with at least 1,299 women. One of his conquests said, "He should be in a jar at the Harvard Medical School."

SELECTED HITS (and Misses)

FILM: *Splendor in the Grass* (1961), *The Roman Spring of Mrs. Stone* (1961), *Lilith* (1964), *Mickey One* (1965), *Promise Her Anything* (1966), *Bonnie and Clyde* (1967), *McCabe and Mrs. Miller* (1971), *The Parallax View* (1974), *Shampoo* (1975), *The Fortune* (1975), *Heaven Can Wait* (1978),* *Reds* (Oscar for Best Director—1981),* *Ishtar* (1987), *Dick Tracy* (1990), *Bugsy* (1991),* *Love Affair* (1994), *Bulworth* (1998), *Town and Country* (1999), *Mr. Hughes* (2000).

*Also directed by Beatty.

TV SERIES: *The Many Loves of Dobie Gillis* (1959–60).

QUICKIE BIO

Family friends called him "the Kid," but best buddy Jack Nicholson knew him as "the Pro." The football-playing high school heartthrob, Warren Beatty followed the trail blazed by his sister, Shirley MacLaine, to New York City, where he hit it big with actresses Joan Collins and Natalie Wood, and, oh yeah, did some acting. Beatty neither drank nor did drugs. He has saved all his energy for chasing women, and, oh yeah, making movies. According to actress Britt Ekland, "He could handle women as smoothly as operating an elevator. He knew exactly where to locate the top button." However, singer Carly Simon probably came closer to the truth when she wrote a hit song that was rumored to be all about Beatty. The title? "You're So Vain." Beatty, himself, has often complained that the media depicts him as a playboy. He can't figure out why.

WARREN BEATTY
DOES THE DUMBEST THINGS

⭐ As a teenager in Washington, DC, Beatty obtained his first job at the National Theatre. More precisely, behind the theatre. He worked in the alley scaring away rats.

⭐ On the set of *Splendor in the Grass* (1961), Warren wasted so much time looking at himself that the director, Elia Kazan, ordered his assistants to cover up all the mirrors.

⭐ At a charity event, Beatty was overheard in the bathroom saying, "You look wonderful. God, you're handsome!" He was talking to a mirror.

⭐ During a 1962 interview, the actor opened a suitcase. Thirty-five uncashed checks fell out. Beatty shrugged, "I can't be bothered with things like this."

⭐ Warren allegedly held up filming of the psychological drama *Lilith* (1964) for three days while he argued vehemently with director Robert Rossen over whether his character should say, "I've read *Crime and Punishment* and *The Brothers Karamazov*" or "I've read *Crime and Punishment* and half of *The Brothers Karamazov*."

⭐ Also on the set of *Lilith*, the screen stud refused to talk with visiting reporters, insisting that he had to discuss a crucial matter with the director. Beatty went to him and asked, "Do you think my hair is too long behind the ears?"

⭐ For the potential assignment of playing John F. Kennedy in the film *PT 109* (1963), movie studio boss Jack L. Warner suggested that Warren go to Washington and visit President Kennedy to soak up the atmosphere. "If the president wants me to play him," Beatty complained, "tell him to come here and soak up some of my atmosphere." The part of JFK eventually went to Cliff Robertson.

⭐ Beatty later fell to the ground in front of Jack L. Warner, grabbed the mogul's knees, and told the moviemaker that he would kiss his shoes, even lick them, if Warner gave him money for *Bonnie and Clyde* (1967). "What the f*** you doin'?" said an embarrassed Warner. "Get off the f***in' floor." Then he gave Beatty $1.6 million to make the gangster saga.

⭐ When not on the set for *Bonnie and Clyde,* Warren spent time in his Winnebago camper. A procession of girls went in and out of the star's motor home at all hours. When the camper was a-rockin', the crew didn't bother knockin'.

Beatty became politically active in the 1960s, but sometimes politics bored him. On a visit with an Italian director, the conversation turned to the topic of communism. Beatty excused himself and disappeared into a bathroom with an actress. They emerged together fifteen minutes later.

⭐ Warren and his then girlfriend actress Natalie Wood were eating at swank Chasen's in Beverly Hills. Beatty excused himself for a minute, but never returned to the table. A week later, Beatty arrived at Wood's house to pick up his things. Wood told her maid to tell him that there was nothing to pick up. She had burned all his clothes.

Sometimes Beatty liked to share his girlfriends with actor pal Jack Nicholson and his other buddy, producer Robert Evans. One woman claimed that she heard the three guys bragging about how often they had had her. The woman decided to get even. First she went to Evans' house and screwed him. Next, she went to Nicholson's house and screwed him. Then she went to Warren's house. After Beatty satisfied her orally, the woman began to laugh and told him that Evans and Jack had recently been visiting the same location. At first Warren was mad, then he thought it was funny.

⭐ When TV talk-show host Arsenio Hall asked Madonna, "What does Warren Beatty have that we don't have?" Madonna answered, "About a billion dollars."

★ After his affair with Madonna ended, Beatty sent the Material Girl a life-size cardboard cutout of himself from the movie *Dick Tracy* (1990). Warren sent along a note with the cutout asking, "Remember me?" Madonna promptly sent back the cutout with a reply note attached to it that said, "Yes."

John Belushi

FACTS OF LIFE (and Death)

ORIGIN: Born January 24, 1949, Chicago, Illinois; died March 5, 1982, in Los Angeles after receiving a hefty injection of cocaine and heroin.

FORMATIVE YEARS: Graduated from the College of DuPage, a two-year junior college in Glen Ellyn, Illinois.

FAMILY PLANNING: Married Judy Jacklin (high school sweetheart), December 31, 1976.

ROMANTIC INTERESTS: John "partied" with an assortment of drug-buddy females including his last such pal Cathy Evelyn Smith.

SELECTED HITS (and Misses)

FILMS: *National Lampoon's Animal House* (1978), *Going South* (1978), *1941* (1979), *Old Boyfriends* (1979), *The Blues Brothers* (1980), *Neighbors* (1981), *Continental Divide* (1981).

TV SERIES: *Saturday Night Live* (1975–79).

QUICKIE BIO

The son of an Albanian immigrant who spent years serving cheeseburgers for a living, Belushi started his acting career in 1967, performing in a theatre near his hometown of Wheaton, Illinois. After working with Chicago's Second City improvisational theater group, Belushi hit the fast track as an original member of The Not Ready for Prime Time Players on NBC's *Saturday*

Night Live (1975–79). Belushi's disturbing portrayals of Marlon Brando, Joe Cocker, the samurai warrior, and the bumble bee (which he hated) made him an instant star. As his fame grew, so did his waistline—and his drug habit. "You've got to understand," explained Belushi to concerned friends before he died from an overdose of cocaine and heroin, "it's my lifestyle." Belushi's lifestyle was later immortalized in the book and 1989 movie *Wired*. John's younger brother, James Belushi, also became an actor and carried on the Belushi tradition of portraying overweight louts on-camera.

JOHN BELUSHI
DOES THE DUMBEST THINGS

⭐ One Thanksgiving weekend, Belushi started partying in the apartment of Lorne Michaels, the creator/producer of NBC's *Saturday Night Live*. Belushi lit up a cigarette, passed out, and set the place on fire.

⭐ After the incendiary episode, the comedian sought help from a doctor. The therapist asked Belushi to honestly describe his drug use. The actor obliged. The doctor took the following notes: "Smokes three packs a day. Alcohol: drinks socially. Medication: Valium occasionally. Marijuana: four to five times a week. Cocaine: snorts daily, main habit. Mescaline: regularly. Acid: ten to twenty trips. No heroin. Amphetamines: four kinds. Barbiturates: habit[ual]." On his way out the door, Belushi confessed that he was also addicted to Quaaludes. The doctor wrote him a prescription for thirty of them. Later, John started doing heroin.

⭐ Belushi backed off coke for a brief period. However, in 1979, Rolling Stones' guitarist Keith Richards rolled into town and invited Belushi to party. The two spent most of the night snorting blow. When John stumbled into the NBC television studio for a *Saturday Night Live* dress rehearsal the next morning, he was totally unable to function. A doctor examined him and said that if he performed there was "a 50-50 chance he'll die." Producer Lorne Michaels, who badly needed Belushi on camera, quipped, "I can live with those odds."

⭐ One of Belushi's favorite party games was "cocaine chicken." To play, John took a quarter ounce of coke and cut it into one line several feet long. Then he and his opponent started snorting from opposite ends of the line and raced to the middle. Belushi usually won the contest.

⭐ Escorted by his enormous bodyguard, Belushi bragged to a gang hanging out on the New York City streets that they used real coke for the skits on NBC's *Saturday Night Live*. As the bodyguard attempted to get him away from the belligerent gang members, John whipped out his own member and took a leak. When a car drove by and a passenger shouted, "Hey, it's John Belushi peeing." The comedian yelled, "F*** you, faggot," and chased the car down the street.

✪ John was a big fan of punk rock. One night at an after-hours club, he entertained stodgy producers by playing the song "Too Drunk to F***" by the Dead Kennedys. Not long after, Belushi went out with several Playboy bunnies, but found that he himself was too drunk to, uh, perform.

✪ A strung-out Belushi once barged into the office of powerful talent agent Michael Ovitz, delivered an overdue script, and rambled incoherently. When he tried to leave, he was so blasted that he couldn't find his way out of the building. Ovitz had to summon a couple of mail room workers to help John successfully navigate his way to the street exit.

✪ Two weeks after Belushi's death in March 1982, his friend Cathy Evelyn Smith appeared on national TV and explained why John was drinking the night he died. "He was working on a screenplay that had to do with vintage wine-making," she sniffed, "so he was drinking wine."

✪ In one classic *Saturday Night Live* skit, Belushi visited the graves of his costars. Wandering amongst the tombstones, he said, "They all thought I'd be the first to go. I was one of those, 'Live fast, die young, leave a good looking corpse' types, you know. I guess they were wrong . . ." In reality, Belushi *was* the first of the original cast of *Saturday Night Live* to go. One thousand mourners attended Belushi's funeral at the Cathedral of Saint John the Divine in New York City. Instead of a eulogy for his fallen friend, Dan Aykroyd stunned the crowd by playing a tape of the Ventures' song "The 2,000 Pound Bee."

Marlon Brando

DUMBEST QUOTES

"I'm fascinated about anything.
I'll talk for seven hours about splinters."

"The most repulsive thing you could ever imagine is
the inside of a camel's mouth. That and watching a
girl eat octopus or squid."

"The viscosity of some people's saliva is remarkable."

FACTS OF LIFE

ORIGIN: Born Marlon "Bud" Brando Jr., April 3, 1924, Omaha, Nebraska.

FORMATIVE YEARS: Expelled from Shattuck Military Academy in Faribault, Minnesota, reportedly either for faking an injury to get out of an inspection or for having sex with one of the cadets.

FAMILY PLANNING: Married Anna Kashfi (actress), October 11, 1957 (Brando thought she was an exotic Asian woman, but she turned out to be Joan O'Callaghan, the daughter of an Irish factory worker); divorced 1959; married Movita Castaneda (actress), January 4, 1960; annulled 1968. Brando eventually fathered between nine and thirteen children by at least four different women.

ROMANTIC INTERESTS: Stella Adler (acting coach), Rita Moreno (actress), Marilyn Monroe (actress), Liliane Montevecchi (actress), Montgomery Clift (actor), Barbara Luna (actress), Tarita Tumi Teriipaia (dishwasher), Pat Quinn (actress).

SELECTED HITS (and Misses)

FILMS: *The Men* (1950), *A Streetcar Named Desire* (1951), *Viva Zapata!* (1952), *Julius Caesar* (1953), *On the Waterfront* (Oscar for Best Actor—1954), *The Wild One* (1954), *Guys and Dolls* (1955), *The Teahouse of the August Moon* (1956), *Sayonara* (1957), *The Young Lions* (1958), *The Fugitive Kind* (1960), *One-Eyed Jacks*

(1961),* *Mutiny on the Bounty* (1962), *The Ugly American* (1963), *Reflections in a Golden Eye* (1967), *The Godfather* (Oscar for Best Actor—1972), *Last Tango in Paris* (1973), *The Godfather Part II* (1974), *Superman* (1978), *Apocalypse Now* (1979), *The Freshman* (1990), *Don Juan DeMarco* (1995), *The Island of Dr. Moreau* (1996), *The Brave* (1997), *Free Money* (1998), *Autumn of the Patriarch* (1999).

*Also directed by Brando.

QUICKIE BIO

Born to hard drinking theater fans in Nebraska, Brando got tossed out of several schools and played drums in a band called Bud Brando and the Keg Lines before he wound up on the New York stage in the 1940s. A pioneer of the natural "method" acting style, Marlon quickly earned critical raves and sexual favors. The Mallomar-munching sex symbol scaled the Hollywood hierarchy, mooning fans and coworkers as he handled what he referred to as his "noble tool." Brando became a huge star—literally. His performances in his later films caused many to believe him when he confessed, "I hate acting."

MARLON BRANDO
DOES THE DUMBEST THINGS

✪ While acting on Broadway, Brando performed with girlfriends backstage, between his entrances. Said a costar: "For him, sex was like eating or going to the bathroom."

✪ Brando rarely used birth control. According to his lover Sondra Lee, he paid for hundreds of abortions—and this while he was still in his twenties. In the 1950s, when abortion was still illegal, Marlon basically kept two doctors on retainer.

In the winter of 1948, the star and a female companion had an "abortion party" in a New York City apartment. Brando sat playing his bongos while his companion walked around the party holding a paper cup, pointed to a bloody mass in the cup, and introduced it to partiers with the words, "How do you do? This is . . ."

✪ Brando later described rape as "assault with a friendly weapon."

✪ At a dinner party with friends, Marlon ordered everybody to strip naked. Everybody agreed except for one woman who left the room in tears. Brando got up and chased her. He paused next to a vase, pulled out a lily, and stuck it in his butt.

⭐ When the daughter-in-law of a French government official was introduced to Brando, the actor simply sat on a sofa and said, "Take my finger." The confused woman did. Marlon commanded, "Tirez" ("Pull"),
which she did—he then let out what one onlooker described as a
"Wagnerian" fart.

⭐ Marlon prided himself on being a "method" actor. So if his character
was supposed to be drunk, Brando got drunk. For a scene in *Viva Zapata!* (1952), where he played the self-made Mexican ruler, Brando
downed a bottle of vodka in preparation, but got so drunk he couldn't
do the scene. This behavior went on for six consecutive weeks. Finally,
the crew abandoned the soused Brando in Mexico, and that particular
sequence was never completed.

⭐ For *Mutiny on the Bounty* (1962), Brando was supposed to be badly
burned in one scene. He did research and found that such a person
feels much like a person who is frozen. To achieve the "perfect mood"
for the scene, Brando laid down on a bed of cracked ice, covered with a
sheet, until he got "death tremors." Then he tried to do the scene. The
partially frozen actor couldn't remember his dialogue, so the crew
wrote them on his costar's forehead with a grease pencil. Thereafter,
Brando caught a cold, closing down production for three days.

🗩 Marlon also couldn't remember his lines for *Last Tango in Paris* (1973).
So he hit upon the idea of writing his words on the bottom of his shoe,
then taking the shoe off during the scene and reading the dialogue. He
purposely limped through the shot because he was afraid walking
would erase words from the shoe.

⭐ The production of *One-Eyed Jacks* (1961) ran way behind schedule
because of Brando, who was directing the western as well as acting in it.
Typical of the holdups was the time that Marlon sat on a rock on the
seashore, waiting for the surf to be "just right." The star waited and
waited, as did the crew. He continued to look at the surf through his
director's view finder, and complained about the "little piddly, bubbly
things coming up, no white." The assistant director then noticed that
Brando was looking through the wrong end of the viewfinder. "Holy
s***," Brando chuckled, "No wonder I'm a week late."

🖼 About this time Brando began to balloon upward in size. So much so
that the costume director for *One-Eyed Jacks* was forced to make Marlon's costumes out of elasticized material. Brando still split eighteen
pairs of pants during filming. At one point, cast members posted a sign
reading, "Don't Feed the Director."

⭐ One morning, during the shooting of *The Missouri Breaks* (1976), another western, Brando plucked a live frog from a stream, took a bite out of it and tossed it back.

⭐ Brando's eating binges were impressive and routine. He would consume half a cheesecake and a pint of ice cream in one sitting, or maybe two whole chickens at a time. On other occasions, he donned sunglasses and a large floppy hat and drove off in the middle of the night to a food stand, where he would gorge himself on six or more hot dogs.

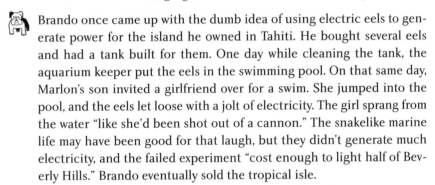 Brando once came up with the dumb idea of using electric eels to generate power for the island he owned in Tahiti. He bought several eels and had a tank built for them. One day while cleaning the tank, the aquarium keeper put the eels in the swimming pool. On that same day, Marlon's son invited a girlfriend over for a swim. She jumped into the pool, and the eels let loose with a jolt of electricity. The girl sprang from the water "like she'd been shot out of a cannon." The snakelike marine life may have been good for that laugh, but they didn't generate much electricity, and the failed experiment "cost enough to light half of Beverly Hills." Brando eventually sold the tropical isle.

Richard Burton

FACTS OF LIFE (and Death)

ORIGIN: Born Richard Walter Jenkins Jr., November 10, 1925, Pontrhydyfen, Wales; died August 8, 1984, Geneva, Switzerland.

FORMATIVE YEARS: Dropped out of Oxford University, Oxford, England.

FAMILY PLANNING: Married Sybil Williams (drama student), February 5, 1949; divorced 1963; married Elizabeth Taylor (actress), March 15, 1964; divorced 1974; married Elizabeth Taylor (again), October 10, 1975; divorced (again) 1976; married Susan Hunt, July 3, 1983.

ROMANTIC INTERESTS: Zsa Zsa Gabor (actress), Claire Bloom (actress), Tammy Grimes (actress), Susan Strasberg (director's daughter), Jean Simmons (actress). Burton described himself as "a great womanizer—knocking off everyone in sight."

SELECTED HITS (and Misses)

FILMS: *The Last Days of Dolwyn* (1949), *Green Grows the Rushes* (1951), *My Cousin Rachel* (1952), *The Robe* (1953), *Prince of Players* (1954), *Alexander the Great* (1956), *Sea Wife* (1957), *Look Back in Anger* (1959), *Ice Palace* (1960), *The Longest Day* (1962), *Cleopatra* (1963), *The V.I.P.s* (1963), *Becket* (1964), *The Night of the Iguana* (1964), *The Spy Who Came in from the Cold* (1965), *Who's Afraid of Virginia Woolf?* (1966), *The Taming of the Shrew* (1967), *Boom!* (1968), *Where Eagles Dare* (1968), *Staircase* (1969), *Anne of the Thousand Days* (1970), *Bluebeard* (1972), *The Assassination of Trotsky* (1972), *The Klansman* (1974), *Equus* (1977), *The Wild Geese* (1978), *The Medusa Touch* (1978), *Wagner* (1983), *1984* (1984).

QUICKIE BIO

Richard Jenkins was the twelfth child born to a hard drinking Welsh coal miner. Son Richard followed in his dad's footsteps—not into the coal mines, but into the bottle. Young Jenkins took the name of his acting teacher at Oxford, dropped out to join the Royal Air Force in World War II, and wound up a star of stage and screen—and Elizabeth Taylor's husband. It was a marriage so "nice," they did it twice. After regal and extravagant Liz got through with him, Dick wasn't much good for anything else. As a public relations man said to reporters eager to speak with Burton in the 1970s, "If you want to interview a drunk and watch a drunk fall in the camellia bushes, come ahead." *Time* magazine declared, "Richard Burton, once an actor, now performs as a buffoon."

RICHARD BURTON
DOES THE DUMBEST THINGS

 After his first sexual encounter, young Burton and his conquest fell asleep in front of a fire at the girl's home. He was soon awakened by the smell of his own feet smoldering. "I thought I was in hell fire," Burton recalled, "but it was just my socks smoking."

★ Burton's royal voice and kingly demeanor made him a favorite for epic theatrical dramas. "I don't want to do them. I don't like them, I hate getting made up for them, I hate my hair being curled up in the mornings, I hate tights, I hate boots, I hate everything," Richard snarled.

While their relationship was still a bit of a mystery, a tipsy Burton burst into a dinner party at Elizabeth Taylor's home. Taylor's husband Eddie Fisher appeared and asked what the Welsh actor was doing there. "I'm in love with that girl over there," Burton replied, pointing at Liz. Fisher reminded Dick that he was still married. Burton responded by saying they (his wife and Liz) were "both my girls." He turned to Taylor and asked, "You're my girl aren't you?" Taylor answered, "Yes." Burton then pushed it even further. "If you're my girl come over here and stick your tongue down my throat." With hubby Fisher looking on, Taylor went over and kissed Burton.

★ Days later, when Eddie Fisher called "home," Burton picked up the phone. Eddie asked what he was doing there. "What do you think I'm doing?" Dick said rhetorically. "I'm f***ing your wife."

★ While vacationing at his villa in Puerto Vallarta, Mexico, Burton invited the American consul and his wife over for dinner. Burton entertained his guests by acting out a script based on the memoirs of Winston Churchill.

That is, Burton entertained until he fell asleep in mid-sentence. The American consul's wife quickly decided, "We'd better be going."

⭐ Richard Burton liked to perform soliloquies from Shakespeare at the dinner table. Everyone loved it but Liz, who often interrupted her husband by saying, "Would you shut the f*** up?"

⭐ "It sounds strange to say that at heart I am a communist," Dick once proclaimed. At the time, the actor was making more than a million dollars per movie.

⭐ Richard and Liz became known as "The Battling Burtons." Richard liked to refer to his spouse as "Miss Tits" or "Fatty." He declared Liz's mammaries "apocalyptic, they would topple empires before they withered." Dick once drunkenly demanded Liz "turn off the motherf***ing television." When she refused, he kicked the set in—and seriously cut his foot. It took Liz almost an hour to stop the bleeding.

⭐ Burton tried to pick up costar Joan Collins on the set of *Sea Wife* (1957) in Jamaica. Burton kissed her, but she didn't respond. "Richard," Collins said, "I do believe you would screw a snake if you had the chance." He countered, "Only if it was wearing a skirt, darling. It would have to be a female snake."

⭐ While filming Edna Ferber's saga *Ice Palace* (1960) in Alaska, Burton shared his philosophy of filmmaking with fellow actor Jim Backus, the voice of Mr. Magoo. "Here we are sitting on top of the world, having a drink at three in the morning with the sun out and the dogs barking, making this piece of s***," Dick reflected. "If they want to pay us, let them."

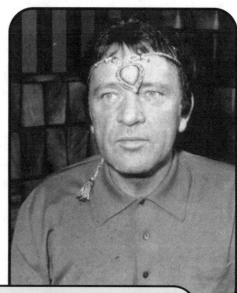

"I am not quite sure whether I am [an alcoholic] or not," observed Richard Burton, who once drank an entire bottle of vodka during a matinee performance of the play *Camelot*, then drank another bottle during the evening performance.
[photo courtesy of Express Newspapers/Archive Photos]

Jim Carrey

FACTS OF LIFE

ORIGIN: Born James Eugene "Jimmy Gene the String Bean" Carrey, January 17, 1962, Newmarket, Ontario, Canada.

FORMATIVE YEARS: Dropped out of high school.

FAMILY PLANNING: Married Melissa Womer (waitress), March 28, 1987; divorced 1994; married Lauren Holly (actress), September 23, 1996; divorced June 1997.

ROMANTIC INTERESTS: Linda Ronstadt (singer).

SELECTED HITS (and Misses)

FILMS: *The Sex and Violence Family Hour* (1983), *Peggy Sue Got Married* (1986), *The Dead Pool* (1988), *Earth Girls Are Easy* (1989), *The Mask* (1994), *Dumb & Dumber* (1994), *Ace Ventura, Pet Detective* (1994), *Batman Forever* (1995), *Ace Ventura: When Nature Calls* (1995), *The Cable Guy* (1996), *Liar Liar* (1997), *The Truman Show* (1998), *Man on the Moon* (1999), *Me, Myself and Irene* (2000), *How the Grinch Stole Christmas* (2000).

TV SERIES: *The Dutch Factory* (1984), *In Living Color* (1990–94).

QUICKIE BIO

Alrighty then. Born to a frustrated Canadian musician father in a suburb of Toronto, Ontario, ten-year-old Jim Carrey sent his résumé to TV's *The Carol Burnett Show* and started doing stand-up comedy at age sixteen. Carrey made a name for himself with imitations that combined the genius of Jerry

Lewis and Curly of the Three Stooges. Carrey zoomed to big screen success before he began to act dumb and dumber with his *Dumb & Dumber* (1994) costar Lauren Holly, and compared himself to Chaplin—size-wise, anyway. Spank you, Jim. Spank you very much.

JIM CARREY
DOES THE DUMBEST THINGS

⭐ Teenager Carrey made his stage debut at a Toronto comedy club dressed in a yellow polyester suit. When the audience started booing, the venue's owner played the chorus from the musical *Jesus Christ Superstar*—"Crucify him! Crucify him!"

⭐ As the white guy on TV's *In Living Color* in the early 1990s, Jim created the character Fire Marshal Bill, a man who set fires while giving safety lessons. Fire prevention groups were furious, but cops congratulated Carrey. Why? Because after years of cop jokes, the firemen were finally getting it.

💬 On the set of *In Living Color*, lanky Jim didn't like a certain script. When producer/director/writer comedian Keenen Ivory Wayans, the guiding force on the comedy variety series, insisted that Carrey read the script, Carrey turned around, pulled down his pants, bent over, put his hands on his butt, and read the pages through his rear end.

⭐ Carrey played an alcoholic in the TV movie *Doing Time on Maple Drive* (1992). "One thing I hope I'll never be is drunk with my own power," he later explained. "And anybody who says I am will never work in this town again."

⭐ Jim takes his roles seriously—sometimes too seriously. While making *Man on the Moon* (1999), a biopic about comedian Andy Kaufman (1948–1984), Carrey recreated a scene from Kaufman's life in which Kaufman tangled with professional wrestler Jerry Lawler and suffered a serious neck injury. While shooting this recreation, Carrey spit in Lawler's face. Lawler got angry, grabbed Jim by the hair, and jerked his neck. Carrey returned to the set in a neck brace.

⭐ Carrey keeps a chef on the set of his pictures to cook special dishes—for his dog.

⭐ On the set of *Ace Ventura: When Nature Calls* (1995), Jim paid half the cost of a personal chef for his pet iguana. The film producers paid the other half.

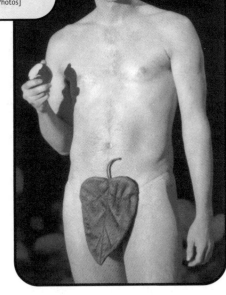

"Until *Ace Ventura*, no actor had considered talking through his ass," **Jim Carrey pronounced.** [photo courtesy of Reuters/Jeff Christensen/Archive Photos]

 Jim hired a masseuse to come to his home three times a week to give a forty-five minute massage to his Labrador retriever.

⭐ Carrey bought a $20,000 three-room house with a plush sofa, just for his dog.

⭐ On the MTV Movie Awards, the comedian won as best villain for playing the Riddler in *Batman Forever* (1995). He accepted the prize and said, "I'll remember this not as an award, but as undeniable proof that I am a bada** motherf***er." Then he stepped to the side of the stage and made a lewd jerking hand gesture in front of his crotch. Host Mike Myers said of the show, "I don't think it was sexually explicit enough. I like my comedy porno."

⭐ Carrey appeared at the twentieth anniversary of the Comedy Store in Los Angeles wearing nothing but a sock on his privates.

⭐ According to reporters, Jim Carrey allegedly tried to mellow himself out with "every mood stabilizer from Prozac to colonic irrigation." The comedic star said he particularly liked colonic irrigation because "sometimes you find old jewelry."

⭐ When a psychic told the comedian to find the missing colors of his aura, Carrey drove all over Los Angeles looking for colored ribbons. Observed a friend, "He's very spiritual."

⭐ After a tourist on a Caribbean island spotted honeymooners Jim Carrey and Lauren Holly, he whipped out his video camera and began taping.

Witnesses allege that an irate Carrey dumped a pitcher of ice water on the video guy and bonked him on the head with the empty pitcher.

★ Jim married actress Lauren Holly, then divorced her after ten months, then got back together with her in the summer of 1998 for a six-month trial reunion. The couple reportedly agreed to have sex only once a week, to prove that there was more to their relationship than mere lust. And Carrey promised not to make funny faces when he passed a mirror. Holly claimed the faces scared her. The test rematch didn't work. Maybe Jim just couldn't stop with those faces.

★ On the set of *Me, Myself and Irene* (2000) Jim sometimes walked around with a coat pulled over his head. At one point, he grabbed a bagel, took a bite, and screamed, "Who's trying to poison me?" Carrey spit the bagel mess into a napkin and walked about the set asking, "Is it you? What about you?"

★ When asked why beautiful women fell for comedians, Carrey explained "A surface-to-air missile-type d***."

Charlie Chaplin

FACTS OF LIFE (and Death)

ORIGIN: Born Charles Spencer Chaplin, April 16, 1889, London, England; died December 25, 1977, Vevey, Switzerland.

FORMATIVE YEARS: Quit school as a child to join a troop of clog dancers.

FAMILY PLANNING: Married Mildred Harris (actress), October 23, 1918; divorced 1920; married Lita Grey (actress), November 24, 1924; divorced 1927; married Paulette Goddard (actress), June 1936; divorced 1942; married Oona O'Neill (actress), June 16, 1943.

ROMANTIC INTERESTS: Alla Nazimova (actress), Mabel Normand (actress), Marion Davies (actress), Pola Negri (actress), Joan Barry (actress), Lupe Velez (actress), Hedy Lamarr (actress).

SELECTED HITS (and Misses)

FILMS (as actor/director): *Tillie's Punctured Romance* (1914),* *The Tramp* (1915), *Carmen* (1916), *The Immigrant* (1917), *Easy Street* (1917), *A Dog's Life* (1918), *Shoulder Arms* (1918), *The Kid* (1921), *The Pilgrim* (1923), *The Gold Rush* (1925), *The Circus* (Special Oscar at the first Academy Awards ceremony— 1927–28), *City Lights* (1931), *Modern Times* (1936), *The Great Dictator* (1940), *Monsieur Verdoux* (1947), *Limelight* (1952), *A King in New York* (1957), *A Countess from Hong Kong* (1967).

*Directed by Mack Sennett.

QUICKIE BIO

The son of impoverished British show biz types who separated when he was one year old, Chaplin first portrayed his little tramp character on-screen in the 1914 silent short subject *Kid Auto Races at Venice*. Adults and children loved his comic creation, and the little tramp loved children—maybe a bit too much. "The most beautiful form of human life," Chaplin rhapsodized was "the very young girl just starting to bloom." Charlie married a nineteen-year-old, an eighteen-year-old, and two sixteen-year-olds. One of the most original of movie stars, as well as co-founder of his own film production studio, Chaplin was never an American citizen and was banned from the United States for twenty years because of the government's belief that he was a communist. The British knighted him, and Hollywood finally gave him a special Oscar for Lifetime Achievement in 1972. Why did Sir Charles refer to himself as the "Eighth Wonder of the World"? Read on . . .

CHARLIE CHAPLIN
DOES THE DUMBEST THINGS

- ✪ As a young man, Chaplin caught the eye of gold-digging Ziegfeld Follies girl Peggy Hopkins Joyce. On their first date, Peggy inquired, "Is it true what all the girls say—that you're hung like a horse?"

- 💬 Charlie referred to his johnson as the "Eighth Wonder of the World." He claimed he could have sex five or six times in short order with just a few minutes rest in between. His brother Sydney (1885–1965) was equally sex crazed. He considered having sex with four different women in a day about average.

- ✪ Although he was voracious, Charlie was rather shy about his sex life. In his autobiography, he referred to his buxom conquests as having "upper regional domes immensely expansive."

- ✪ Chaplin was furious when producer Louis B. Mayer promoted films featuring his ex-wife as Mildred Harris Chaplin. When the screen's Little Tramp confronted Mayer, the movie mogul screamed, "You filthy pervert!" and punched Chaplin.

- ✪ Lillita MacMurray started acting with Chaplin when she was only six years old. Chaplin performed with her for ten years, then began an affair with her when she was barely a teen. Her mother approved and changed the girl's name to Lita Grey.

- ✪ Charlie called condoms "aesthetically hideous" and didn't use them while cavorting with Lita Grey. When she got pregnant, Chaplin offered her $20,000 to marry someone else. After threats of a paternity suit and statutory rape charges, Chaplin agreed to wed her in Mexico. On the journey from Los Angeles to south of the border, the movie star suggested that his young bride-to-be throw herself from the train.

★ Lita's mother, "Nana," moved in with the newlyweds on the grounds that her daughter was still a youngster. The ever-alert mother-in-law kept a diary of life with the Chaplins, which included intimate details of pillow talk. Among the dirt was the fact that Charlie wanted little Lita to perform oral sex. Lita described the act as an "abnormal, against nature, perverted, degenerate and indecent act." Charlie tried to talk her into it by saying "Relax, dear, all married people do it." Lita's uncle published the diary which became a bestseller—and the subject of several stag films.

Charlie Chaplin was so convinced that iodine would prevent venereal disease that he painted his poker bright red before participating in an orgy.

★ When the bills for actress Joan Barry's abortions started adding up, Chaplin cut his costar's salary from one hundred dollars per week to twenty-five dollars. She retaliated by dancing naked under the sprinklers in front of his Beverly Hills mansion.

★ Joan once stormed Chaplin's house with a pistol. Her wild threats made Charlie horny, and the two ended up humping on the fur rug before his fireplace with the gun nearby. "Well, this is a new twist," he said of the weapon's presence.

★ The jury at Charlie's 1944 trial for sexual misconduct with a minor was definitely star struck. One juror claimed Chaplin could not have been guilty because he was an artist, and therefore could never have sex on his mind. Another jury member brought photos of her fourteen-year-old daughter to the trial, hoping that Charlie might be interested. Chaplain was found not guilty.

★ Strolling around Paris, happy that no one recognized him, Chaplin was attacked with a vicious stomach cramp. Desperate to find a bathroom, Chaplin approached a porter for directions. The silent movie star didn't know French, so he grunted, squatted, and rolled his eyes around. The porter thought he was mad and ran away. Chaplin hailed a cab driver, and repeated the performance. The cabbie started laughing. Soon a crowd formed around the groaning comedian. Finally a cheese vendor came to the door of his shop and called out in English, "Do you want a job? You could draw in the customers." Chaplin shouted, "Not a job. A toilet." The cheese vendor invited Chaplin in. As the movie star entered the store, the crowd recognized his famous tramp walk and started shouting "Charlot! Charlot!" As the mob rushed forward, Chaplin ran into the bathroom and bolted the door. The crowd broke down the walls of the building. Chaplin escaped, as the mob fought for souvenir bits of the bathroom.

★ After residents of Catalina Island in Southern California watched Charlie and a girlfriend cavorting naked on the beach, they began calling the native goats "Charlies" in honor of the well-endowed actor.

★ Chaplin's daughter Geraldine said she and her siblings never could figure out how many wives her father had until he wrote *My Autobiography* (1964). "And then we heard that they were maybe very young girls, that was even more fascinating," Geraldine gushed. "You find the dark side of someone you love, especially a parent, and you're certainly quite proud of it."

★ Body snatchers made off with Chaplin's corpse from his grave near Vevey, Switzerland, in 1978, and demanded a huge ransom for its return. It was almost three months before the coffin was found intact near Lake Geneva.

Cher

DUMBEST QUOTE

"I've never written a check."

"Anything that deals with normal life I'm not good at."

"I believe in God, but I think I made him up to suit myself. . . . I talk to him all the time."

"I am not ashamed of *The Sonny and Cher Show*. I don't think it's *Gone with the Wind*. Actually, I don't think *Gone with the Wind* is *Gone with the Wind*."

"F*** everybody."

"What am I, f***ing Kreskin?"

"I've been up and down [professionally] so many times that I feel as if I'm in a revolving door."

FACTS OF LIFE

ORIGIN: Born Cherilyn Sarkisian, May 20, 1946, El Centro, California.

FORMATIVE YEARS: High school dropout.

FAMILY PLANNING: Married Salvatore "Sonny" Phillip Bono (singer/musician), 1964; divorced 1974; married Gregory "Gregg" Lenoir Allman (musician), June 30, 1975; divorced 1978.

ROMANTIC INTERESTS: Warren Beatty (actor), David Geffen (entertainment mogul), Val Kilmer (actor), Richie Sambora (musician), Gene Simmons (musician), Sean Penn (actor), Robert Camilletti (bartender/bagel maker), Ray Liotta (actor).

SELECTED HITS (and Misses)

FILMS: *Wild on the Beach* (1965), *Chastity* (1969), *Come Back to the 5 and Dime, Jimmy Dean, Jimmy Dean* (1982), *Silkwood* (1983), *Mask* (1985), *The Witches*

of Eastwick (1987), *Moonstruck* (Oscar for Best Actress—1987), *Mermaids* (1990), *Faithful* (1995), *Tea with Mussolini* (1999).

TV SERiES: *The Sonny and Cher Comedy Show Hour* (1971–74, 1975–77), *Cher* (1975–76).

QUICKIE BIO

C her is living proof that you don't have to be blonde to do dumb things. When she was sixteen, the chisel-faced southern California brunette moved in with a twenty-eight-year-old aspiring record promoter/per-former/producer named Sonny Bono. Young Cher believed Sonny Bono when he told her he was a descendant of Napoleon. She also believed that Mt. Rushmore was a natural phenomenon. Copping a Carnaby Street-goes-Checkerboard Square look, the clean-cut hipsters scored hit records and modeled furry vests on America's most popular TV variety series in the early 1970s. From her perch atop the pop universe, Cher dumped Sonny and focused her energies on movies, plastic surgery, a Las Vegas act, and infomer-cials hawking Gothic home furnishings. Meanwhile, ex-husband Sonny was elected to Congress and died in 1998 when he skied into a tree. The beat goes on. Yeah, baby.

CHER DOES THE
DUMBEST THINGS

✪ "When I was four, my parents took me to see *Dumbo*," Cher confessed. "And I was never quite the same." Cher didn't want to miss any of the animated film, so she peed in her seat. Years later, Cher bragged, "I gave up everything for my art!"

✪ Cher claimed that she lost her virginity to actor Warren Beatty when she was sixteen and scoffed, "I wasn't the least bit satisfied!"

✪ In her early days as a backup singer, Cher showed up at a recording stu-dio one day. Piano player Leon Russell also arrived, drunk. Producer Phil Spector got angry at Leon and asked, "Leon did you ever hear of the word 'respect'?" Leon snarled, "Hey, Phil, have you ever heard of the word 'f*** you'?" "When I think back on it," Cher wrote years later, "those days were some of the happiest ones I can remember."

✪ In the midst of early Beatlemania, Cher took the name Bobbie Jo Mason and released a song entitled "Ringo, I Love You." Sonny told his wife to take the fake name because he thought the song was so stupid. DJs thought that Bobbie Jo Mason was really a gay guy who had a crush on Ringo.

✪ Sonny and Cher began hosting a weekly television variety series in 1971. Three years later the show (and the marriage) fell apart. In 1976, Cher teamed up with her estranged husband for another go at a TV series, but the program was canceled after only a few months. During a rehearsal for one of the last episodes of *The Sonny and Cher Comedy Hour,* Sonny delivered the line, "Mother Nature, what is the secret of life?" Cher ad-libbed, "Go f*** yourself." Cher found it difficult to cuddle up to Sonny when she was pregnant with someone else's child.

✪ That someone else was Gregg Allman, a musician with the Allman Brothers Band. Cher married Gregg soon after she divorced Sonny. Nine days later, Cher filed for divorce from the man she called "Gui Gui." Then they reconciled. Their union lasted until 1977, when Gregg passed out and fell face first into a plate of spaghetti at an awards banquet.

✪ When the press gave her a hard time about dating bartender/bagel maker Robert Camilletti (whom Cher nicknamed Mook), the brunette snipped, "I hate the phrase 'boy toy.' It's so demeaning." Later, she bought Camilletti a video game for his twenty-eighth birthday and giggled, "I bought a game boy for my bagel boy!"

✪ When Cher first split from Sonny, she celebrated her independence with her first tattoo—a flower and butterfly design spreading across the top of her butt. Cher later described the decoration as "pretty stupid."

✪ That didn't stop her from later getting at least five other tattoos on her arms, ankle, waist, and crotch. In addition, Cher altered her five-foot-seven inch body with a boob job, a tummy tuck, a nose job, a dental makeover, and a chemical facial peel. However, she vehemently denied that she had any ribs removed in the beautification process.

✪ Cher dissed her daughter Chastity when the girl announced that she was gay. "It must be tough having a beautiful mother like Cher and being named Chastity," veteran movie queen Ava Gardner observed. "I guess the only thing worse would be being beautiful and being named Slut."

✪ Cher described Republicans as "old, stupid, nerdy, bulls*** dressing, pinchy-face, golfing, bad-hair-day people." However, when her ex-husband Republican congressman Sonny Bono died in 1998, Cher jumped into the mourning spotlight. "I never stopped loving him," Cher sobbed. One of her associates asked in amazement, "Can everyone else have forgotten how much she hated his guts?"

- ⭐ After Sonny's death, Cher wondered, "How hard can dying be?" Then she viewed Sonny's corpse, and decided she really wanted to talk to him, though she hadn't spoken to him for the last two years of his life. She communicated with Sonny through spiritual medium James Van Praagh. Sonny's spirit advised Cher about her diet and her movie roles. Cher exclaimed, "I know it's Sonny's spirit because he's still trying to run my life."

- ⭐ Cher missed Sonny so much that she sued his estate in 1998 for $1.66 million in unpaid alimony.

- ⭐ Cher was fascinated by Armenia because, in her words, "it was the only place I'd ever been where everyone looked like me."

"I'm not afraid to look ridiculous," Cher confessed after she appeared at the 1986 Academy Awards ceremony in a Mohawk inspired Bob Mackie outfit. Cher later decided, "It was chic in a very bizarre way."
[photo courtesy of Bob Scott/Fotos International/Archive Photos]

Joan Collins

FACTS OF LIFE

ORIGIN: Born May 23, 1933, London, England.

FORMATIVE YEARS: Studied acting at the Royal Academy of Dramatic Arts, London, England.

FAMILY PLANNING: Married Maxwell Reed (actor), May 24, 1951; divorced 1956; married Anthony Newley (writer/composer), May 27, 1963; divorced 1971; married Ronald Kass (executive), March, 1972; divorced 1983; married Peter Holm (manager), October, 1985; divorced 1986.

ROMANTIC INTERESTS: Sydney Chaplin (son of the movie star), Arthur Loew Jr. (son of a movie mogul), Nicky Hilton Jr. (son of a hotel baron), Warren Beatty (actor), Robert Wagner (actor), Ryan O'Neal (actor).

SELECTED HITS (and Misses)

FILMS: *I Believe in You* (1953), *The Good Die Young* (1954), *Land of the Pharaohs* (1955), *The Virgin Queen* (1955), *The Girl in the Red Velvet Swing* (1955), *The Opposite Sex* (1956), *The Wayward Bus* (1957), *Island in the Sun* (1957), *Sea Wife* (1957), *The Bravados* (1958), *Seven Thieves* (1960), *Warning Shot* (1966), *Can Hieronymus Merkin Ever Forget Mercy Humppe and Find True Happiness?* (1969), *Empire of the Ants* (1977), *The Stud* (1978), *The Bitch* (1978), *Game for Vultures* (1979), *Sunburn* (1979), *Decadence* (1993), *In the Bleak Midwinter* (1995), *The Flintstones in Viva Rock Vegas* (1999), *The Clandestine Marriage* (1999).

TV SERIES: *Dynasty* (1981–89), *Pacific Palisades* (1997).

QUICKIE BIO

The daughter of a London talent agent, young Joan Collins was hailed as the "Global Glamour Girl" and the "Pouting Panther" in the 1950s, but watched her career fizzle in the 1960s as critics said she looked too much like Elizabeth Taylor. Collins recaptured the magic when she found her inner bitch as Alexis Carrington on TV's *Dynasty* (1981–89). According to novelist Jackie Collins, her sister Joan "always lived her life like a man." At least Joan could keep up with the boys. After all, she once spent an evening with Marlon Brando discussing the pros and cons of a "vomitorium"—a designated barfing area used by Romans during feasts.

JOAN COLLINS
DOES THE DUMBEST THINGS

✪ On her first date with older actor Maxwell Reed, the seventeen-year-old Collins was taken by Reed to his apartment, where he handed her a book of sex pictures and then drugged her. When Joan fell asleep, Reed had sex with her. After the fact, Max asked, "Did you like it?" she looked at him "dumbly." "*Like* it?" she wrote years later, "I *hated* it. . . . Were there actually women who *liked* this sort of thing? No wonder some of them got paid for it." She later married the British performer.

✪ At one point, Collins flew to Palm Springs to meet her boyfriend, actor Sydney Chaplin. However, he didn't pick her up at the airport. A furious Joan finally found him at a local bar with several friends. They were sampling the bar's inventory in alphabetical order. They had made it to vodka by the time Joan showed up. She yelled at Sydney, "F*** you, Sydney. F*** you. F*** you. F*** you. F*** you!" "And f*** you, too," Sydney responded as he keeled over. "Well, that will be the last time you will *ever* f*** me again, Sydney," Joan said. And it was.

✪ Collins's beau Arthur Loew Jr. visited her on location in Jamaica where she was making *Island in the Sun* (1957). One day a crew member asked "Where's Joan?" His buddy answered, "She's laying Loew."

✪ Collins broke up with Arthur Loew at a New Year's Eve party. He said, "You are a f***ing bore." She snapped back, "You are a boring f***."

✪ While filming in Japan, Joan went on a date with a man called Charles. He took her to a live sex show. A young girl took the stage and massaged herself. Then two men joined in the fun. She arched her back and bent her head to a ninety-degree angle. One man made love to her with "rabbit rapidity" while she pleasured the other. Charles put his hand on

Collins' thigh and breathed in her ear, "What do you think?" Collins mused, "I wonder if she can cook."

✪ "I think I'm pregnant," Joan Collins told her boyfriend Warren Beatty. "Pregnant?" asked Warren, who had given Collins an engagement ring. "How could that happen?" "The butler did it," Joan snapped, "or maybe it's an immaculate conception." Beatty later dumped her.

✪ Collins fell in love with producer George Englund, husband of actress Cloris Leachman. When Joan caught him fooling around, she was shocked. "He had lied to me," Collins snorted. "The bastard was cheating on me—with his wife!"

✪ Collins's second spouse was British actor/writer/composer Anthony Newley. After a few years of married life, Newley wrote a semi-autobiographical film entitled *Can Hieronymus Merkin Ever Forget Mercy Humppe and Find True Happiness?* (1969). Characters in the movie included Filigree Fondle, Trampolina Wham Bang, and Maidenhair Fern. Joan was cast as Polyester Poontang.

✪ Before her first nude scene on-camera, Collins drank a half bottle of brandy and put an X of bright blue duct tape on her nipples. During the scene, her Italian costar fell asleep. The director screamed, "You woman, he boy—ees beree beree beeg thrill for you." Collins described it as "squirm, squirm—wriggle, wriggle—pant, pant. . . ." The tape stuck to her costar's chest. "We were Siamese twins," Collins said.

✪ Joan's big breakthrough came with *The Stud* (1978), written by her sister Jackie. Then Joan starred in *The Bitch* (1978). The producer advertised the movie with an airplane trailing the banner, "Joan Collins Is *The Bitch.*"

✪ While slipping into her limo in London one night, Collins's wig came off. When a fan took pictures of the scene, Joan forked over five hundred dollars for the telltale negatives.

🐶 Visiting the magical duo Seigfried and Roy backstage, Collins tossed her $50,000 mink coat on the couch. One of the illusionists' white tigers hopped onto the couch and onto the mink. Joan tried to coax the cat off her fur, calling, "Here kitty kitty." The tiger didn't budge. So Collins gently tugged at the coat. The tiger let out a roar that sent a frightened Collins speeding across the room.

✪ In 1989, Collins arrived at a charity ball in Monaco only to discover that she wasn't seated at a celebrity table. "There's been some mistake," she screamed to the maitre d', "I'm Joan Collins. I'm very famous."

Kevin Costner

FACTS OF LIFE

ORIGIN: Born January 18, 1955, Lynwood, California.

FORMATIVE YEARS: Graduated with a degree in marketing from California State College at Fullerton.

FAMILY PLANNING: Married Cindy Silva (Snow White at Disneyland), 1978; divorced 1994; fathered a child by Bridget Rooney.

ROMANTIC INTERESTS: Angie Everhart (model), Courtney Cox (actress), Michelle Amaral (hula dancer), Mira Sorvino (actress), Joan Lunden (TV show host), Bridget Bloxom (model).

SELECTED HITS (and BIG Misses)

FILMS: *Sizzle Beach, USA* (1974—released in 1986), *Night Shift* (1982), *Testament* (1983), *Fandango* (1984), *Silverado* (1985), *The Untouchables* (1987), *No Way Out* (1987), *Bull Durham* (1988), *Field of Dreams* (1989), *Dances with Wolves* (Oscars for Best Director and Best Picture—1990),* *JFK* (1991), *Robin Hood: Prince of Thieves* (1991), *Waterworld* (1995), *Tin Cup* (1996), *The Postman* (1997),* *Message in a Bottle* (1999), *For Love of the Game* (1999) *Thirteen Days* (2000).

*Also directed by Costner.

QUICKIE BIO

Kevin Costner grew up in Los Angeles and modeled tuxedos as he worked his way up the show biz food chain. After appearing as a corpse in *The Big Chill* (1983), he started picking up parts with actual lines. Costner became a Hollywood heavyweight with hits like *Dances with Wolves* (1990). Then there were the major flops of *Waterworld* (1995) and *The Postman* (1997), the former a futuristic thriller about water, and the latter a futuristic thriller about mail delivery. The public came to think so little of Costner that a rock band distributed form letters begging the actor to retire. The missives began, "Dear Kevin, Hello my name is ____ and I urge you to stop making and/or appearing in films. All the movies you have been in have sucked. You have sucked in them."

KEVIN COSTNER DOES THE DUMBEST THINGS

✪ Costner quit his first "real" job just thirty days after starting. He came home and told his wife Cindy that he was going to be an actor and a writer. She tossed a pile of papers at him and screamed, "A writer? But you can't even spell."

✪ Kevin tried to buy the rights to a 1974 movie called *Malibu Hot Summers* (later *Sizzle Beach, USA*). The film featured Kevin in a shirtless love scene. Costner not only failed to get the rights, but the producers eventually cut the old scene with Kevin into a new movie.

✪ While staying at a Washington, DC, hotel, Costner paid a room service waiter $300 to keep his suite stocked with Twinkies, Ding Dongs, and Ho Hos.

✪ Inspired by the men's movement detailed in the book *Iron John* (1990) by Robert Bly, Costner took a trip with ten male friends to the Wyoming woods. The group lived off the land, beat drums, primal screamed, and danced around naked in order to feel more like guys.

✪ After seeing a photo of model Angie Everhart in a magazine, the agog Costner contacted her New York agency and found she was on a shoot in Mexico. He then phoned her for a date. She agreed. So he hired a private plane, loaded it with flowers, and sent the plane to Mexico to fly her back to Los Angeles. Then Kevin appeared and took her to dinner at an exclusive eatery. The cost of the date? $15,000. Afterward, Everhart chose to spend the night with friends.

✪ During the making of the golfing story *Tin Cup* (1996), Costner hit on a cute blonde in a local bar. When he left briefly to relieve himself, costar Don Johnson moved in on her. Johnson and Costner got into an argument, and the woman got up and left.

✪ At the editing phase of *Robin Hood: Prince of Thieves* (1991), the director of photography was kept out of the editing room because he had cut out too many of Kevin's close-ups.

"I never got over being short," Kevin Costner moaned.
(photo courtesy of Frank Edwards/Fotos International/Archive Photos)

★ Like other movie stars, Costner complained about the press invading his private life. But after an employee at a British nightclub blabbed to the press that Kevin had "made love with such passion that he brought tears to [my] eyes," Costner arranged for close-ups of himself to appear in the British tabloids.

★ Kevin had such a reputation for picking up women in Aspen, Colorado, that he earned the nickname "Dances with Foxes." Eventually, he got so annoyed by press reports of his womanizing that he ordered employees, and even friends, to sign a strict confidentiality agreement which barred them from discussing his love life.

★ In Madonna's documentary *Truth Or Dare* (1991), Costner is shown greeting the star backstage after one of her concerts. Kevin told Madonna that he thought her sex-laden show was "neat." Right after Costner left, the material girl demonstrated her feelings for him by putting her fingers down her throat and making a gagging sound.

★ During the making of *Message in a Bottle* (1999), Kevin tried again and again on-camera to put on a sport coat without getting his arm caught in the sleeve. Costner finally threw the sport coat to the ground and shouted, "You're fired!"

Joan Crawford

FACTS OF LIFE (and Death)

ORIGIN: Born Lucille Fay Le Sueur, March, 23 1904, San Antonio, Texas; died May 10, 1977, New York City, New York.

FAMILY PLANNING: Married James Welton (musician), 1924; divorced 1925; married Douglas Fairbanks Jr. (actor), June 3, 1929; divorced 1933; married Franchot Tone (actor), October 11, 1935; divorced 1940; married Phillip Terry (actor), July 21, 1942; divorced 1946; married Alfred Steele (businessman), May 10, 1955; widowed 1959.

ROMANTIC INTERESTS: Howard Hughes (producer), Clark Gable (actor), Jackie Cooper (actor), Yul Brynner (actor).

SELECTED HITS (and Misses)

FILMS: *Pretty Ladies* (1925), *The Unknown* (1927), *Our Dancing Daughters* (1928), *Our Modern Maidens* (1929), *Our Blushing Brides* (1930), *This Modern Age* (1931), *Letty Lynton* (1932), *Grand Hotel* (1932), *Rain* (1932), *Dancing Lady* (1933), *Sadie McKee* (1934), *The Gorgeous Hussy* (1936), *The Last of Mrs. Cheyney* (1937), *The Women* (1939), *Strange Cargo* (1940), *A Woman's Face* (1941), *Above Suspicion* (1943), *Mildred Pierce* (Oscar for Best Actress—1945), *Humoresque* (1946), *Possessed* (1947), *Flamingo Road* (1949), *Goodbye, My Fancy* (1951), *Sudden Fear* (1952), *Johnny Guitar* (1954), *Queen Bee* (1955), *Autumn Leaves* (1956), *The Best of Everything* (1959), *What Ever Happened to Baby Jane?* (1962), *Strait-Jacket* (1964), *I Saw What You Did* (1965), *Berserk* (1967), *Trog* (1970).

QUICKIE BIO

Hollywood executives thought the name Le Sueur sounded like sewer, so they held a nationwide contest to name the new star of the silent screen. The winning choice was Joan Crawford. For the next half century, Joan thrived as a Hollywood luminary, living her entire life as if it were on-screen. Her adopted daughter Christina eventually demonized her mother in the tell-all book (1978) and screen biography *Mommie Dearest* (1981). However, Joan was truly one of the lucky ones whose star never completely faded. "Too many actresses today are little more than tramps and tarts," sniffed aging celebrity Joan. Perhaps she forgot that she, herself, was rumored to have made her movie debut dancing the Charleston nude and supposedly once performed in a stag film entitled *The Casting Couch*.

JOAN CRAWFORD
DOES THE DUMBEST THINGS

⭐ Joan stripped naked in front of the producer in order to get the lead role in *Our Dancing Daughters* (1928). When the decision maker told Joan that the director was in charge of casting, Joan went to his office, repeated her performance, and got the part.

⭐ While auditioning for *Torch Song* (1953), a movie in which the veteran star donned black face, the nearly fifty-year-old Joan Crawford paraded naked before director Charles Walters. When asked if she herself had ever gone the way of the casting couch, Joan snapped, "Well, it sure beat the hard, cold floor."

⭐ Like Marlene Dietrich would do, Crawford had her back teeth removed to achieve that sunken cheek look.

💬 "They went to heaven" was her way of talking about sexual intercourse. She called female breasts "ninny pies."

⭐ Joan once gave actor Henry Fonda a jockstrap decorated with rhinestones, gold sequins, and red beads.

⭐ Thirty-something Joan had a brief affair with seventeen-year-old actor Jackie Cooper. "She would bathe me, powder me, cologne me," Cooper explained. "Then she would do it all over again."

 Crawford was rumored to have had lesbian affairs with a number of women including wide-mouth comedian Martha Raye, later of denture advertising fame. Joan's maid was so worried about her sexually active boss that she locked her bedroom at night.

✪ In the early 1940s, Joan concluded that raising kids would help her fading screen image. So she decided to adopt a few, even though she wasn't married at the time. Since it was illegal then for a single woman to adopt a baby in California, Joan reportedly contacted her friend, mob boss Meyer Lansky. Sure enough, Lansky arranged for her to adopt a daughter on the black market. First Joan called her Joan Crawford Jr., then changed the youngster's name to Christina Crawford.

✪ Meyer Lansky supposedly helped Joan adopt baby number two, a boy rechristened Christopher Crawford. Things got complicated when a woman recognized "Christopher Crawford" as having the same birth date as the baby taken from her. The woman showed up at the Crawford home demanding—and getting—her baby back. Joan, then married to actor Phillip Terry, ordered another baby boy and named him Phillip Terry Jr. When Joan and Phillip divorced, Joan changed Junior's name to . . . Christopher Crawford.

✪ Not satisfied with Christina and Christopher, Crawford adopted two more babies through her underworld connections. She called these "the twins," though they were not twins and were not even born on the same day.

✪ Joan forced Christina and her siblings to refer to her as Mommie dearest. Mommie dearest once called the children out in their nightclothes to chop down trees. On another night, Christina awoke to find Mommie dearest tearing through her closet. Joan brandished a closet hanger in Christina's terrified face and screamed, "No wire hangers!"

✪ For Christopher, Mommie dearest devised a particularly torturous device she called a "sleep safe." It was a sort of harness that strapped her son to his bed. Sister Christina risked being beaten when she freed her brother in order to let him go pee.

✪ Anxious to blot out her impoverished past, Joan stayed away from her own mother. Finally, Crawford let her mom see her grandchildren, but only through a screen door.

✪ Crawford was equally uncharitable to her brother Hal. When the would-be actor came around once too often asking for money, Joan had him committed to a mental institution.

✪ On a date with actor Kirk Douglas, Joan Crawford seduced him by taking off her dress as soon as they returned to her Brentwood (California) home. They had sex on the floor. Then Joan took him upstairs to check on Christina and Christopher. After Kirk saw the children "safely" strapped to their beds he recalled, "I got out fast."

✪ When Joan's son Christopher brought his newborn daughter to see her famous grandmother, Granny Joan sneered, "It doesn't look like you. It's probably a bastard."

✪ Crawford always rode in her limousine to photo sessions on the MGM lot, even though the portrait studio was just a few yards from her dressing room. When the limo driver didn't show up one day, Crawford canceled the session. When the photographer asked her why she didn't just walk over, Crawford explained, "It's in my contract that I have a limousine. . . ."

✪ In her last feature film, *Trog* (1970), Joan played opposite a prehistoric creature onscreen and shared beauty tips with a reporter off-camera. "Dump a tray of ice in your wash basin and splash ice water on your bazooms," Joan suggested. "It keeps them firm."

✪ Just hours after the star's death in 1977, daughter Christina Crawford received a call from a longtime Joan fan. The fan expressed deep sorrow, explained that the news crews were coming to his place to film his Crawford clothing collection, and, by the way, might he have Miss Crawford's dog?

Bette Davis

FACTS OF LIFE (and Death)

ORIGIN: Born Ruth Elizabeth Davis, April 5, 1908, Lowell, Massachusetts; died October 6, 1989, Paris, France.

FORMATIVE YEARS: Studied drama at John Murray Anderson's Dramatic School in New York City, but was fired from her first acting job.

FAMILY PLANNING: Married Harmon Nelson Jr. (trumpeter), August 18, 1932; divorced 1939; married Arthur Farnsworth (hotelier), December 31, 1940; widowed 1943; married William Sherry (boxer), November 30, 1945; divorced 1950; married Gary Merrill (actor), July 28, 1950; divorced 1960. An unsatisfied Bette recalled, "None of my four husbands was ever man enough to become Mr. Bette Davis."

ROMANTIC INTERESTS: Howard Hughes (producer), Franchot Tone (actor), Henry Fonda (actor), George Brent (actor), Gig Young (actor), Johnny Mercer (songwriter), Anatole Litvak (director).

SELECTED HITS (and Misses)

FILMS: *Bad Sister* (1931), *Waterloo Bridge* (1931), *The Man Who Played God* (1932), *The Cabin in the Cotton* (1932), *The Working Man* (1933), *Of Human Bondage* (1934), *Dangerous* (Oscar for Best Actress—1935), *The Petrified Forest* (1936), *That Certain Woman* (1937), *It's Love I'm After* (1937), *Jezebel* (Oscar for Best Actress—1938), *Dark Victory* (1938), *The Old Maid* (1939), *The Private Lives*

of *Elizabeth and Essex* (1939), *The Letter* (1940), *The Great Lie* (1941), *The Little Foxes* (1941), *The Man Who Came to Dinner* (1941), *Now, Voyager* (1942), *Mr. Skeffington* (1944), *The Corn Is Green* (1945), *A Stolen Life* (1946), *Beyond the Forest* (1949), *All About Eve* (1950), *Payment on Demand* (1951), *The Star* (1952), *The Virgin Queen* (1955), *The Catered Affair* (1956), *A Pocketful of Miracles* (1961), *What Ever Happened to Baby Jane?* (1962), *Hush . . . Hush Sweet Charlotte* (1964), *The Nanny* (1965), *The Anniversary* (1968), *Bunny O'Hare* (1971), *Burnt Offerings* (1976), *Death on the Nile* (1978), *The Watcher in the Woods* (1980), *The Whales of August* (1987), *Wicked Stepmother* (1990—released after her death).

QUICKIE BIO

With eyes so buggy they wrote a song about them, Bette Davis was hardly a classic Hollywood beauty. In fact, upon arriving in Tinseltown, the studio rep sent to greet her left the passenger train station because he didn't see anyone who looked like a star. Despite the inauspicious beginning, Davis enjoyed six decades of stardom and a reputation as a ruthless heartbreaker. One of Davis's rivals described her as "a greedy little girl at a party table who had to sample other women's cupcakes." Bette knew better. "Until you're known in my profession as a monster," she declared, "you're not a star."

BETTE DAVIS
DOES THE DUMBEST THINGS

⭐ Bette's temperamental disposition manifested itself in a number of ways. When she was performing in a play, the producer received a call from Davis's sister Bobbi, saying that Bette was ill. When asked if Bette had seen a doctor, Bobbi replied that her sibling was "too sick to see a doctor."

⭐ When Bette Davis filed for divorce from William Grant Sherry in 1950, she told everyone—except him! Davis publicly ridiculed her ignorant ex by entertaining friends with a comic reading of a heartfelt letter in which he expressed his love and desire to reconcile.

⭐ Davis carried on a secret love affair with her *All About Eve* (1950) costar Gary Merrill until an inebriated Merrill publicly declared his passion for Bette—in front of his then wife. The irate woman filed for divorce the next day.

⭐ "We had tremendous fights," Bette recalled about her stormy relationship with Merrill. "He used his fists more than his mouth." They did a lot of shouting too. "You haven't laid me in years," Bette screamed at

Merrill. "The only time you touch me is when you beat me up." "What are you bitching about?" Merrill yelled back. "Getting slapped around is the only thing you enjoy. . . ."

✪ Bette told Gary Merrill that one time during her affair with billionaire weirdo producer Howard Hughes they consummated their passion on a bed of gardenias. Merrill wasn't impressed. "He f***ed every two-bit twat in Hollywood and you're proud of holding out for ten bucks worth of gardenias?"

✪ Bette also claimed that Howard Hughes liked to talk obscenely, close his eyes, and pretend she was a man while she was, um, entertaining him.

✪ After Douglas Fairbanks Jr. met Bette Davis, he thrust his hand down her blouse and informed her she should use ice cubes to keep her nipples hard "the way Joan Crawford does."

✪ Bette knew that Joan Crawford always had affairs with her movie directors so that she would get better exposure on-camera. Davis wouldn't commit to costarring with Crawford in *What Ever Happened to Baby Jane?* (1962) until she talked with director Robert Aldrich. Davis asked, "Have you ever slept with Miss Crawford?" "No," the director answered. Davis took the part. However, the filmmaker was lying. Bette later claimed that Joan Crawford "slept with every male star at MGM except Lassie."

✪ For the dramatic ending of *What Ever Happened to Baby Jane?*, Joan's character died on the beach. Joan chose a particularly pointy pair of falsies for the scene. Bette bellowed, "When a woman lies on her back, her bosoms do not stand straight up!"

✪ Later in the scene, Bette fell on top of the prone Joan. Bette claimed it knocked the breath out of her. "It was like falling on two footballs," she griped. Davis later said about costarring with Joan Crawford, "The scenes I most enjoyed were the ones where I had to beat the crap out of her!"

✪ "One area of life Joan should never have gotten into was children," Bette later lectured. "She bought them. . . . Joan was the perfect mother in front of the public but not behind the front door. She wanted this image that wasn't meant for her. I've never behaved like that—Well, I doubt that my children will write a book." Bette was wrong. Her daughter did write a book about how bad a mother she was. The book was called *My Mother's Keeper* (1985).

The aging Davis became so unpredictable that she dropped a cigarette on the floor and set her apartment on fire. When her secretary located the cigarette, the star observed, "Oh, that's where it went."

⭐ Bette Davis star-tripped to the end. During the filming of *The Whales of August* (1987), her co-lead, the legendary Lillian Gish (1899–1993), had a hearing problem and was prompted through a headset. The cast and crew were most cooperative, but Bette fussed incessantly. "You try working with a deaf mute," Davis complained. Later, the seventy-nine year old Betty wryly observed, "That bitch has been around forever, you know."

Sammy Davis Jr.

FACTS OF LIFE (and Death)

ORIGIN: Born December 8, 1925, Harlem, New York; died May 16, 1990, Beverly Hills, California.

FORMATIVE YEARS: "Haven't spent a single day in school in my whole life," Sammy claimed.

FAMILY PLANNING: Married Loray White (dancer), January 10, 1958; divorced 1959; married May Britt (actress), November 13, 1960; divorced 1968; married Altovise Gore (showgirl), May 11, 1970.

ROMANTIC INTERESTS: Kim Novak (actress), Romy Schneider (actress).

SELECTED HITS (and Misses)

FILMS: *Anna Lucasta* (1958), *Porgy and Bess* (1959), *Ocean's Eleven* (1960), *Sergeants Three* (1962), *Convicts Four* (1962), *Robin and the Seven Hoods* (1964), *The Threepenny Opera* (1965), *Salt and Pepper* (1968), *Sweet Charity* (1968), *One More Time* (1970), *Stop the World—I Want to Get Off* (1978), *The Cannonball Run* (1981), *Cannonball Run II* (1984), *Moon over Parador* (1988), *Tap* (1989).

TV SERIES: *The Sammy Davis Jr. Show* (1966).

QUICKIE BIO

Billed as "the greatest entertainer in the world," Sammy Davis Jr. was one of the coolest cats ever to hit the big screen. Sammy began his stage career at the age of one, became a full-time professional song and dance man at age three, ran into some "prejudiced cats" in the Army who busted his nose twice, played the vaudeville circuit, and finally hit it big at Ciro's nightclub in Hollywood in 1951. Frank Sinatra adopted Sammy as the Rat Pack's black guy. For much of the next three decades, Sammy sang and danced while Frank, Dean Martin, and Peter Lawford playfully made fun of him. With his trademark cigarette and tux, Sammy became a fixture in the Las Vegas firmament, even after he lost an eye in a car wreck. The women all knew him as "the Carpenter" because he "nailed every girl he met." That's entertainment, baby. You dig?

SAMMY DAVIS JR.
DOES THE DUMBEST THINGS

⭐ Sammy's dad and uncle, both entertainers, took him on the road when he was an infant. He was so good in the act that they never let him attend school. When child welfare authorities came by, they glued whiskers to Sammy's face and insisted he was a midget.

⭐ During the Rat Pack years, Davis claimed that "sex wasn't the point." Confessed Sammy, "Two or three people would get into bed with you and you'd fall asleep."

⭐ Frank Sinatra loved to tease his little, black buddy. Once, when Sammy started to sing "What kind of fool am I . . .", Frank yelled from offstage, "Keep smiling so they can see you, Smokey." Another funny Sinatra line was, "Hurry up, Sam, the watermelon's getting warm."

⭐ Sammy told tough guy Sam Giancana that he shouldn't force movie star Shirley MacLaine to eat spaghetti if she was on a diet. Giancana belted Davis in the stomach and threw cherry bombs under his chair.

⭐ The black press accused Sammy of having an affair with blonde bombshell screen-star Kim Novak. Sammy was furious at first, then went ahead and had a relationship with her. Kim's studio boss, Harry Cohn, was so upset by the interracial affair that he hired mobsters who threatened to put out Sammy's good eye. Within twenty-four hours, Sammy announced his marriage to African-American dancer Loray White.

 Davis liked to wear three different colognes—Lactopoine, Hermes, and Eau Savage—all at the same time.

⭐ In the late 1960s, Sammy got into a hippie groove. He wore Nehru jackets and beads. One night, he ate pot brownies and walked out on stage. Davis sang one song, then thanked the crowd and walked off. He spaced out during the entire performance.

"You don't hug the President of the United States," explained Sammy after he gave President Richard Nixon a big hug at the 1972 Republican National Convention in Miami, Florida. "That's bad taste."

⭐ The multi-talented Davis was enjoying the Hollywood high life when he got into a car wreck and lost his left eye. A short time later, he tried to commit suicide by driving his car off a cliff. When that didn't work, he converted to Judaism. After his conversion, Sammy always referred to God as "The Cat Upstairs," and claimed that his spiritual home was Las Vegas.

⭐ After Sammy married Swedish actress May Britt, the newlyweds made their Hollywood social debut at a dinner hosted by comedian Jack Benny. Sammy and May wore matching tuxedo hot pants. Television comedian Milton Berle cracked, "How did an old Jew like you get such a gorgeous young wife?"

⭐ "I've never even spent a whole night in bed with a woman. Never," Sammy confessed to his spouse May Britt. "When it was time to sleep, either they'd go home or I'd fall asleep on the couch or the floor."

⭐ Sex goddess–star Ava Gardner once drove up to Harlem to see Sammy perform. Later that night, Davis donned a Santa Claus suit and went to Gardner's hotel suite. Sammy explained, "I'm proud to be black, but I don't want my blackness to be a burden to me."

⭐ When *Roots* author Alex Haley asked Sammy, "Have you ever wished you weren't Negro?" Davis answered, "Well, not professionally, anyway."

⭐ "Nobody enjoys luxuries more than I do," Sammy said in the mid 1960s, when his expenses were running about $17,000 per week. "I've got a limousine that costs $25,000 with all the fixtures. I sit there, I press a button, a television comes up. Ain't no other pleasure in the world like that for me." After his death in 1990, Sammy's widow found that her husband's estate was five million dollars in debt. Here come da judge!

James Dean

FACTS OF LIFE (and Death)

ORIGIN: Born James Byron Dean, February 8, 1931, Marion, Indiana; died September 30, 1955, in a car accident near Cholame, California.

FORMATIVE YEARS: Attended Santa Monica (California) Junior College and UCLA in Los Angeles.

FAMILY PLANNING: He was just too neurotic.

ROMANTIC INTERESTS: Elizabeth McPherson (gym teacher), Elizabeth Sherican (dancer), Rogers Brackett (director), Lilli Kardell (actress), Pier Angeli (actress).

SELECTED HITS (and Misses)

FILMS: *Has Anybody Seen My Gal?* (1952), *Trouble Along the Way* (1953), *East of Eden* (1955), *Rebel without a Cause* (1955), *Giant* (1956).

QUICKIE BIO

The rebel James Dean lived weird and died young. Rude, crude, and moody, Dean grew up mostly in Los Angeles, where he studied drama and entertained his classmates by sculpting anatomically correct phallic candle holders. He played bit parts on TV and tested stunts for game shows before impressing the industry with his mumbling style in the Broadway play *The Immoralist* (1954). Though he only starred in three feature films (one of which was released after his death), Dean, like Elvis Presley, has become posthumously popular. Thousands of fans visit his grave site every year even though he's been dead for decades. One devoted fan has dedicated herself to wiping the lipstick off Dean's gravestone.

JAMES DEAN
DOES THE DUMBEST THINGS

★ Dean's early days in Hollywood were not too shabby after he moved in with "sugar daddy" Rogers Brackett, a TV director with a fancy Hollywood home. Dean reportedly explained, "He said we could have twin beds."

★ One night, Dean's girlfriend, Arleen Sacks, invited him over for an "orgy." The boys and girls took off their shirts and cuddled under a blanket until Dean started to play with himself. The girlfriend observed this action and said, "This is not what I wanted to happen."

★ When Dean started going with actress Lilli Kordell, the two wore matching outfits and had their hair cut the same way.

★ James Dean liked to hang around a rough Hollywood bar called "The Club." When he was drunk and sexed up, he would ask his pals to snuff out cigarettes on his chest. His buddies obliged, and James earned the nickname "The Human Ashtray."

★ Uncle Sam came calling and James Dean went balling. He told the Selective Service that he was homosexual. When gossip columnist Hedda Hopper asked Dean how he avoided the draft, he said, "I kissed the medic."

★ When the rebel actor was at the Warner Bros. studio cafeteria, he spit at the framed photos of legendary movie stars James Cagney, Paul Muni, and Humphrey Bogart. When the studio put a picture of James Dean on the celebrity wall, Dean tore it into little pieces and screamed, "Don't ever put my f***ing picture in here! Nobody owns me!"

★ Dean once sat in the Warner Bros. cafeteria pouring spoonful after spoonful of sugar into his coffee. When the cup was full of sugar, he left.

★ Dean was more than ill-behaved and rude, he was irresponsible. He stuffed money into his mattress, let his sex life interfere with filming mooched off his friends rather than rent his own apartment.

★ Dean once called up a friend in the middle of the night and invited him over. When the man arrived, he found a drunk James Dean with a towel wrapped around his head entertaining a one-legged girl while he talked on the phone.

★ Dean dated Italian import Pier Angeli and called her "Miss Pizza." When the film actress married singer/actor Vic Damone in November 1954, Dean drove his motorcycle to the church and sat outside during the ceremony, revving the engine.

⭐ On the first day of shooting *Rebel without a Cause* (1955), Dean tried out his sophisticated method-acting techniques. When someone on the set announced, "Quiet, we're going to shoot now," James curled up into the fetal position, and gave a soft whistle. When the director said, "Action!" Dean yelled out a swear word, stood up, and went to work. Jim Backus, his costar, burst out laughing.

⭐ On the set of *Rebel without a Cause,* Dean stayed in character between scenes, scratching his crotch. There was a more precise reason he was itching: James Dean had contracted a nasty case of crabs.

⭐ At a Hollywood dinner party, James picked up the steak he had been served and tossed it out the window.

⭐ Dean once tried to avoid a journalist by pretending he was deaf.

⭐ James starred in a commercial for the National Highway Committee with fellow actor Gig Young. Dean's last line of dialogue was, "And, remember, drive safely because the life you save might be . . . mine." After he died in a car crash, officials exhibited the wreck of his Spyder Porsche to encourage safe driving.

⭐ Numerous young women killed themselves after Dean died, and continued to do so as late as 1965. At one time, a group calling itself the James Dean Death Club held a race like the one in *Rebel without a Cause.* Two young men died in the ensuing crash.

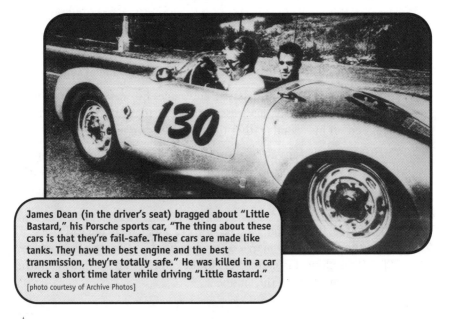

James Dean (in the driver's seat) bragged about "Little Bastard," his Porsche sports car, "The thing about these cars is that they're fail-safe. These cars are made like tanks. They have the best engine and the best transmission, they're totally safe." He was killed in a car wreck a short time later while driving "Little Bastard."
[photo courtesy of Archive Photos]

Johnny Depp

FACTS OF LIFE

ORIGIN: Born John Christopher Depp III, June 9, 1963, Owensboro, Kentucky.

FORMATIVE YEARS: Claims to have graduated from Mirimar High School, Mirimar, Florida. Later took acting lessons at the Loft Studio in Los Angeles.

FAMILY PLANNING: Married Lori Ann Allison (makeup artist), 1983; divorced 1985.

ROMANTIC INTERESTS: Winona Ryder (actress), Kate Moss (supermodel), Sherilyn Fenn (actress), Jennifer Grey (actress), Tally Chanel (actress), Vanessa Paradis (singer and mother of his child).

SELECTED HITS (and Misses)

FILMS: *A Nightmare on Elm Street* (1984), *Private Resort* (1985), *Cry-Baby* (1990), *Edward Scissorhands* (1990), *Arizona Dreamer* (1991—released in 1993), *Benny & Joon* (1993), *What's Eating Gilbert Grape?* (1993), *Ed Wood* (1994), *Nick of Time* (1995), *Don Juan DeMarco* (1995), *Dead Man* (1996), *The Brave* (1997),* *Fear and Loathing in Las Vegas* (1998), *The Astronaut's Wife* (1999), *The Source* (documentary, 1999), *Sleepy Hollow* (1999), *The Ninth Gate* (1999).

TV SERIES: *21 Jump Street* (1987–90)

*Also directed by Depp.

QUICKIE BIO

When his middle-class parents divorced, Johnny Depp fell under the spell of his fundamentalist-preaching uncle and started to play the electric guitar. He moved to Los Angeles to be a rock star, and eventually found an agent. One audition later, Depp was on his way to becoming a movie star. He became a teen idol on TV's *21 Jump Street* and did interviews for (in his words), *"Sixteen! Teen Beat! Teen Dream! Teen Poop! Teen P***! Teen S***!"* After the show's run, Depp returned to the silver screen, and became part owner of the infamous Viper Room in Los Angeles, the club in front of which River Phoenix died in 1993. Depp is working presently to expand the club's franchise—perhaps as a combination bar/funeral parlor?

JOHNNY DEPP
DOES THE DUMBEST THINGS

✪ "I would love to buy Bela Lugosi's old house," Depp said. "Or Errol Flynn's. Or Charlie Chaplin's. I want some old, depressing history to call my own. Plus, I love the idea of a view." Depp did buy Bela Lugosi's house and moved in with his collection of insects and guns.

✪ As a result of his tenure on TV's *21 Jump Street* in the late 1980s, Depp's teen-heartthrob stock went through the roof. Johnny, however, quickly began to loathe the series and intentionally became a jerk in hopes of getting fired. He once suggested that his TV series character (Tom Hanson) had become obsessed with peanut butter. Depp was never fired, but he was never happy. "The only thing I have in common with Tom Hanson is that we look alike," he whined.

✪ To protest that fact that no one had cleaned up his *21 Jump Street* trailer, the young star set fire to his underwear on the set.

✪ Johnny's actress-girlfriend Winona Ryder snapped some ultra-risqué pics of him. They took the photos to a one-hour film processor, thinking that no one would see them because machines did all the processing. However, when the couple returned for their pics, the teenager working the drive-thru window told the actor, "I loved your pictures."

✪ To celebrate his love for sweetheart Winona Ryder, Depp had "Winona Forever" tattooed on his arm. When the two broke up, he changed the tattoo to "Wino Forever."

✪ Johnny cuts himself on his arm to mark memorable occasions in his life. He explains, "In a way, your body is a journal and the scars are sort of entries in it."

✪ Depp believes in ghosts and insists that he has been visited by them at various times in his life. When he stayed in the room where famed gay English writer Oscar Wilde died, he said of the experience, "I was a little paranoid that I might be buggered by his ghost at 4:00 A.M."

✪ Johnny was insulted when someone suggested that he was fixated on white women. "I ain't f***ing white, that's for sure," Depp snarled. "Kate [Moss] is definitely not. She's about the furthest thing from white there is. She's got that high-water booty."

✪ In September 1994, Depp reportedly trashed his $2,200-a-night Presidential suite at New York's Mark Hotel. He offered to pay for the damages on the spot, but when he refused to check out, he was arrested. Johnny spent the night in three different jail cells and was mobbed by women cops at all three locations. Oddly enough, the hotel guest who first complained about Depp was none other than musician Roger Daltrey of The Who, the band that authored the unofficial handbook on methods of hotel room destruction.

✪ Tired of talking about the incident, Depp began telling inquirers that the hotel damage was caused by animals running amok in the room. First it was a dachshund. Then it was an armadillo. Then it was a cockroach the size of a baseball. "I was chasing a huge rat in the hotel room and I just kept swatting at it," Johnny said. "I couldn't catch it and it just jumped out the window."

✪ Asked by a magazine interviewer why he trashed a hotel room, Depp said he became extremely upset when he noticed that someone had written an unfriendly transcription inside his copy of the autobiography of Marlon Brando. According to Depp, it read, "F*** you, Johnny Depp. You're an a**hole." However, a witness alleged that Depp's girlfriend, supermodel Kate Moss, may have started the ruckus when she commented, "You know what your problem is . . ." and reportedly made reference to his supposedly undersized willy.

✪ At a chic London hangout, a photographer accidentally picked up the wrong drink at the bar—one that belonged to Depp. The picture-taker soon found both of his ears in Johnny's grasp and his head being forced to the floor. The man responded by informing Depp that this "was not the customary way of greeting people in England."

✪ Johnny had to dress in drag for the title role in *Ed Wood* (1994). Director Tim Burton was a bit nervous until he saw his star; "He looks great in women's clothes," a relieved Burton admitted. Costume designer Colleen Atwood had a similar fear and reaction. "The first time we put him in angora we were saying, 'God, he looks beautiful.'"

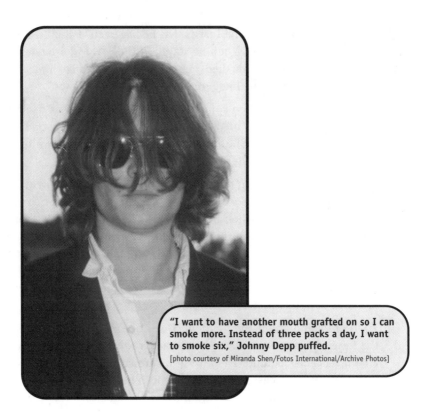

"I want to have another mouth grafted on so I can smoke more. Instead of three packs a day, I want to smoke six," Johnny Depp puffed.
[photo courtesy of Miranda Shen/Fotos International/Archive Photos]

⭐ It may have been Depp's cross-dressing that attracted the attention of a crazed transvestite who claimed to be married to the movie star. The disturbed fan telephoned Depp's Viper Room nightclub in Los Angeles and told the staff that he was "Johnny's wife." He also announced that he was flying into town and wanted Johnny to meet him at the airport. When the individual arrived at the club by taxi, the police hauled him away. Another Depp fan stalked the actor and claimed that he was Edward Scissorhands. Depp nonchalantly commented, "I just attract a lot of oddness."

⭐ As Johnny escorted his pregnant girlfriend Vanessa Paradis into a fancy London restaurant, he snarled at onlookers, "There won't be any pictures tonight or there'll be a fight." When Depp and Paradis came out, there were pictures, and there was a fight. Depp swung a club at photographers screaming, "I'll f***ing kill you!" What was Depp doing in London? Working on a film called *Sleepy Hollow* (1999).

 On an airplane flight to Vancouver, Johnny shouted out, "I f*** animals!" An accountant seated next to him, leaned over and asked, "What kind?"

Marlene Dietrich

FACTS OF LIFE (and Death)

BORN: Marie Magdelene Dietrich, December 27, 1901, Schoneberg, Germany; died May 6, 1992, Paris, France.

FAMILY PLANNING: Married Rudolf Sieber (casting director), May 17, 1923; widowed 1976.

ROMANTIC INTERESTS: Josef von Sternberg (director), Gary Cooper (actor), Maurice Chevalier (actor), Mercedes De Acosta (actress), Douglas Fairbanks Jr. (actor), Jimmy Stewart (actor), Jean Gabin (actor), Edith Piaf (singer), Colette (writer), John Wayne (actor), Gen. James Gavin (U.S. Army general), Gen. George S. Patton (U.S. Army general), Edward R. Murrow (newsman), Orson Welles (actor), Fritz Lang (director), Frank Sinatra (actor), Burt Bacharach (musician).

SELECTED HITS (and Misses)

FILMS: *The Tragedy of Love* (1923), *Café Electric* (1927), *The Blue Angel* (1930), *Morocco* (1930), *Dishonored* (1931), *Shanghai Express* (1932), *The Scarlet Empress* (1934), *The Devil Is a Woman* (1935), *Desire* (1936), *Angel* (1937), *Destry Rides Again* (1939), *Seven Sinners* (1940), *The Flame of New Orleans* (1941), *Manpower* (1941), *The Spoilers* (1942), *Follow the Boys* (1944), *Kismet* (1944), *Golden*

Earrings (1947), *A Foreign Affair* (1948), *Stage Fright* (1950), *Rancho Notorious* (1952), *Witness for the Prosecution* (1958), *Touch of Evil* (1958), *Judgment at Nuremberg* (1961), *Paris When It Sizzles* (1964), *Just a Gigolo* (1979).

QUICKIE BIO

Fifteen-year-old Marlene Dietrich was so stunning that her violin teacher was dismissed for having an affair with her. Marlene broke into show business as a cabaret singer in Germany, and gained attention by playing a musical saw while showing off her underwear. She was discovered (and bedded) by director Josef von Sternberg and became the essence of Berlin transsexual decadence before migrating to Hollywood in 1930. When Adolf Hitler requested that she return to Germany, Marlene refused, became an American citizen, and later hit it big in Las Vegas as a chanteuse. Though she had dozens of male and female lovers, she described sex as "an inescapable burden that women had to endure." Dietrich endured it for decades.

MARLENE DIETRICH DOES THE DUMBEST THINGS

✪ In 1929, director Josef von Sternberg was casting *The Blue Angel* in Berlin. Future Nazi propaganda filmmaker Leni Riefenstahl competed for the key lead part with Dietrich. Riefenstahl saw her rival sitting with some young actresses. Leni recalled that Marlene said loudly, "Why must we always have beautiful bosoms? Why can't they hang a little?" Then she lifted up one of her breasts and played with it.

✪ While shooting *The Blue Angel* (1930), Marlene went overboard on one production number. "You sow," director von Sternberg shouted. "Pull down your [hot] pants. Everyone can see your pubic hair."

✪ Vanity, thy name is Dietrich: Marlene Dietrich's legs were insured for $1 million. In order to emphasize her hollow cheeks, she had some of her back teeth removed, just like Joan Crawford had done earlier.

✪ In the days before birth control pills, Marlene religiously douched with ice water and vinegar, ordering Heinz brand vinegar by the case.

✪ A clean freak, Dietrich carried disinfectant and cleaning supplies with her whenever she traveled. She made a point of cleansing the hotel bathroom herself.

✪ When Marlene met famed playwright George Bernard Shaw, she dropped to her knees and entertained him orally. "I had to do it before we could talk," she claimed.

★ Dietrich fell in love with actress Mercedes De Acosta and sent her tulips, roses, carnations, and orchids. She sent so many flowers she drove Mercedes to distraction. De Acosta said, "I was walking on flowers, falling on flowers, and sleeping on flowers. I finally wept and flew into a rage." Mercedes told Marlene that if she sent any more flowers, she would throw her into the pool. So Marlene began sending her female lover men's clothing.

★ Marlene once found herself competing with lover/director/mentor Josef von Sternberg for the company of a young extra on the set of *The Scarlet Empress* (1934). Marlene was so taken with the girl, that when she noticed von Sternberg's interest, she said, "Want to share?"

★ Besides French singer Edith Piaf and Mercedes De Acosta, Marlene Dietrich's girlfriends were rumored to include Errol Flynn's wife Lili Damita, actress Claudette Colbert, and heiress Jo Carstairs. All of these women adopted Dietrich's habit of dressing like a man.

★ During World War II, Marlene did her part for the Allied war effort by getting drunks in nightclubs to write checks for war bonds. She then sat on their laps while government agents called the customers' banks to make sure their checks would clear. "We're grateful to you," President Roosevelt told her after summoning her to the White House. "But I won't allow this sort of prostitution technique."

★ While shooting *Golden Earrings* (1947), Dietrich decided she didn't like her costar, Ray Milland. So she added "realism" to her role as a gypsy by eating a fish head, sucking out the eye, and spitting out the rest of the head. When the take was finished, she made herself vomit.

★ To further disgust Milland, Dietrich explained, "I would itch my crotch. All gypsies have lice." Dietrich complained that Milland stank, so she decided to stink too. "I didn't take any baths during filming," Marlene growled, "and he had to do love scenes with me."

★ She later had an affair with Ray Milland and instructed her daughter Maria to stand guard outside the dressing room while they "rehearsed." Marlene then made her daughter change the "rehearsal" sheets on the bed.

★ Dietrich held movie actor Fernando Lamas in such low esteem that she named her suppositories after the South American actor.

★ When Marlene's grandchild was born physically handicapped, she blamed it on her daughter's appearance on a cerebral palsy telethon. When the second grandchild was born normal, Marlene was mystified that the newborn child was "unmarked by that telethon thing."

⊗ In her later years, Marlene took up with a young male writer. He complained that her body was so bound up with bandages to keep her trim that he had to unwind her like a mummy before they made love. His head was later chopped off by a helicopter rotor blade.

⊗ One night Dietrich ran into Sir John Gielgud and invited him up to her place to listen to her "latest record." Gielgud sat there as Dietrich played a twenty-minute tape of applause.

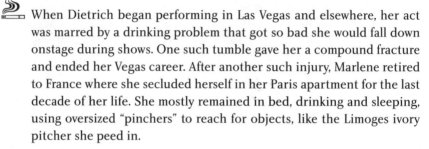 When Dietrich began performing in Las Vegas and elsewhere, her act was marred by a drinking problem that got so bad she would fall down onstage during shows. One such tumble gave her a compound fracture and ended her Vegas career. After another such injury, Marlene retired to France where she secluded herself in her Paris apartment for the last decade of her life. She mostly remained in bed, drinking and sleeping, using oversized "pinchers" to reach for objects, like the Limoges ivory pitcher she peed in.

Divine

FACTS OF LIFE (and Death)

ORIGINS: Born Harris Glenn Milstead, October 19, 1945, Baltimore, Maryland; died March 7, 1988, Los Angeles, California, of an enlarged heart.

FORMATIVE YEARS: Graduated from the Marinella Beauty School in Baltimore, Maryland.

FAMILY PLANNING: Planned not to have one.

ROMANTIC INTERESTS: "I become very possessive and jealous when I'm having an affair. . . . It makes you crazy. So I actually hope it never happens to me again. I'd rather decorate or something."

SELECTED HITS (and Misses)

FILMS: *Eat Your Makeup!* (1968), *Multiple Maniacs* (1970), *Mondo Trasho* (1970), *Pink Flamingos* (1972), *Female Trouble* (1974), *Polyester* (1981), *Trouble in Mind* (1985), *Lust in the Dust* (1985), *Out of the Dark* (1988), *Hairspray* (1988).

QUICKIE BIO

Hailed by *People* magazine as the "Drag Queen of the Century," Divine grew up as Glenn Milstead in a house outside of Baltimore, Maryland, that was once home to acclaimed writer F. Scott Fitzgerald. Glenn wanted to be famous, but he didn't go to Hollywood. Instead, he teamed up with high-school chum director John Waters and took the gutter to the top. Donning full drag, the zaftig one-time hairdresser starred in most of Waters' early trashy epics, and earned the title "The Most Beautiful Woman in the World. Almost." Divine grew along with his success, until he passed away of causes related to obesity, ill-health, and all-around trashy living. Divine's demise occurred the day before he was scheduled to make a guest appearance on the TV series *Married . . . . . . with Children.*

DIVINE DOES THE DUMBEST THINGS

⭐ Divine filled his bra with lentils—that is, until his heavy fake boobs started causing him back problems.

⭐ At his first disco club gig, Divine received a thousand dollars for standing on stage for fifty seconds and shouting "F*** you" to the audience.

⭐ Divine liked to rent banquet halls at the swankiest hotels and host huge sit-down dinners with an open bar. Divine often paid for the parties by writing a bad check or by charging it to his father's credit card. At other times, Divine would rent a luxury apartment for his extravagant celebrations. The soirees often wound up with everyone taking LSD and planning burglaries. Divine once talked a partygoer into being lowered by his feet out a seventh story window in order to break into the apartment below.

⭐ While on LSD, Divine wrapped his head in a towel and did marathon Dionne Warwick impersonations.

⭐ Divine constantly relocated in an attempt to dodge bill collectors. While hiding out, he quit his job, ate heavily, and put on enormous amounts of weight. According to Waters, "He got so lethargic that when the toilet broke, he s*** in the tub and beat the turd down the drain with a stick."

⭐ After a show in Atlanta, Georgia, Divine was signing autographs. One young man came up, turned around, and dropped his pants. Divine obliged and signed the fan's rear end. Everyone else in line began to follow suit. One man didn't turn around, and instead brandished his erection in Divine's face. Divine made his manager hold the man's johnson and gave new meaning to the term "John Hancock."

⭐ Divine spent much of his spare time in New York City at The Gaiety, a male "entertainment" joint in Times Square. For the floor show, a dozen or so young men all took the stage buck naked. Backstage, Divine would help the boys prepare for their finale. He professed, "It's the only time in my life that I wished I had more than two hands and one mouth."

⭐ In *Female Trouble* (1974), Divine played a male role in addition to the female lead. In one scene, Dawn, played by Divine, was raped by Earl,

"If my performing career fails, I can always be a stewardess," Divine once noted.
[photo courtesy of Tim Boxer/Archive Photos]

played by Divine. Years later, when Divine performed at disco clubs, hecklers shouted, "Go f*** yourself." Divine replied, "I've done that already."

Giddy over his success, Divine's fans in Holland gave him two bulldog puppies as a gift. Divine named them Beatrix and Klaus, after the Queen of the Netherlands and her husband, and brought them back with him to the United States. They flew first class of course.

 "God, I wanted to be famous so bad," the hefty Divine once confessed. "I wanted it so bad I used to say I could taste it." And he had to. Director John Waters convinced his oversized star to eat dog doo on camera for the final scene of *Pink Flamingos* (1972). In order to get the scene just right, the crew locked up a poodle for three days and fed it steak. When the time came, they let the dog loose to do his business. Waters rolled the cameras, and in one continuous shot (so no one could accuse him of faking the scene) Divine picked up the poop and put it in his mouth. Afterward Divine rushed to a friend's house and used her toothbrush.

✪ At the wrap party for *Pink Flamingos,* someone snickered, "I think you can get sick from eating s***." A worried Divine called a hospital and in a disguised voice asked, "My son ate some dog feces and I'm wondering if he can get sick." After Divine hung up the phone he informed the cast and crew, "She said he'll probably be okay, but it's a possibility he could get the white worm."

✪ Other on-screen festivities included Divine eating an old cow's heart, and a "rosary job" in which the religious item was placed lovingly in Divine's "most private parts."

Robert Downey Jr.

FACTS OF LIFE

ORIGIN: Born April 4, 1965, New York City, New York.

FORMATIVE YEARS: Dropped out of high school.

FAMILY PLANNING: Married Deborah Falconer (actress), May 1993; separated 1996.

ROMANTIC INTERESTS: Farrah Fawcett (actress), Sarah Jessica Parker (actress), Uma Thurman (actress).

SELECTED HITS AND MISSES

FILMS: *Pound* (1970), *Greaser's Palace* (1972), *Up the Academy* (1980), *Firstborn* (1984), *Tuff Turf* (1985), *Back to School* (1986), *Less Than Zero* (1987), *The Pick-up Artist* (1987), *Johnny Be Good* (1988), *True Believer* (1989), *Chances Are* (1989), *Air America* (1990), *Soapdish* (1991), *Chaplin* (1992), *Heart and Soul* (1993), *Restoration* (1994), *Only You* (1994), *Natural Born Killers* (1994), *Home for the Holidays* (1995), *Danger Zone* (1996), *One Night Stand* (1997), *The Gingerbread Man* (1998), *U.S. Marshals* (1998), *Two Girls and a Guy* (1998), *Friends & Lovers* (1999), *Black and White* (1999), *In Dreams* (1999), *Bowfinger* (1999).

QUICKIE BIO

Robert Downey Jr. inherited his father's yen for the cinema and a taste for drugs. Young Robert started using drugs while he was in elementary school, explaining that, in the Downey home, recreational drug use was "as casual as it would be having a glass of white wine with Thanksgiving." Robert Sr. cast his five-year-old son as a dog in the film *Pound* (1970). Robert's first words on film were, "Got any hair on your balls?" In the mid-1980s, the burgeoning actor parlayed his show business contacts into a season on NBC's *Saturday Night Live* and some serious film roles, before launching his own career of drug abuse, arrests, jail time, and tabloid headlines. "I was pulling 360s in the Universal parking lot and disappearing for three days for things one needs blood transfusions to recuperate from," Downey recalled. He eventually served 113 days in the Los Angeles County Jail, during which time he garnered a busted face and several lucrative job offers.

ROBERT DOWNEY JR. DOES THE DUMBEST THINGS

✪ As a young actor starting out, Downey said that he was willing to do a nude scene, but that he was worried. "I hope I don't get a hard on—it would be distracting to the crew and I'd be embarrassed because, s***, maybe it's not as big as I want it to be."

✪ Downey was out front with his bizarre sexual history. "One of my cousins sucked my d*** when I was nine," the actor recalled. "It was for about four seconds, and I said I would do it back to him, but I reneged."

✪ When no girls were available, high school student Robert used to make out with his best friend "as a last resort."

✪ Fifteen-year-old Downey had an experience with a transsexual, or "trannie" as he put it, at a screening of *The Rocky Horror Picture Show* (1975) in New York City. "Her name was International Crisis," Downey confessed, "and I was sure that she was a white girl with a p***y . . . but then there was more." The actor claimed that he was attracted to International Crisis for drugs not sex: "I was there actually for the pot, not the surprise member."

✪ Robert was sleeping at a male friend's house, when he felt a strange slurping down below. The awakened actor wondered, "Did he think that I'd wake up and suddenly find him wildly attractive? I never looked at him the same way."

✪ Downney liked to hang out with a soap opera star who "was really cool" and had "lots of blow." But when the unshaven guy tried to kiss Robert, Downey said the scratchy sensation "didn't work for me."

✪ In the mid-1990s, a hot young director stood behind Downey. The film-maker wore a Royalton hotel robe "that had a big boner pushing it up." Robert Jr. wasn't interested, so he immediately began calling up hookers "to come over just to get a buffer between this, uh, potential intrusion."

✪ In Italy, Downey told a friend that in Rome, "a four-star-rated restaurant was like a D-rated greasy spoon in Detroit." His pal got sick on a piece of fish, and then the two went to a gay bar to look for cocaine. Out on the street in front of the club, Downey kissed his friend's fishy mouth. "I was drunk," the movie star sighed, "and it just felt right."

✪ "I could not get over her butt," Downey said of ex-wife Deborah Falconer, "so I married her."

🚬 In 1996, Robert was arrested for allegedly driving under the influence, for possession of crack cocaine, powder cocaine, and black-tar heroin, and for supposedly having a concealed .357 Magnum. Less than a month later, Downey got toasted, wandered into a neighbor's home in Malibu, and passed out in a child's bed. His action became known as "the Goldilocks incident."

✪ Three days later, Downey walked away from a rehab center in Los Angeles and was arrested again.

✪ Robert pleaded no contest and was freed on bail with three years probation. His probation was revoked in 1997 when he went on a four-day binge. He ended up being sentenced to six months in the Los Angeles County Jail.

✪ One day out of rehab, Downey stopped by a friend's house and asked, "Can I just get a line?" The two buddies reportedly started snorting coke and turned on the TV. Downey, who was high as a kite, watched himself on *The Tonight Show,* bragging about his sobriety.

✪ Who should walk into Downey's jail cell but convicted rock and roll wife-beater Tommy Lee. "Hey, man," Downey said, "It's good to see ya!" "This isn't really where I want to say hi, you know," Tommy Lee hesitated. "Yeah, I knew you were coming," Downey enthused. "I saw it on TV."

✪ After Tommy Lee left his cell, Downey bragged about his sexual conquests to his fellow inmates. While scrubbing toilets with another prisoner, Robert muttered something in German. The inmate asked for a translation: "Be patient, it won't be long before you find love." The prisoner looked at the movie star like, "Sure, Robert, but not with you!" On another occasion, Downey wore a yellow flower stuck behind his ear. A fellow inmate noted, "Jail's not the best place to wear a flower in your hair."

⭐ Robert allegedly smoked crack in jail and frequently acted like a jerk. One day he was cornered by a gang of inmates who punched him in the face. The movie actor screamed "Deputy! Help!" He had a deep cut on his face, and was allowed out of jail to visit a special plastic surgeon. Then he was sent into solitary confinement for his own protection.

⭐ Downey went back to jail in August 1999 after he apparently failed to show up for mandatory drug tests and for violating his probation. In sentencing Robert the judge sighed, "There is something going on here that I can't understand." Downey,s arrest came shortly after he dropped out of the animated TV series *God, the Devil, and Bob*.

⭐ Downey often has referred to his devilish side as the "goat-boy." "The goat-boy is out only for instant gratification," he confessed. "If you repress the goat, he will nail you." At one point, the actor brayed like a goat for his father and explained, "That's my goat-boy, that's who I really am."

Clint Eastwood

FACTS OF LIFE

ORIGIN: Born Clinton Eastwood Jr., May 31, 1930, San Francisco, California.

FORMATIVE YEARS: Studied business at Los Angeles City College.

FAMILY PLANNING: Married Maggie Johnson (model), December 19, 1953; divorced 1983; married Dina Ruiz (TV news anchor), December 29, 1995.

ROMANTIC INTERESTS: Barbara Minty (widow of Steve McQueen), Dani Janssen (widow of David Janssen), Sondra Locke (actress), Frances Fisher (actress).

SELECTED HITS (and Misses)

FILMS: *Revenge of the Creature* (1953), *The First Traveling Saleslady* (1956), *Lafayette Escadrille* (1958), *A Fistful of Dollars* (1964), *For a Few Dollars More* (1965), *The Good, The Bad and The Ugly* (1966), *Coogan's Bluff* (1968), *Where Eagles Dare* (1969), *Paint Your Wagon* (1969), *Two Mules for Sister Sara* (1970), *Play Misty for Me* (1971),* *Dirty Harry* (1971), *High Plains Drifter* (1973),* *The Eiger Sanction* (1974),* *The Outlaw Josey Wales* (1976),* *The Enforcer* (1976), *The Gauntlet* (1977),* *Escape from Alcatraz* (1979), *Any Which Way You Can* (1980), *Bronco Billy* (1980),* *Firefox* (1982),* *Honkytonk Man* (1982),* *Sudden Impact* (1983),* *Tightrope* (1984), *City Heat* (1984), *Pale Rider* (1985),* *Heartbreak Ridge* (1986), *The Dead Pool* (1988), *Pink Cadillac* (1989), *White Hunter, Black Heart* (1990),* *Unforgiven* (Oscars for Best Picture and Best Director—1992),* *In the*

Line of Fire (1993), *A Perfect World* (1993),* *The Bridges of Madison County* (1995),* *Absolute Power* (1997),* *True Crime* (1999),* *Space Cowboys* (2000).*

TV Series: *Rawhide* (1959–64).

*Also directed by Eastwood.

QUICKIE BIO

When Eastwood's army buddies encouraged him to try acting in 1954, Clint felt lucky. He landed bit parts in horror films like *Tarantula* (1955) before hitting the trail as Rowdy Yates in the hit western TV series *Rawhide* (1959–64). Eastwood didn't like being Rowdie, so he agreed to star in a low-budget Western being made in Spain by an Italian director, Sergio Leone. *A Fistful of Dollars* (1964) and its spaghetti western follow-ups made lanky, laconic Eastwood a legend. Over the following three decades, squint-eyed Eastwood's movies grossed over two billion dollars and he came out as a Republican and won election as the mayor of Carmel, California. However, Eastwood's personal life went from good to bad to really ugly when he split from his long-time, live-in girlfriend Sondra Locke. Actress Locke wrote a tell-all book about Dirty Harry*The Good, the Bad, and the Very Ugly: A Hollywood Journey* (1997), and won a big court settlement. It certainly made Locke's day.

CLINT EASTWOOD
DOES THE DUMBEST THINGS

✪ Eastwood asked his much younger girlfriend Sondra Locke to call him "Daddy."

✪ In 1985, Eastwood was asked by *Rolling Stone* magazine if he would ever run for political office. "That's something nobody has to worry about," he replied. About six months later, in January of 1986, Eastwood dropped off his nominating petition for mayor of Carmel, California, and won the election.

✪ Clint didn't like it when people parked in his studio lot space, nor did he wait for a tow truck to remedy the situation. On one occasion he was so annoyed, he reportedly took a sledgehammer to the windshield of a car stashed in his private space.

✪ Eastwood had a security system installed in his Jeep. The system played a recorded message that said, "Make my day."

✪ When his longtime girlfriend Sondra Locke was looking at houses for Eastwood and herself, the real estate agent introduced Locke to prospective sellers as Mrs. Anderson. On a few occasions Eastwood came along and introduced himself as Mr. Anderson.

✪ Eastwood went on a mega vitamin kick when he costarred with an orangutan for *Any Which Way You Can* (1980). Clint cooked up his own vitamin recipe from a variety of powders, which he then packed into enormous gelatin capsules. When the overstuffed capsules didn't fit together, Eastwood threw a hissy-fit, yelling, "These f***ing capsules are crap," and threw them across the room. When a friend suggested letting someone else pack the capsules, Eastwood went ballistic, "I don't want anybody else's hands touching this stuff."

✪ At one point, Eastwood took so much carotene that his hands turned orange.

✪ On another occasion Clint's hands turned red. He got mad at the closet doors in his Las Vegas hotel room after they stuck, so he punched his fists through it. Later that night at dinner, a palm reader looked at Clint's upturned hands and spoke, "You are a very tranquil man." The other side of his hands were still bleeding from earlier in the day.

✪ Eastwood was downright anal about the food he kept in his office refrigerator. One day he was going to make himself a tuna fish sandwich for lunch, but his mayonnaise jar was empty. He came flying out of his office and yelled at his secretary, "Who's been in my mayonnaise? I know there was more than this in the jar. How many times do I have to tell you to leave my mayonnaise alone."

In the mid-1980s, Eastwood had hair transplants. Shortly after the surgery, some of his children dropped in for an unexpected visit. Eastwood, head wrapped in bandages, sat at the table talking with his kids as if there was nothing out of the ordinary. Finally his daughter asked, "What's wrong with your head, Dad?" Eastwood responded, "Oh, I had a bicycle accident."

✪ Eastwood once fired a shot over the head of a fan who didn't leave the set of his film fast enough.

✪ Clint turned down a lead role in *Apocalypse Now* (1979), which was later taken by Martin Sheen. When he heard that the budget for the picture was more than $35 million, Republican Eastwood was surprised. "For that sort of money," he said, "we could have invaded somewhere."

✪ In addition to having children by his two wives, Eastwood "The Man with No Name" fathered offspring with Frances Fisher (actress), Roxanne Tunis (actress), and Jacelyn Reeves. And this from a guy who once said, "Sex can be overrated."

Mia Farrow

FACTS OF LIFE

ORIGIN: Born Maria de Lourdes Villiers Farrow, February 9, 1945, Santa Monica, California.

FORMATIVE YEARS: Attended Marymount High School (Los Angeles). Graduated finishing school, Cygnet House (London, England).

FAMILY PLANNING: Married Frank Sinatra (singer/movie star), July 19, 1966; divorced 1968; married Andre Previn (conductor), September 10, 1970; divorced 1979; girlfriend of Woody Allen (director/movie star) for twelve years (1980–92) and had a child by Allen.

ROMANTIC INTERESTS: Salvador Dali (artist), William Goldman (screenwriter), Peter Sellers (actor), John Phillips (musician), Kirk Douglas (actor), Tom Stoppard (playwright).

SELECTED HITS (and Misses)

FILMS: *John Paul Jones* (1959), *Guns at Batasi* (1964), *Rosemary's Baby* (1968), *Secret Ceremony* (1969), *See No Evil* (1971), *High Heels* (1972), *The Great Gatsby* (1974), *The Haunting of Julia* (1976), *Death on the Nile* (1978), *The Hurricane* (1979), *Broadway Danny Rose* (1984), *The Purple Rose of Cairo* (1985), *Hannah and Her Sisters* (1986), *Radio Days* (1987), *September* (1987), *Crimes and Misdemeanors* (1989), *Alice* (1990), *Husbands and Wives* (1992), *Bullets Over Broadway* (1994), *Widow's Peak* (1994), *Miami Rhapsody* (1995), *Reckless* (1995), *Agnes Mooney Dies Again* (1997), *Miracle at Midnight* (1998), *Coming Soon* (1999).

TV SERIES: *Peyton Place* (1964–66).

QUICKIE BIO

Although she made her movie debut at age fourteen in a film directed by her father, John Farrow, the rail-thin daughter of screen and stage actress Maureen O'Sullivan claimed that she made her own way into show business. She went from stage to soap, with a two-year stint on TV's *Peyton Place*, before creating her own personal Peyton Place by marrying Frank Sinatra. Following her split from the crooner, Mia turned mystic and discovered "a mathematical formula for mind expansion." After a marriage to Andre Previn, Farrow's mind expanded toward comic genius Woody Allen. They made love and thirteen movies together, but when Woody got woody with Farrow's adopted daughter Soon-Yi Previn, Mia went berserk and charged Allen and Soon-Yi of numerous crimes and misdemeanors. "Maybe she didn't understand what a mother was," mama Mia sighed. However, maybe it was Mia who didn't understand.

MIA FARROW
DOES THE DUMBEST THINGS

✪ As a child, Mia was attracted to the mysteries of the Catholic Church. Explained Farrow, "I decided that a nun would be a groovy thing to be." Farrow later became disenchanted. "I thought I would be able to levitate and stuff and have visions," she sighed.

✪ Still in her teens, Mia became fast friends with surreal artist Salvador Dali. Farrow complained to Dali that she had fallen into a rut. The artist proposed a cure. He suggested she wear her left shoe on her right foot for a couple of days. A few days later Farrow ran into Salvador and told him that the experiment had provided her with a unique perspective.

✪ Dali invited Farrow to a hip Greenwich Village party. When they arrived, Mia discovered to her horror that all of the guests were naked. Mia said of the orgy, "I honestly still don't know exactly what they were all doing."

✪ Mia soon figured out about the birds and the bees. To catch Frank Sinatra's eye on the set of *Von Ryan's Express* (1965), Farrow started hanging around in a sheer nightgown she borrowed from studio wardrobe.

✪ A friend of Farrow's approached Sinatra at a nightclub and asked him if he had any grass. Boozin' Frank replied, "Yeah, pal, I got plenty of grass. It's all at home—on my lawn." When the singer and his bodyguards tried to force their "square" attitude on Farrow, Mia hid in the ladies' room and got high with her pals.

⭐ Mia wooed her second husband, Andre Previn, away from his wife Dory. Mia had twins by Previn while he was still married to Dory. Farrow later bragged: "It's marvelous being a seductress." Dory wrote a song about the experience, "Beware of Little Girls."

⭐ Farrow went to India to meet the Maharishi Mahesh Yogi and to meditate with the Beatles. Mia chanted, "I'm leaving myself in the hands of God." She wound up in the hands of the Maharishi, who allegedly made a pass at her.

⭐ After fleeing the Maharishi, Farrow joined up with a party of American hunters in India. She left when she realized that the hunters were actually going to kill an animal. Farrow then hooked up with a group of nice young beggars. When Mia realized that they were lepers, she jumped into the Ganges, one of the world's most polluted rivers, to scrub herself clean.

💬 Farrow caused a scene in a London municipal court after she was arrested for telling two police officers what to do with themselves as they escorted her out of a local night spot. In court, the magistrate told Farrow to come forward. Mia asked if she should take her clothes off first. The magistrate then asked Farrow if she had used foul language with the law enforcers. Farrow explained that "f***" was not a dirty word because it was the nicest thing she could wish the judge.

⭐ For Valentine's Day 1992, Farrow sent Woody Allen a romantic homemade card. It was a big red heart with a family photo glued to it. Skewers (real ones) bore through the children in the picture, and a knife (also real) pierced Farrow's heart. Mia had crossed out the words "love and joy" and scribbled in the word "pain."

⭐ After learning that Allen was having an affair with her adopted daughter Soon-Yi, Farrow tacked a sign on her bathroom that read: "CHILD MOLESTER. MOLDED THEN ABUSED ONE SISTER. NOW FOCUSED ON YOUNGEST SISTER." Woody was eventually cleared by the courts of all child molestation charges.

⭐ After Allen began an affair with her adopted daughter, and after Farrow accused Allen of molesting another daughter, Farrow still fully expected Allen to hire her for his 1993 feature, *Manhattan Murder Mystery*. He didn't. Diane Keaton got the acting assignment.

⭐ Mia attended Frank Sinatra's funeral in 1998 with Frank's daughter Nancy ("These Boots Are Made for Walking") Sinatra. Mia approached the open casket, took a silver ring from her finger, and slipped it into the breast pocket of Frank's coat. Nancy had already spent six days cluttering the coffin with Tootsie Rolls, wild cherry flavor Lifesavers, chewing gum, and cotton balls soaked in cologne. Sinatra's wife Barbara called Mia and Nancy "two wackos who understand only each other."

★ Mia once claimed she'd make a great Peter Pan because she had been to Never Never Land numerous times.

Errol Flynn

DUMBEST QUOTE

"I think I can truthfully say that my behavior in whorehouses has been exemplary."

FACTS OF LIFE (and Death)

ORIGIN: Born Errol Leslie Thomson Flynn, June 20, 1909, Hobart, Tasmania, Australia; died October 14, 1959, Vancouver, British Columbia, Canada.

FORMATIVE YEARS: Was expelled from school for having sex with a girl on a pile of coal.

FAMILY PLANNING: Married Lili Damita (actress), June 19, 1935; divorced 1942; married Nora Eddington (policeman's daughter), August 1943; divorced 1948; married Patrice Wymore (actress), October 23, 1950.

ROMANTIC INTERESTS: Tuperselai (twelve-year-old Melanesian maid), Ting Ting O'Connor (prostitute), Eva Peron (dictator's wife), Beverly Aadland (aspiring actress). Flynn estimated that he had spent between 12,000 and 14,000 nights making love.

SELECTED HITS (and Misses)

FILMS: *Captain Blood* (1935), *The Charge of the Light Brigade* (1936), *The Prince and the Pauper* (1937), *The Dawn Patrol* (1938), *The Adventures of Robin Hood* (1938), *Dodge City* (1939), *The Private Lives of Elizabeth and Essex* (1939), *The Sea Hawk* (1940), *They Died with Their Boots On* (1941), *Gentleman Jim* (1942), *Edge of Darkness* (1943), *Objective, Burma!* (1945), *San Antonio* (1945), *Cry Wolf* (1947), *Silver River* (1948), *Adventures of Don Juan* (1949), *That Forsyte Woman* (1949), *Kim* (1951), *Against All Flags* (1952), *The Master of Ballantrae* (1953), *The Warriors* (1955), *Istanbul* (1957), *The Sun Also Rises* (1957), *Too Much, Too Soon* (1958), *The Roots of Heaven* (1958), *Cuban Rebel Girls* (1959).

TV SERIES: *Errol Flynn Theatre* (1957).

QUICKIE BIO

Errol Flynn was the original Tasmanian Devil. From New Guinea to Hong Kong to Calcutta to Paris, Flynn explored sex around the globe before arriving in Hollywood in the 1930s. The swashbuckling rake wound up portraying, you guessed it, swashbuckling rakes. When he beat a rap for statutory rape in 1943, "in like Flynn" became the phrase young men used when their chances of scoring a babe (and getting away with it) were high. Flynn balanced his desire for women with his appetite for opium, marijuana, cocaine, and morphine, and spent his last years living on his yacht in Jamaica with his teenage girlfriend. Flynn achieved his most cherished goal—to die broke. The title of Flynn's 1959 autobiography (published after his death in 1960) says it all: *My Wicked, Wicked Ways.*

ERROL FLYNN
DOES THE DUMBEST THINGS

- ✪ Flynn got a job in the Australian outback castrating sheep. "All I had to do was stick my face into the gruesome mess and bite off the young sheep's testicles," Flynn bragged. Then he seduced the sheep rancher's daughter.

- ✪ A society woman in Australia introduced handsome Errol Flynn to the joys of oral sex. After she gobbled his jewels, Flynn stole *her* jewels and left town.

- ✪ Flynn appreciated a woman with talent. "Lupe [Velez] had a unique ability to rotate her left breast," Flynn observed. "Not only that, she could counter-rotate it, a feat so supple and beautiful to observe that you couldn't believe your eyes."

- ✪ On the set of *Adventures of Don Juan* (1949), Flynn was late for a scene. The director stormed into his dressing room and found Flynn stark naked lying under a woman in full costume.

- Errol Flynn once put out to sea on his yacht and noticed his dog was missing. Flynn called the Coast Guard, which discovered the pooch's waterlogged corpse. Flynn was so upset, he asked the Coast Guard to send him just the collar of his dog, which he buried. A reporter wrote up the incident, and accused Errol of not caring for his pooch. A few weeks later, Flynn saw the newsman in a nightclub, smacked him, and knocked him to the floor, at which point the newsman's wife stabbed Errol in the ear with a fork. The journalist sued the movie star, but they settled out of court and later became friends. "Your wife has good table manners," Flynn complimented the reporter. "She used the right fork."

- Flynn didn't care very much about other animals. He glued one dog's eyelids shut. He also clipped the feathers off a parrot's wing, set it on a hot metal tub, and watched it dance.

- Errol loved to sail aboard his yacht. An admiring fan got herself invited aboard and Errol showed her the view from below the deck. The fan's husband angrily boated out to the yacht and demanded his spouse. The wife dove off Errol's yacht and started to swim to her mate's boat. Before she made it, hubby sailed off. So did Errol. The woman had to swim two miles to shore.

- So much sex went on aboard his yacht that Errol flew the insignia FFF for "Flynn's Flying F***ers." Flynn kept track of everyone's activities in a score book, and presented worthy performers with a badge that flamboyantly depicted a woody with a set of balls.

- Flynn, who called under-aged girls "jail bait" or "San Quentin quail," wound up facing charges for statutory rape in 1943. One of Flynn's accusers claimed that the movie star didn't even take his shoes off before he had his way with her. Flynn had five shots of vodka before taking the stand, and denied everything. The jury found him not guilty. Perhaps the court should have screened one of Errol's past hits. The title? *They Died with Their Boots On* (1941).

- During the trial, Flynn fell for the barely legal eighteen-year-old girl who worked at a cubicle selling cigarettes and gum in the entrance of City Hall. Her name? Nora Eddington—daughter of Captain Jack Eddington of the Los Angeles County Sheriff's Office. Flynn eventually married her.

- In an attempt to seduce (yes, seduce!) actress Olivia de Havilland, Flynn put a dead snake in her panties.

- Errol's main interest was obvious in his house. A mural painted for his fish tank depicted fish with oversized glands performing amazing sexual feats. His bar had a bullfighting motif. Opening the liquor cabinet required squeezing a pair of bull testicles. Certain chairs were rigged so that willies popped out from cushions with the touch of a button. Even Flynn's lighters were designed like wangers.

- Sometimes on film sets, Flynn squirted oranges full of vodka with a hypodermic needle and sucked the juice/vodka out of them.

- Before making love, Flynn liked to put a dab of cocaine on the end of his penis. According to the mighty lover, it helped if "you're quick on the trigger."

○ While starring in *The Sea Hawk* (1940), Flynn had a problem with the script. He couldn't figure out how to say the line "England . . ." Flynn asked the screenwriter, "You want me to say 'dot, dot, dot'?" "No," said the screenwriter. "I want you to say 'England.' You can act out the rest with your feelings. "I can't," Flynn smiled. "You see, I'm not an actor."

✪ Errol liked to pose nude for his male friends. He had two-way mirrors installed in his home so he could peep at his pals while they dallied. At the climax, Flynn applauded.

✪ Flynn visited Truman Capote at his tiny, walk-up apartment. The two had sex, sort of. "If it hadn't been Errol Flynn," Capote said, "I wouldn't even have remembered."

✪ At a lesbian bar in Paris, Flynn's fifteen-year-old girlfriend started slow dancing with a tough-looking woman. Errol jumped in between them and picked a fight. The woman decked the swashbuckler. "If they hear about this in Hollywood," Flynn gasped from the floor, "I'm finished." He was literally finished (dead) a short time later.

Jane Fonda

FACTS OF LIFE

ORIGIN: Born Jane Seymour Fonda, December 21, 1937, New York City, New York.

FORMATIVE YEARS: Dropped out of Vassar College (Poughkeepsie, New York) to study painting at the Sorbonne in Paris, France. She later confessed, "I went to Paris to be a painter, but I lived there for six months and never even opened my paints."

FAMILY PLANNING: Declared that marriage was "obsolete" in 1961. Then she married Roger Vladimir Plemiannikov (director Roger Vadim), August 14, 1965; divorced 1973; married Tom Hayden (politician), January 19, 1973; divorced 1990; married Ted Turner (media mogul), December 21, 1991.

ROMANTIC INTERESTS: Timothy Everett (actor), Andreas Voutsinas (aspiring producer), Alain Delon (actor), Fred Gardner (screenwriter/political activist), Donald Sutherland (actor), Barry Matalon (hairdresser), Lorenzo Caccialanza (soccer player).

SELECTED HITS (and Misses)

FILMS: *Tall Story* (1960), *Walk on the Wild Side* (1961), *The Chapman Report* (1962), *Sunday in New York* (1963), *La Ronde [Circle of Love]* (1964), *Cat Ballou* (1965), *The Chase* (1966), *Any Wednesday* (1966), *Hurry Sundown* (1967), *Barefoot in the Park* (1967), *Barbarella* (1968), *They Shoot Horses, Don't They?* (1969), *Klute* (Oscar for Best Actress—1971), *A Doll's House* (1974), *The Bluebird* (1976), *Fun with Dick and Jane* (1977), *Coming Home* (Oscar for Best Actress—

1978), *The China Syndrome* (1980), *Nine to Five* (1981), *On Golden Pond* (1981), *Agnes of God* (1985), *The Morning After* (1986), *Old Gringo* (1989), *Stanley and Iris* (1990).

QUICKIE BIO

Lady Jane Fonda grew up in the Los Angeles compound of her famous actor-father Henry Fonda, survived the suicide of her mother (Frances Seymour Brokaw) in 1950, and graced the cover of *Vogue* magazine in 1959. Her film career began the following year. Later, lanky Jane transformed from a sex goddess to a radical. "Hanoi Jane" traveled to North Vietnam and giggled with the enemy. The sexy revolutionary became a sexy millionaire when she released a series of exercise videos in the 1980s. After marrying cable TV magnate Ted Turner, Jane gave up the clenched fist salute of the 1960s for the tomahawk chop of the Atlanta Braves and retired from acting. Go for the burn, Jane!

JANE FONDA
DOES THE DUMBEST THINGS

⭐ While attending prep school, Jane came up with her first weight-loss plan. She went into the bathroom, turned on the tap, put her fingers down her throat, and made herself vomit.

📓 When a reporter visited her in 1961, Jane munched on food constantly. "I have to be eating something all the time," Jane said. "Do I have a weight problem? Oo! Ee! . . . I don't do any exercises per se. They have to be in terms of something. Like I lie down to do exercises and I end up chewing my fingernails. I forget why I'm there."

⭐ While working on the tawdry drama *Walk on the Wild Side* (1962), Jane refused to wear underclothes and smacked her costar during a fight scene. Jane explained, "I've gotten over the feeling that everyone has to love me." "No one can reach twenty-three and be quite as repulsive," one of Jane's costars observed. "It's not possible."

⭐ Fonda fell in love with French director Roger Vadim. She was so hot for him that she ran through the rain in a transparent negligee to meet him at a bar. But when they hit the sack, Vadim reportedly couldn't perform because of Jane's aggressive behavior. After three weeks, Vadim got used to the overly active American, and the couple stayed in bed for forty-eight hours.

⭐ Vadim got bored of sex with Jane. So he brought in other lovers to spice things up. "She seemed to understand," Vadim recalled, "and as always went all out—all the way."

✪ Jane appeared nude in Vadim's romantic drama *La Ronde [Circle of Love]* (1964). When a New York theatre owner erected a huge billboard of a nude Jane in Times Square to promote the feature, Fonda sued. So the theatre owner draped a large piece of canvas over Jane's king-sized butt.

✪ Fonda went to a party at director Roman Polanski's house in the late 1960s. The housekeeper tried to get into the bathroom and pounded on the locked door. Jane walked out of the restroom accompanied by a male guest. She complained to her husband Vadim, "I hate it when something's half finished."

✪ Young Jane was named "Miss Army Recruiting of 1962." A thrilled Fonda wore a red, white, and blue outfit and gave a speech praising the military. Later, radical Jane traveled across the country with an anti-war review entitled "FTA" which stood for "F*** the Army."

✪ Jane appeared on TV's *Dick Cavett Show* in the late 1960s. She gave a clenched fist salute, and then explained that the only reason Americans were pursuing the Vietnam "war" was because Vietnam had valuable deposits of "tung and tinsten." When someone pointed out that there was no such thing as "tung and tinsten," Jane reportedly explained, "I didn't have time to sit down with books and get a historical analysis and put it all into perspective."

✪ After a trip to Canada in 1970, Jane was busted by U.S. Immigration officials at Cleveland's airport. Fonda asked to go to the bathroom. When the officer said she'd have to wait for prison guards to escort her, she took a swing at one officer, kicked another, and screamed, "Get the f*** out of here, you pig!" All charges were later dropped.

On a trek to North Vietnam, Jane was photographed, while smiling, next to an anti-aircraft gun used to shoot down American planes. Years later, Jane explained that she wasn't beaming in support of the North Vietnamese, she was smiling because she was singing "Yankee Doodle Dandy."

✪ When asked about rumors that her visit harmed American POWs, Jane snapped, "I think they're lying. . . . It was not a policy of the North Vietnamese to torture prisoners." Wrong. John McCain, who later served as a U.S. senator from Arizona, was in a North Vietnamese prison camp at the time. McCain had his arms broken because he wouldn't pose for pictures with the Hollywood radical.

✪ Jane devoted herself to helping her husband Tom Hayden's political career and his organization, the Campaign for Economic Democracy

(CED). While Tom was quoted as saying "abolish private property," Jane said that she wanted to make enough money to "get the CED off my f***ing back."

★ "I'm really appalled by what I see going on in plastic surgery in this country," exclaimed fitness guru Fonda. "You can spot an inflated breast a mile away." A year later, Jane had the fat around her eyelids removed. Then she had $5,000 worth of breast implants and reportedly had two ribs sawed off to make her look slimmer. "I never said I would never have plastic surgery," Jane later explained. "I said you have to make friends with the aging process and with your wrinkles, and you have to do everything you can."

★ While conducting an interview with a reporter in her apartment in the late 1960s, Jane asked, "You don't mind if I turn on, do you?" The journalist didn't mind, so Jane lit up a joint. "Doctors, lawyers, politicians— I don't know anyone who doesn't turn on," Jane puffed, "except maybe in the South. I guess the South is still fifty years behind." When she heard her father Henry Fonda knocking at the door, she quickly opened the windows of the room to hide the marijuana smoke.

★ In 1998, Jane dissed the South once again, comparing parts of Georgia to "developing countries" where children were "starving to death." The governor of Georgia commented, "Maybe the view from your penthouse apartment is not as clear as it needs to be." Jane later apologized for her stringent comments.

"I didn't have any political understanding of what was going on . . ." confessed sixties radical Jane Fonda, pictured here being arrested for handing out anti-war leaflets.
[photo courtesy of Archive Photos]

Clark Gable

FACTS OF LIFE (and Death)

ORIGIN: Born William Clark Gable, February 1, 1901, Cadiz, Ohio; died November 16, 1960, Hollywood, California.

FORMATIVE YEARS: Dropped out of school and worked as a mule skinner, a lumberjack, and a wildcatter.

FAMILY PLANNING: Married Josephine Dillon (acting instructor), December 13, 1924; divorced 1931; married Maria "Ria" Langham (socialite), June 29, 1931; divorced 1939; married Carole Lombard (actress), March 29, 1939; widowed 1942; married (Lady) Sylvia Ashley (chorus girl/wife of nobility), December 20, 1949; divorced 1952; married Kay [Williams] Spreckels (actress), July 11, 1955.

ROMANTIC INTERESTS: Joan Crawford (actress), Jean Harlow (actress), Loretta Young (actress), Millicent Rogers (heiress), Nancy Reagan (actress), Ava Gardner (actress), Grace Kelly (actress).

SELECTED HITS (and Misses)

FILMS: *Forbidden Paradise* (1924), *Dance, Fools, Dance* (1931), *The Secret Six* (1931), *Red Dust* (1932), *Strange Interlude* (1932), *No Man of Her Own* (1932), *The White Sister* (1933), *It Happened One Night* (Oscar for Best Actor—1934), *The Call of the Wild* (1935), *Mutiny on the Bounty* (1935), *San Francisco* (1936), *Parnell* (1937), *Test Pilot* (1938), *Idiot's Delight* (1939), *Gone with the Wind* (1939), *Boom Town* (1940), *Honky Tonk* (1941), *Somewhere I'll Find You* (1942), *Adventure* (1945), *The Hucksters* (1947), *Command Decision* (1948), *Homecoming* (1948), *To Please a Lady* (1950), *Across the Wide Missouri* (1951), *Lone Star* (1952), *Mogambo* (1953), *Betrayed* (1954), *The Tall Men* (1955), *Band of Angels* (1957), *Teacher's Pet* (1958), *Run Silent, Run Deep* (1958), *It Started in Naples* (1959), *The Misfits* (1961).

QUICKIE BIO

Who would throw away five hundred dollars of our money on that big ape?" movie mogul Jack L. Warner scoffed in the early 1930s. "Just look at those big, bat-like ears!" studio boss Irving Thalberg crowed. Yes, it took a lot of fixing up to make Clark Gable a leading man. However, the actor with a head "like a taxi cab with its doors open" (as Howard Hughes said) became the King of Hollywood in the 1930s (at least according to a newspaper poll). After the love of his life, actress Carole Lombard, died in 1942, Gable fought valiantly in World War II, and went out with women who closely resembled his former wife. There was only one problem: Hollywood's greatest sex symbol wasn't very good, at, um, sex. Clark's secret to wooing women? "I don't open doors for them. They open doors for me." Frankly, Gable just didn't give a damn.

CLARK GABLE
DOES THE DUMBEST THINGS

✪ Gable's teeth were rotten and the studios demanded he have dental work done. The first dentist who capped his teeth did such a bad job he had to have them pulled and wear dentures. Thereafter, when women hit on him, one of his favorite party tricks was to flash his toothless grin. Vivien Leigh, Gable's costar in *Gone with the Wind* (1939), sighed that he was "not that romantic. His dentures smelled something awful."

✪ Clark Gable and Grace Kelly got carried away in the jungle during the filming of *Mogambo* (1953) in Africa. "Would you like a nibble of my *ndizi*?" Kelly offered. "I'd never turn down an offer like that," Gable answered. *Ndizi* meant banana in Swahili. After their torrid affair cooled off, Grace said, "His false teeth were too much."

✪ It is rumored that Clark's first wife, acting coach Josephine Dillon, used to sit on Gable's head to flatten his protruding ears.

✪ Joan Crawford and Clark Gable had a steamy affair that lasted until the bosses at MGM studio broke it up. When asked what Clark's appeal was, Joan said bluntly, "Balls. He had them." Though Gable had testosterone, Crawford also claimed, "He wasn't a satisfying lover."

✪ Clark shaved his armpits and chest. His favorite method of lovemaking? No necking, no foreplay, just one minute from start to finish.

✪ Actress Lupe Velez, "the Mexican Spitfire," tried to put the make on Clark Gable, but he ran away from her. The reason? According to Gable, "She'll be blabbing it all over town the next day what a lousy lay I am."

✪ Gable could not keep up with his stage-star lover Pauline Frederick, although she was older than him by twenty years. To keep him going, Frederick fed Gable oysters until he ate so many he got ill.

✪ Clark got off to a rocky start with wife number four (actress Kay Spreckels). It was rumored that on one of their first dates Gable suggested, "Why don't you go upstairs and get undressed?" Kay retorted, "Why don't you go s*** in your hat?"

✪ After Gable slapped actress Norma Shearer in *A Free Soul* (1931), the studio got thousands of letters from women volunteering to let Clark slap them.

✪ In *It Happened One Night* (1934), Clark Gable took off his shirt to reveal the shocking truth—he was not wearing an undershirt. Almost overnight, the sale of undershirts dropped. Underwear manufacturers went to the makers of the movie and begged them to cut the scene. They refused.

✪ One night Gable escorted screen star Myrna Loy to her home. While she was unlocking her door, Gable gave her a "monkey bite" on the back of her neck. Myrna pushed Clark off the porch and into a hedge.

✪ Clark Gable and actress Loretta Young costarred in *The Call of The Wild* (1935). Apparently, a shortage of blankets on the Alaska set forced Gable and Young to bed down together. Right after filming ended, Young took a long leave of absence, and then returned to acting, having "adopted" a baby girl named Judy. According to one Hollywood insider, "All I know is Loretta disappeared when the film was finished and showed up with a daughter who had big ears."

✪ One year for Christmas, Gable's wife Carole Lombard gave him a hand-knitted penis warmer.

✪ Clark liked to impress Carole with stories of his sexual conquests. "It's hard to do in a swimming pool," Clark observed. "Yes, isn't it?" Carole knowingly agreed. Clark went ballistic and yelled. "How dare you do a thing like that and have the nerve to tell me about it!"

✪ "God knows I love Clark, but he's the worst lay in town," Carole Lombard once declared. "If Clark had one inch less, he'd be 'the queen of Hollywood' instead of 'the King.'"

Greta Garbo

FACTS OF LIFE

ORIGIN: Born Greta Lovisa Gustafsson, September 18, 1905, Stockholm, Sweden; died April 15, 1990, New York City, New York.

FORMATIVE YEARS: Studied at the Royal Dramatic Theatre Academy, Stockholm, Sweden.

FAMILY PLANNING: Never married. She preferred to be alone.

ROMANTIC INTERESTS: Max Gumpel (businessman), John Gilbert (actor), Mercedes De Acosta (actress), Lilyan Tashman (actress), Fifi D'Orsay (actress), Leopold Stokowski (conductor), Gaylord Hauser (health enthusiast), George Schlee (businessman), Cecil Beaton (photographer).

SELECTED HITS (and Misses)

FILMS: *Peter the Tramp* (1922), *The Story of Gösta Berling* (1924), *The Torrent* (1926), *Flesh and the Devil* (1927), *Love* (1927), *The Divine Woman* (1928), *The Kiss* (1929), *Wild Orchids* (1929), *Anna Christie* (1930), *Romance* (1930), *Susan Lennox: Her Fall and Rise* (1931), *Grand Hotel* (1932), *Mata Hari* (1932), *Queen Christina* (1933), *The Painted Veil* (1934), *Anna Karenina* (1935), *Camille* (1937), *Conquest* (1937), *Ninotchka* (1939), *Two-Faced Woman* (1941). Awarded special Oscar for lifetime achievement in 1954.

QUICKIE BIO

The Scandinavian sphinx grew up dirt poor in Stockholm, Sweden, and worked as a "lather girl" in a barber shop before breaking into silent films as a hat model in the 1922 promotional short, *Mr. and Mrs. Stockholm Go Shopping*. The eighteen-year-old Garbo headed for Hollywood along with the flamboyantly gay forty-year-old Swedish director Mauritz Stiller. Garbo went on to become the hottest lover on the silent screen, famous for her "ambidextrous" appeal. When she appeared in her first sound film (*Anna Christie*) in 1930, headlines blared, "Garbo talks!" The Hollywood hermit never talked much to the press, but her silence gained her even more publicity. The gloomiest Scandinavian since Hamlet spent the last years of her life in New York City, introducing herself only as Harriet Brown.

GRETA GARBO
DOES THE DUMBEST THINGS

★ Lovisa Gustafsson took the stage name Greta Garbo in Sweden. However, when she came to America, publicity honchos wanted to change it because "Garbo sounds too much like garbage."

★ MGM studio boss Louis B. Mayer met Garbo in Berlin and offered her a job *only* if she shed some weight. The rotund mogul asked an interpreter to explain: "Tell her that in America we don't like fat women."

★ Cecil Beaton referred to his girlfriend Garbo as "Dear Boy," or "Dear Young Man." Greta confessed that she wanted to play the male lead role in the movie *The Picture of Dorian Gray*, and asked writer Aldous Huxley to produce a screenplay with her in the role of St. Francis of Assisi. "What," Huxley asked, "complete with beard?"

★ When Greta dressed in men's clothing and walked down the street with her gal pal Mercedes De Acosta, the headlines screamed, "Garbo in pants!" De Acosta later confessed, "I do not understand the difference between a man and a woman."

★ After arriving at a crowded Hollywood party, Garbo announced to the hostess in German, "Ich bin ganz und gar besoffen!" Translation? "I am stinking drunk."

★ Gazing out the window of her swanky Los Angeles home, Greta enjoyed staring at a small dead tree in the backyard. "This tree is my one joy in Hollywood," the morose Scandinavian sighed. "I imagine that the cold has made it leafless and that soon there will be snow on its branches."

★ Garbo began to follow the dietary teaching of Pasadena, California, doctor Harold Bieler in the 1930s. She gushed, "I believe in him like I do Buddha."

★ After her weight dropped dramatically, Greta forgot about Buddha and took up with Gaylord Hauser, author of the 1936 best-selling book *Eat and Grow Beautiful*. "I am convinced that you can never win a victory over your complexion if your intestines are against you," observed Hauser who recommended that Garbo ingest large doses of laxatives, and referred to constipation as "the sin of sins."

✪ After Hauser became Garbo's lover, a neighbor complained that "the skinny Swedish actress and her fancy boyfriend are always running around naked in their backyard."

✪ Although Greta once told a reporter, "I don't like to see my soul laid bare upon paper," she did like to swim, garden, and sunbathe in the nude. When she learned that one of her servants was charging people to view her activities from a window, she laughed.

✪ Garbo said that she wanted "to travel to India and become wise." Instead she went on a picnic in Los Angeles with Hindu philosopher Krishnamurti, philosopher Bertrand Russell, actor Charlie Chaplin, and other celebrities. The spiritual searchers ate lunch then crawled under a nearby chain link fence. Their adventure was soon halted by a groundskeeper who pointed to a "No Trespassing" sign and asked, "Doesn't anyone in this group know how to read?"

✪ Later, Garbo led another group on a search for a medicinal spring in the desert. The healing spring turned out to be a pipe with a faucet. Underneath the faucet Greta discovered a battered old bathtub in which a bearded derelict was relaxing.

✪ Garbo did not care for her illustrious but self-absorbed costar Fredric March on the set of *Anna Karenina* (1935). So before their love scenes, Greta munched on garlic.

✪ Garbo accepted an invitation to go to actress Tallulah Bankhead's house for dinner. She arrived at Bankhead's place with a black wig, a Chinese dress, and Orientalized eyes. "So solly," Greta slurred in a Sino-Scandinavian accent, "but Miss Garbo will not be able to join you. She send me instead."

✪ High fashion photographer/designer Cecil Beaton asked Greta if he could take her passport picture. He took the photo and sold it to *Vogue* magazine. Greta was furious and didn't speak to the Britisher for almost two years. Then she went to bed with him and made ecstatic love. Later, the bisexual Beaton admitted, "Ecstasy is revolting."

Judy Garland

FACTS OF LIFE (and Death)

ORIGIN: Born Frances Ethel Gumm, June 10, 1922, Grand Rapids, Minnesota; died June 22, 1969, London, England.

FORMATIVE YEARS: Attended MGM's school for child actors in Culver City, California.

FAMILY PLANNING: Married David Rose (bandleader), July 28, 1941; divorced 1945; married Vincente Minnelli (director), June 15, 1945; divorced 1952; married Sid Luft (producer), June 8, 1952; divorced 1965; married Mark Herron (actor), November 14, 1965; divorced 1966; married Mickey Deans (waiter), March 15, 1969.

ROMANTIC INTERESTS: Artie Shaw (musician), Greg Bautzer (lawyer), Joseph L. Mankiewicz (director), Tyrone Power (actor), Glenn Ford (actor), Mario Lanza (actor), Eddie Fisher (singer), Prince Aly Khan (royalty).

SELECTED HITS (and Misses)

FILMS: *Pigskin Parade* (1936), *Thoroughbreds Don't Cry* (1938), *Listen, Darling* (1938), *Everybody Sing* (1938), *Love Finds Andy Hardy* (1938), *The Wizard of Oz* (Oscar for Best Juvenile Performance—1939), *Babes in Arms* (1939), *Strike Up the Band* (1940), *Ziegfeld Girl* (1941), *Life Begins for Andy Hardy* (1941), *For Me and My Gal* (1942), *Girl Crazy* (1943), *Meet Me in St. Louis* (1944), *The Clock* (1945), *The Harvey Girls* (1946), *The Pirate* (1948), *Easter Parade* (1948), *In the Good Old Summertime* (1949), *Summer Stock* (1950), *A Star Is Born* (1954), *Judgment at Nuremberg* (1961), *Gay Purree* (voice only, 1962), *I Could Go on Singing* (1963).

TV SERIES: *The Judy Garland Show* (1963–64).

QUICKIE BIO

Poor Frances Gumm—she died not long after she hit the stage at the age of two and a half. In her place rose the Hollywood creation—Judy Garland. She regulated her weight (with a movie studio prescribing her a diet of pep pills and sleeping pills) to help her become the perfect innocent in the hi-tech musical smash *The Wizard of Oz* (1939). However, when drug-addled Judy finally fell apart in 1950, the studio fired her, and the career of the enormously talented singer went slowly downhill. Later, Judy became the queen of camp and a pill-popping maternal menace. "Watch this," Judy warned her daughter Liza Minnelli. "I'm gonna have to do something crazy." Did she ever!

JUDY GARLAND
DOES THE DUMBEST THINGS

⭐ After putting pudgy young Judy under contract, MGM studio boss Louis B. Mayer ordered that the lot's commissary serve her nothing but chicken soup. When his demands did not result in a skinny Judy, the MGM doctor gave teenage Judy amphetamines. He then prescribed sedatives to help her sleep.

⭐ In 1946, the studio put a psychiatrist on the payroll. He was one of three such mental doctors Garland saw every day during that period.

⭐ Judy was bullied constantly by the studio. She let them tell her what to eat, wear, drink, and even who to date. MGM made her break up with fellow actor Tyrone Power, saying he was bad for her image. After she eloped with composer David Rose and became pregnant, she was pressured by the studio into having an abortion. Garland later told friends that her first marriage fell apart because Rose refused to satisfy her orally.

⭐ According to Hollywood gay lore, Garland was first seduced by a young publicist named Betty Asher and later allegedly had affairs with Broadway luminary Ethel Merman and singer/vocal coach/writer Kay Thompson. It was rumored that Judy married director Vincente Minnelli so that they each might engage in unusual extramarital affairs.

⭐ During the filming of MGM's *Annie Get Your Gun* (1950), Judy's pill-popping was so bad, she was literally falling down. Finally, after one too many of these collapses, the crew simply walked off and left her lying in a heap. She had recorded the entire soundtrack, but was still replaced by Betty Hutton, who was borrowed from Paramount Pictures.

✪ After she was suspended from MGM in 1950, Garland locked herself in the bathroom, broke a mirror, and tried, unsuccessfully, to cut her throat. Fellow Metro-Goldwyn-Mayer star Katharine Hepburn sent Judy a get-well card after the incident. Hepburn wrote "So glad you cut your throat. All the other girl singers need that kind of break." Judy read the note aloud to a visiting friend and declared, "Isn't that sweet?"

✪ Judy gave throat cutting a second try just after daughter Lorna's birth in 1952. This incident was more serious than the first, requiring stitches. Days later, Garland performed at a Christmas charity wearing a high collar dress.

✪ Garland tried slashing her wrists too. The doctor said he didn't understand why she didn't just slash her ankles. "I can't," she said, "because I am a dancer."

✪ As a child, Liza Minnelli had to mother her own unstable mom. Among her "jobs" was replacing Judy's pills with sugar substitutes. Mother Judy was so devious about hiding her drugs that she sewed them in the linings of draperies and hid them in powder, in the bed, and under rugs.

✪ At one time Garland hired a chauffeur, who proved to be a drunk. However, she liked him too much to fire him. So she made elder daughter Liza drive her siblings to school, even though Liza was too young to have a driver's license.

✪ Judy had taken so many pills one time that she fell asleep with a burning cigarette and third husband Sid Luft had to save her from the resultant fire.

✪ During the custody battle between Judy and Sid Luft, it was claimed Judy tried to commit suicide twenty-three times, and that in 1961 she ran naked around a hotel room, trying to jump out the window.

✪ By the mid-1950s, Judy was very broke and in severe debt to the Internal Revenue Service. She tried to save money by sneaking out of hotels without paying her bills. Garland dressed herself and her children in up to five layers of clothes to avoid carrying suitcases as they ran out of the lobby.

💰 Despite ongoing money troubles, the singing star kept a bag filled with about $28,000 in cash in the house. When she got too blotto, she'd forget where she hid it and would accuse everyone of stealing it.

✪ Judy liked to go bowling with actor Peter Lawford. Her favorite trick was to throw the bowling ball high in the air with an underhand toss. She thought that a gutter ball meant the ball went down someone else's lane.

⭐ A Garland maid recalled that she once prepared a tray of shrimp creole for Judy to eat in bed. When presented with the meal, Judy commented on how pretty the tray looked, then threw it across the room, and told the maid to get out.

⭐ Judy once called her children's governess "a Texas bitch." "I'm not from Texas," the governess said. At that point, Judy chased her out of the room with a hot iron. Quite sensibly, the children's caretaker quit.

⭐ Judy married her fourth husband, the mysterious actor Mark Herron, on November 14, 1965, in a Buddhist ceremony. They separated six months later. In her divorce deposition, she claimed the union with Herron had never been consummated.

Whoopi Goldberg

FACTS OF LIFE

ORiGiN: Born Caryn Elaine Johnson, November 13, 1949 (or November 13, 1955), New York City, New York.

FORMATIVE YEARS: Studied at the Deloux School of Cosmetology, San Diego, California.

FAMiLY PLANNiNG: Married Alvin Martin (drug counselor), 1971; divorced 1973; married David Claessen (filmmaker), September 1, 1986, divorced 1988; married Lyle Trachtenberg (union organizer), October 1, 1994; divorced 1995.

ROMANTiC iNTERESTS: Brent Spiner (actor), Eric Bogosian (actor), Timothy Dalton (actor), Ted Danson (actor), Frank Langella (actor).

SELECTED HITS (and Misses)

FiLMS: *The Color Purple* (1985), *Jumpin' Jack Flash* (1986), *Burglar* (1987), *Fatal Beauty* (1987), *Clara's Heart* (1988), *Homer and Eddie* (1989), *Ghost* (Oscar for Best Supporting Actress—1990), *The Long Walk Home* (1990), *Soapdish* (1991), *The Player* (1992), *Sarafina!* (1992), *Sister Act* (1992), *Made in America* (1993), *Sister Act 2: Back in the Habit* (1993), *The Lion King* (voice only, 1994), *Corrina, Corrina* (1994), *Boys on the Side* (1995), *Moonlight and Valentino* (1995), *Eddie* (1996), *Bogus* (1996), *Theodore Rex* (1996), *The Associate* (1996), *How Stella Got Her Groove Back* (1998), *The Deep End of the Ocean* (1999), *Girl, Interrupted* (1999).

TV SERiES: *Star Trek: The Next Generation* (1988–93), *Bagdad Café* (1990–91), *Captain Planet and the Planeteers* (voice only, 1990–93), *The Whoopi Goldberg Show* (1992–93), *Hollywood Squares* (1998–present).

QUICKIE BIO

Caryn Johnson grew up in a black middle-class family and acted on stage in New York before heading to San Diego, California. Taking a cue, perhaps, from Sammy Davis Jr., Johnson adopted the Jewish name Goldberg and hit it big as Whoopi, performing one-woman stage shows in the San Francisco area. She made the jump from the stage to the screen with *The Color Purple* (1985), and goofed her way up the Hollywood ladder, sporting the world's most recognizable set of "do-do" braids, and earning $7.5 million a season for starring on the revival of the classic, campy TV quiz show *Hollywood Squares* in the late 1990s. Whoopi told it like it was when she was paid six million dollars to write a book entitled *Book* (1997). "Everyone gets crusty drawers," Whoopi wrote, "unless we shower after every dump, or walk around with a swab to wipe around the rim." Whoops!

WHOOPI GOLDBERG
DOES THE DUMBEST THINGS

✪ "When I was younger I tried to go down on myself with some success," Whoopi once confessed. "I actually could reach, and I remember thinking that was a big deal, but I couldn't do much down there. . . . I was all curled and rolled into a ball and craning my neck like a long-necked dinosaur in the fetal position."

✪ Early in her career, Whoopi worked as a bricklayer and sheet-rock installer. At one point she even took a job in a strip joint. She claimed that she never took her clothes off because "people were screaming, 'Don't do it.'" Goldberg, mercifully, gave up stripping and started to collect welfare.

✪ Goldberg took cosmetology courses, and got a part-time job at a San Diego mortuary as a cosmetician. Whoopi described the corpses as "big dolls," and made them up to look like Joan Collins or Lucille Ball. Sometimes she taunted the corpses saying, "I'm glad you're dead. You were a creep."

✪ A colleague gave Whoopi her nickname because her farts sounded like joke farts from a whoopee cushion. "Let's consider the fart in all its wonder," Whoopi later reflected. "I always call my farts tree monkeys, 'cause tree monkeys make the same farty sound as I do." Whoopi went

"I don't care if he boned a sheep, if that's his thing," Whoopi Goldberg said about her bosom buddy President Bill Clinton. Whoopi later suggested that "people who pick their noses in cars should be arrested."
[photo courtesy of Reuters/Mike Theiler/Archive Photos]

on to say, "If I'm not dropping air biscuits, something's wrong," and concluded, "Love me, love my farts."

★ To promote the first Comic Relief concert in 1986, organizers Billy Crystal, Robin Williams, and Goldberg stayed in $1,000-a-night suites in a swanky New York City hotel. Comic Relief was a fund-raiser for the homeless.

★ On a trip to Washington, D.C., Whoopi took a train, buying up half of the seats in the club car for herself and her entourage at a cost of $2,500. She went to the nation's capital to testify concerning the effects of budget cuts on the poor.

★ The community around Goldberg's Connecticut home put together a cookbook to raise funds for a local environmental education organization. Luminaries like TV newsman Tom Brokaw submitted recipes. So did Goldberg—for something called "Jewish American Princess Fried Chicken." The recipe read, "Send chauffeur to favorite butcher shop for the chicken. . . . Have cook prepare the rest of the meal while you touch up your makeup."

✪ Goldberg was irked by Hollywood's tendency to cast white people in roles meant to be played by white people. She lobbied hard for the lead in *Single White Female* (1992). "I'm not going to stop doing it," she declared, after she didn't get the part which went to Bridget Fonda.

✪ During the filming of *Sister Act* (1992), Whoopi had a disagreement with Disney, the studio that was producing the screen comedy. An upset Goldberg characterized her appearance in the film as "picking cotton" for Disney. She reportedly showed up on the set one day wearing a T-shirt that read "Nigga-teer."

Whoopi had an affair with actor Ted Danson, her costar in *Made in America* (1993). The Hollywood couple thought it would be funny if boyfriend Ted wore blackface to a Friars Club roast for Whoopi on October 8, 1993, and delivered jokes that Whoopi reportedly wrote. At one point, Danson said, his mother walked in on them and proceeded to lecture Ted and Whoopi on the supposed realities of having mulatto children. One of the parent's supposed "funny" questions: "Who will convince the children if they have diarrhea that they're not melting?" The "funny" reply: "I told her, 'Mom, relax. I'm f***ing her in the a**.'" Whoopi later defended her humor by saying, "Richard Pryor could have delivered the same material on himself and people would have been p***ing themselves in the aisles." Is that a good thing?

✪ Whoopi Goldberg got so angry when a meter attendant gave her a parking ticket that she began to yank on her fake dreadlocks. She screamed, "Don't give me a ticket!" and pulled out half a dozen of her artificial braids, which had taken hours to braid into her real hair. The attendant cracked up and didn't give her a ticket.

Hugh Grant

FACTS OF LIFE

ORIGIN: Born Hugh John Mungo Grant, September 9, 1960, Chiswick, England.

FORMATIVE YEARS: Educated at Oxford University in England.

FAMILY PLANNING: None.

ROMANTIC INTERESTS: Mary Glanville (co-ed), Divine Brown (cross-dressing hooker), Elizabeth Hurley (actress).

SELECTED HITS (and Misses)

FILMS: *Maurice* (1987), *The Lair of the White Worm* (1988), *The Big Man* (1990), *Impromptu* (1991), *Bitter Moon* (1992), *The Remains of the Day* (1993), *Four Weddings and a Funeral* (1994), *Sirens* (1994), *An Awfully Big Adventure* (1994), *Sense and Sensibility* (1995), *Nine Months* (1995), *The Englishman Who Went Up a Hill But Came Down a Mountain* (1995), *Extreme Measures* (1996), *Notting Hill* (1999), *Mickey Blue-Eyes* (1999).

QUICKIE BIO

Grant was born to an upper-middle-class family in the bland and sheltered London suburb of Chiswick. He started acting in high school as a way to meet girls. At Oxford University, he became seriously interested in not being serious, and broke into films. With his dashing good looks and devil-may-care persona, foppish Hugh became the Peter Lawford of the 1990s and hit it big with *Four Weddings and a Funeral* (1994). Grant's most famous role came a year later, when he got too romantic off-camera with a Hollywood hooker. The public was shocked—and couldn't get enough of the naughty Englishman. "I could use a little bad publicity," commented actress Andie MacDowell (Grant's costar in *Four Weddings and a Funeral*) after the incident. "I should go out and do something like that."

HUGH GRANT
DOES THE DUMBEST THINGS

✪ Hugh tried to seduce young ladies with such winning lines as "My girlfriend doesn't understand me." He kept a paperback edition of D. H. Lawrence's classic sex novel *Lady Chatterley's Lover* in his pocket. Grant approached possible conquests with the question, "Do you have the foggiest what D. H. Lawrence is going on about? I don't."

✪ Grant was so convinced that he was going to be offered the lead role in *Greystoke: The Legend of Tarzan* (1984) that he bragged to all his friends and told his teachers at Oxford, "I'm terribly sorry. I may not be able to take my finals. It seems they want me to go off and become a movie star." Grant didn't get the part. Christopher Lambert claimed the jungle assignment.

✪ While "slumming" for acting work, Hugh did a modeling session for the *Secret Love Annual* of a teen fantasy magazine. Grant was profiled as Brian, a romantic hero who rescued a girl from her beer-swilling boyfriend.

✪ The early Grant vehicle *Maurice* (1987) enjoyed decent success in London. Grant casually strolled up and down in front of theatres where the film was playing in hopes of being recognized and fawned over by female fans.

✪ A schoolmate of Hugh's recalled seeing the still-struggling actor standing around in the bathroom at parties, sculpting his hair and "moaning that nobody had asked him whether he was Hugh Grant."

✪ Girlfriend Elizabeth Hurley has confided that Hugh loved nothing more than to see her dressed up in tiny tight hot pants and knee-length white boots. According to Hurley, Grant also liked to wear mint-flavored condoms.

 In June of 1995 in Hollywood, Grant reportedly paid Divine Brown sixty dollars for oral sex. Nearby, cops watched the deal go down in Grant's parked BMW. The law enforcers waited a few minutes more, then interrupted the two in the middle of a "lewd act." The Los Angeles police faxed a report to the newspaper offices of London's *The Times* in a record thirty-three minutes. Brown later revealed that the whole incident could have been avoided if Grant had simply coughed up another forty dollars to go back to her place rather than doing it in the car.

✪ Hugh escaped from the incident with only a few hours of counseling (well, actually, he didn't get off at all). Brown, who was on probation for previous offenses, got slapped with six months in jail, a $1,350 fine, community service, and AIDS counseling. Brown later surfaced as the "spokes-creature" for a porn channel.

✪ After his guest appearance at the police station, Grant's next appearance on *The Tonight Show with Jay Leno* brought talk show maven Leno his highest TV ratings ever.

✪ "I do like making boys wear my high heels and earrings," Grant's girlfriend Elizabeth Hurley confessed. "But not my panties, because that's not going to look very pretty." Hurley spent a lot of her time raising awareness and money for the plight of endangered chimpanzees, and one time told a reporter, "I would prefer a puppy to a baby."

✪ Hugh complained about how badly the press had treated him concerning the hooker incident. He claimed that he was upset because of his family, not himself. "If I'd been a single orphan, I wouldn't have given a monkey's f*** about it." "He's got ears that are very monkeyish," Hurley later observed. "I've always liked things simian."

✪ Grant described his relationship with longtime girlfriend and actress-model Elizabeth Hurley as very "like brother and sister." He added, "Which isn't to say that's not a sexy thing. Because I think the idea of incest is quite titillating."

✪ Grant was on a train in France when he began to suffer discomfort from his first ever hemorrhoid. Curious, Grant retreated to the bathroom, where he stood on the toilet, turned his back to the mirror, pulled his cheeks apart and put his head between his legs to have a look. Unfortunately Grant neglected to lock the door.

✪ After complaining about the press, Grant invited a reporter to a gay club by saying, "Shall we go for a pint of wee-wee?" Indeed Grant stood at the bar of that club and asked the fellow next to him, "Say, I heard one can get a pint of wee-wee here. Do you know if that's true?" The barfly responded, "If you go into the loo and have someone stick their d*** in your mouth, I guess you could, yeah."

⭐ Grant left the bar without tasting wee-wee. As he walked down the street with the reporter, he observed, "They had no idea who the devil I was, did they?"

⭐ Grant claimed he had food fights with Julia Roberts on the set of *Notting Hill* (1999). "She'd come up to me on subsequent days, she'd find some bit of food lying around the set and just quietly press it into the side of my neck," Grant recalled. "Into my ear was one of her favorites."

"If I ate a teaspoon of poo in the morning, how would I feel by teatime?" Hugh Grant pondered.
[photo courtesy of Express Newspapers/Archive]

Jean Harlow

FACTS OF LIFE (and Death)

ORIGIN: Born Harlean Harlow Carpentier, March 3, 1911, Kansas City, Missouri; died June 7, 1937, Los Angeles, California, of kidney disease.

FORMATIVE YEARS: Dropped out of high school.

FAMILY PLANNING: Married Charles Fremont McGrew III (heir), September 21, 1927; divorced 1932; married Paul Bern (studio executive), July 2, 1932; widowed 1932: married Harold Rosson (cinematographer), September 18, 1933; divorced 1936:

ROMANTIC INTERESTS: Howard Hughes (producer), Clark Gable (actor), William Powell (actor), Lew Ayres (actor), Bugsy Siegel (gangster), Jimmy Stewart (actor).

SELECTED HITS (and Misses)

FILMS: *Moran of the Marines* (1928), *Hell's Angels* (1930), *Platinum Blonde* (1931), *The Public Enemy* (1931), *Red-Headed Woman* (1932), *Red Dust* (1932), *Hold Your Man* (1933), *Dinner at Eight* (1933), *Bombshell* (1933), *The Girl from Missouri* (1934), *Reckless* (1935), *China Seas* (1935), *Riff-Raff* (1935), *Wife vs. Secretary* (1936), *Suzy* (1936), *Libeled Lady* (1936), *Personal Property* (1937), *Saratoga* (1937).*

*Harlow died during the filming of this movie. The role was completed by stand-in Mary Dees.

QUICKIE BIO

Sixteen-year-old Harlean Carpentier eloped with a young businessman and wound up in Los Angeles, supporting herself, her cloying mother, and her deadbeat stepfather by working as an extra and bit player in the movies.

Harlean first attracted attention when she wore a sheer negligee for a scene in Laurel and Hardy's short film *Double Whoopee* (1929), and hit it big in Howard Hughes's World War I epic *Hell's Angels* (1930). In the 1930s, the blonde bombshell took her mother's maiden name and evolved into a wise-cracking, on-screen sex pot who stirred the loins of the nation (and the wrath of Hollywood censors) before she died of kidney disease at age twenty-six. Though she proved to be one of Hollywood's most charismatic sex goddesses, Harlow was never sure of her own abilities. "No one expects a great lay to pay all the bills," she once complained. "So why do they expect it of me? Is it because I am not a great lay?"

JEAN HARLOW
DOES THE DUMBEST THINGS

✪ As a little girl, the future Jean Harlow had an unpleasant experience at summer camp. While relieving herself in the wild during a hike, she inadvertently used poison oak leaves as toilet paper.

✪ Jean's first husband, Chuck McGrew, was heir to a small fortune and kept Jean in style. Unfortunately, he was also an alcoholic, and Jean tried to keep up with him. She lost the race when he stayed drunk for two whole days after their first Christmas together.

✪ During the filming of the all-star *Dinner at Eight* (1933), which included John Barrymore, Marie Dressler, and Wallace Beery, Harlow had her blond pubic hair bleached even blonder because it made a shadow behind her filmy costume.

✪ Jean attended a party wearing a revealing gown. The hostess commented that the dress was "down to your waist!" Jean took it as a compliment, slipped the straps from her shoulders and bared her breasts and torso for all to enjoy.

✪ On the set of *The Public Enemy* (1931), James Cagney looked at the ever perky Jean Harlow and asked, "How do you hold those things up?" She responded, "I ice them," which she actually did.

✪ Jean Harlow's second husband was a soft-spoken older MGM producer named Paul Bern. Harlow liked him because, "He's different and doesn't talk f***, f***, f*** all the time."

✪ Paul Bern was different all right. According to some, he was impotent. One night in 1932, he tried to use a mechanical substitute to satisfy Harlow, but they both wound up laughing. A few hours later, Bern committed suicide. Groucho Marx commented, "I would have done the same thing."

Bern had tried to kill himself once before, by drowning himself in the toilet. His head got stuck and a plumber had to come and unscrew the toilet seat. According to one observer, Bern "looked like he just won the derby."

Hollywood insiders feared that Bern's suicide would hurt Harlow's career. It did not. Thanks in part to the scandal, her career thrived. One of her later pictures, *Reckless* (1935), took reality to the celluloid reel. It was about a showgirl whose husband kills himself. The MGM feature was a big hit.

 After her marriage to Bern ended, Harlow considered going out with her stepfather, whom she referred to as "The Sicilian Pimp." Instead, she settled for a string of lovers including a door-to-door salesman and a taxi driver. She waited outside a theatre one evening where her film *Red Dust* (1932) was playing, and picked up a guy who had just seen the jungle-set romance. After they made love, the guy suggested that Jean Harlow get a job as the double for Jean Harlow.

Whatever shortcomings Paul Bern had, close pals called husband number three, cinematographer Harold Rosson, "long dong." Jean filed for divorce from husband Rosson in the mid-1930s on the grounds that Rosson kept her awake at night by reading in bed.

Dennis Hopper

DUMBEST QUOTE

"If you drilled through the Earth
right now you'd reach Tibet; it's like the brains of
the Earth. But the copper is causing an overreaction
and it's pulling the poison out of me."

FACTS OF LIFE

ORIGIN: Born May 17, 1935, Dodge City, Kansas.

FORMATIVE YEARS: Graduated from Helix High School in San Diego, California.

FAMILY PLANNING: Married Brooke Hayward (Hollywood brat), August 9, 1961; divorced 1969; married Michelle Phillips (singer), October 31, 1970; divorced 1971; married Daria Halprin (actress), May 1972; divorced 1976; married Katherine LaNasa, June 1985; divorced 1993.

ROMANTIC INTERESTS: Natalie Wood (actress), Joan Collins (actress), Ursula Andress (actress).

SELECTED HITS (and Misses)

FILMS: *Rebel without a Cause* (1955), *Giant* (1956), *Key Witness* (1960), *The Sons of Katie Elder* (1965), *The Trip* (1967), *Easy Rider* (1969),* *The Last Movie* (1971),* *Mad Dog Morgan* (1976), *The American Friend* (1977), *Reborn* (1978), *Apocalypse Now* (1979), *Out of the Blue* (1980),* *The Osterman Weekend* (1983), *The Inside Man* (1984), *My Science Project* (1985), *Blue Velvet* (1986), *Hoosiers* (1986), *Texas Chainsaw Massacre 2* (1986), *Black Widow* (1987), *Colors* (1988),* *Backtrack* (1989—released in 1991),* *Double-Crossed* (1991), *Super Mario Bros.* (1993), *Boiling Point* (1993), *Red Rock West* (1993), *True Romance* (1993), *Speed* (1994), *Waterworld* (1995), *Carried Away* (1995), *Basquiat* (1996), *Meet the Deedles* (1998), *EdTV* (1999) *The Source* (documentary, 1999), *Straight Shooter* (1999), *Quicksand* (2000).

*Also directed by Hopper.

QUICKIE BIO

"Come the revolution," young Dennis Hopper screamed to a party of Hollywood producers, "this crowd will be dead." Several decades later they were still alive, and, more amazing, so was Hopper. Hopper boogied from his family farm in Kansas to Southern California, where he sampled the drug culture and hit it big on-screen with his actor buddy James Dean. Hopper's drug-induced rages alienated Hollywood. So he made the New York scene, clicked so many photos that friends called him "the Tourist," and painted artwork until everything burned up in a fire. He made film history with the hippie biker saga *Easy Rider* (1969), moved to New Mexico, and went on a bender for more than a decade. His reported daily intake: half a gallon of rum, a few beers, and several grams of cocaine. Hopper eventually straightened up, but looking back on his career, he sighed, "I should really be dead."

DENNIS HOPPER
DOES THE DUMBEST THINGS

✪ As a young boy on the farm in the Midwest with his grandparents, Dennis sniffed gasoline from the tank of his grandfather's truck and tripped out on the clouds. One day he sniffed too much. He went into a violent frenzy and broke the windshield and headlights of the truck with a baseball bat.

✪ As a teenager, Hopper wanted to have an orgy with actress Natalie Wood, actor Nick Adams, and another girl. Natalie Wood had a plan. "To do this right," she said, "we have to have a champagne bath." Dennis and Adams uncorked bottles of champagne, poured them into a bathtub, and yelled out, "Okay, Natalie, let's start the orgy!" Natalie lowered herself into the tub, then jumped out screaming, "I am on fire!" The boys splashed cold water on her and rushed her to a hospital.

✪ Dennis got so drunk so often that he'd fall asleep with lit cigarettes in his fingers and start fires. One time, his first wife, Brooke Hayward, found him lying in bed surrounded by flames. She saved him, but later reflected, "Sometimes I regretted that."

✪ Hopper married his second wife, Michelle Phillips, on Halloween 1970. The groom celebrated by calling his wife a witch, handcuffing her, and smacking her. Michelle ran away. Later she spoke with Dennis on the phone. "I love you," Hopper moaned. Phillips asked, "Have you ever thought of suicide?"

✪ Witnesses on the *Easy Rider* (1969) set in New Orleans described Dennis as being a "semi-psychotic maniac" who was always within easy

"The cocaine problem in the United States is really because of me," bragged Dennis Hopper, pictured here relaxing in 1971. [photo courtesy of Archive Photos]

reach of a loaded gun. Rip Torn was costarring on the set of *Easy Rider*, when he heard Hopper complaining about Texas rednecks. "Take it easy," Torn said. "Not everyone from Texas is an a-hole." Torn offered to shake hands with Hopper, but Hopper knocked his hand away and sneered, "Sit down, you motherf***er." Then Hopper grabbed a steak knife and held it between Torn's eyes. "You wanna have a knife fight?" Hopper asked. "I'll wait for you out in the street . . ." Torn replied. Hopper never showed up, and Torn quit the film.

★ Hopper recalled the incident on a TV talk show in 1994. However, in Dennis's version of the story, Torn had held a knife on him. Torn sued Hopper and won.

★ Hopper wanted to run the credits for *Easy Rider* upside down.

★ After Dennis decided to quit drinking, he went to meetings of Alcoholics Anonymous with half an ounce of coke in his pocket.

★ Jack Nicholson and Hopper got together in Taos, New Mexico, and dropped LSD. They lay in front of the granite tomb of D. H. Lawrence's wife, and watched insects swarm over their heads. Hopper recalled, "We talked about the insects and said that's what we really are."

★ In Peru during the filming of *The Last Movie* (1971), almost every member of Hopper's production crew was doing coke, grass, acid, peyote, or speed. A typical evening: at 2:00 A.M., a girl on a bad trip screamed while women climbed up on the front of the hotel in their nighties. One group held a whipping party. When an actor found a woman chained to a porch post, he pulled a "Joan of Arc" and tried to light a fire around her feet. When authorities told Hopper to keep things under control, he said that Peru was "uptight."

★ After Hopper moved to Taos, New Mexico, in the early 1970s, he was arrested for possession of a deadly weapon, disorderly conduct, verbal assault, and resisting arrest. One day, Hopper and his brother grabbed their guns, drove to the Taos High School, and marched into the student assembly. "Just because these hippies are dropping acid," Hopper reportedly lectured the students, "that doesn't give you the right to rape their women and cut their balls off."

 Hired to play the head of the U.S. Drug Enforcement Agency in a movie, Hopper arrived on the movie set in Mexico completely whacked out. He checked into his hotel, then became convinced that people were being tortured in the basement. Dennis stripped off all his clothes and walked out of town. He insisted he felt snakes and bugs under his skin and saw an alien spacecraft. Then he became his own solar system. When he wandered back into town and friends tried to get him to dress, Dennis yelled, "No, kill me like this!"

★ After being put on a flight out of Mexico, Hopper became convinced that cameras were filming him, so while it was still on the runway he crawled out onto the wing of the airplane.

★ Back in Los Angeles, Hopper grabbed a pair of hedge clippers and began clipping things. He claimed that clipping the shrubbery made the voices in his head shut up. He was diagnosed as paranoid schizophrenic and hospitalized.

★ To promote the film *Out of the Blue* (1980), Hopper recreated something he called the Russian Suicide Death Chair. At a speedway outside Houston, Hopper lay down in a coffin made of paper, surrounded himself with sticks of dynamite, and blew himself up. Nonetheless, he was unhurt.

★ When asked which historical figure he most identified with, Hopper answered, "God."

Whitney Houston

FACTS OF LIFE

ORIGIN: Born August 9, 1963, Newark, New Jersey.

FORMATIVE YEARS: Graduated from Mount Saint Dominick's Academy, Caldwell, New Jersey.

FAMILY PLANNING: Married Bobby Brown (singer), July 18, 1992.

ROMANTIC INTERESTS: Robyn Crawford (school friend), Jermaine Jackson (singer), Eddie Murphy (movie star), Randall Cunningham (football player).

SELECTED HITS (and Misses)

FILMS: *The Bodyguard* (1992), *Waiting to Exhale* (1995), *The Preacher's Wife* (1996), *Scratch the Surface* (documentary, 1997), *Anything for Love* (1999).

QUICKIE BIO

Whitney Houston was born to be a hard-partying star. Her mother was respected, gospel-singing Cissy Houston, and her cousin was the 1960s pop-singing sensation Dionne Warwick. Houston graced the covers of *Seventeen* and *Glamour* as a teenage model, then hit the record charts in 1987 with an album that yielded a record-breaking seven number one hits. Her first feature film, *The Bodyguard* (1992) with Kevin Costner, got bad reviews but sold huge numbers of tickets, and catapulted Whitney into diva-hood. However, success did not keep Whitney from marrying bad-boy singer Bobby Brown and becoming notorious for their public squabbles. For someone who gave generously to charity and ruled as one of the great African-American women of Hollywood, Whitney Houston's bad behavior just seemed so . . . dumb.

WHITNEY HOUSTON
DOES THE DUMBEST THINGS

⭐ Whitney Houston always has worn wigs in public. Explained Houston, "I don't go no place without my hair, honey."

⭐ Robyn Crawford was Whitney's longtime roommate and then her "executive assistant." "No, I'm not a lesbo," Whitney claimed. "Guys that say that about me are the same ones who want to jump into my pants." Mother Cissy Houston attributed the rumors to the fact that "Whitney doesn't wear clothes up to her behind with her tits out, excuse my French."

⭐ Whitney released "The Star-Spangled Banner" as a single cut which went to number one on a wave of Gulf War patriotism in the early 1990s. But another war started after Whitney performed the song at the 1991 Super Bowl. Whitney began to flirt with rapper MC Hammer. Robyn supposedly got jealous, grabbed Whitney and told her to stop. Whitney told Robyn to "go to hell," Robyn reportedly slapped Whitney, and Whitney ran away. Cissy Houston, Whitney's mother, screamed at Robyn, "What the f*** did you put your hands on my baby for?" Then Cissy allegedly slugged Robyn in the jaw and kept on punching her, screaming, "I'll kill you, you stupid-a** bitch!" until onlookers finally separated Whitney's mother from Whitney's best friend.

⭐ Things didn't go much smoother between Whitney and Michael, her brother (and her employee). When Whitney yelled at Michael for being late, Michael yelled, "F*** you, Whitney." Whitney supposedly slapped him across the face, and Michael allegedly slugged his sibling. Then Whitney hit him back. After watching the fight for a while, mama Cissy stepped up to bat, slapped Michael on the head with her cane, and said, "That's enough. Michael, don't you hurt my baby."

⭐ Onstage, Whitney talked like a choir girl. Offstage, she swore like a sailor. Sometimes, she got confused. Appearing for a group of children with AIDS, Whitney hugged them, cried, and posed for the cameras. A few minutes later, a dry-eyed Whitney reportedly hissed under her breath to her bodyguard, "Get me the f*** out of here, away from these musty-a**ed, smelly kids!"

⭐ Whitney and brother Michael were drinking at a hotel bar in Kentucky in 1991, when they got to know the locals. Michael claimed he heard a racist slur and punched a fellow barfly. When another man stepped in to break up the fight, Whitney supposedly punched him. The argument went on until the police came and took Whitney and Michael away. The two men claimed that the Houstons had made "terrorist threats." The charges were later dropped.

⭐ Houston arrived late at the White House for a dinner honoring South African leader Nelson Mandela. When asked why she was two hours tardy, Houston shrugged and said, "I just got off tour." She had—four days earlier.

⭐ When Whitney sang a concert in Sheffield, England, she ordered Chinese food from her favorite restaurant—in London. A cab had to drive 169 miles to pick up the delivery at a cost of $320.

⭐ In 1997, Japanese reporters spied Whitney's husband, singer Bobby Brown, slipping out of the hotel room he was sharing with Houston for a night on the town. Houston found Brown in a club and hauled him out of the joint. An unhappy Bobby threw Whitney's $5,000 wedding ring out the window of the limo on the way back to the hotel.

⭐ Bobby Brown was arrested in Georgia for lewd behavior, and later accused by a teenager of alleged sexual battery in a hotel pool in California. He was arrested for drunk driving in 1996 in Georgia, and that same year crashed his car in Florida and was sentenced to jail time for drunk driving, again. He reportedly showed up to serve his jail time completely inebriated. Whitney sighed, "It hasn't put a strain on our marriage."

⭐ Whitney and Bobby took a romantic cruise on a yacht to the island of Capri. However, when Houston received a two-inch gash on her face and was rushed to a local hospital, it was rumored that hubby Bobby had caused the injury. Not so, Whitney insisted. First she told doctors she cut herself when she swam into a rock. Later she explained that she'd harmed herself when she fell on her yacht, saying, "As I fell I must've hit a plate or something." Or something. Later Whitney confessed, "It was a dumb thing."

★ Whitney and Bobby were spotted screaming at each other in a Honolulu mall parking lot. According to witnesses, Bobby, with a beer in his hand, slapped Whitney. Then she yelled for help. When mall security came to her rescue, the couple said things were cool. Later, her people explained to the press that Bobby hadn't really been fighting with Houston at all. He had actually been fighting with Whitney's sister Donna Houston.

★ Whitney later clarified her tumultuous relationship with husband Bobby. "Contrary to belief, I do the hitting, he doesn't. . . ." She told the press, "When we're fighting, it's like that's love for us. We're fighting for our love."

Bonus Section

(Other) Young Movie Stars
Do the Dumbest Things

DUMBEST QUOTES

Drew Barrymore

"I was born ten years old."

"I always wanted lice."

"I'm obsessed with ice cubes. . . . Ice is very much like flowers. It just dies at a certain point. But you know what's weird? You can bring it back to life. Just by freezing it. Ice, I worship it."

Matt Damon

"I was trying to watch CNN today, like a normal human being, and I'm f***ing all over it."

Claire Danes

"Everyone always has fun bowling."

"I just got my first ATM card and am figuring out how money works."

Cameron Diaz

"Come is coming of age!"

"I hate it when the shrimp has little veins all full of stuff. I can't deal with that."

MORE DUMBEST QUOTES

Salma Hayek
(as official spokesperson for Revlon)

"The secret is that it takes a lot of makeup
to make me look like the kind of woman
who doesn't wear makeup."

Anne Heche

"Want to know why girls turn from straight to gay?
Because the sex is great."

Jennifer Lopez

"All I can say is if they show my butt in a movie,
it better be a wide shot."

Ewan McGregor

"I'm just looking for that moment to drop my Jedi
knickers and pull out my real light saber."

Ryan Phillippe

"My rationale is that an a** is an a**—and that's
one thing everyone has. But it's gotten to
the point where I don't want to become known
as the guy who shows his a**."

Christina Ricci

"Basically, I'm like a whore. I'll give people
whatever they want so they like me."

"Sometimes I think I have Tourette's Syndrome.
I'll read something I've said and think,
'Why the hell did I say that?'"

Winona Ryder

"I think stoner dropouts should be writing
reviews because they're the most accurate."

EVEN MORE DUMBEST QUOTES

Will Smith

"I believe if I set my mind to it, within the next fifteen years, I could be the president of the United States."

Tori Spelling

"My butt fascinates me. So much so that when I dance, I'm always looking back at it."

Matt Stone

"I would love to have a f***ing huge a** for a week."

"Colorado was a really good place for me to live because I'm really conservative and an a**hole."

Catherine Zeta-Jones

"The only thing better than sex is sex with chocolate on top."

Matt Zone

"Condoms allow me to sleep with as many women as possible and not feel bad about it."

Rose McGowan

"I'm sure if lived back in Salem, I would have been burned at the stake."

QUICKIE OVERVIEW

In the old days, we used to hear a lot more dumb stuff about movie stars. But nowadays, with libel lawyers and uptight publicity departments, a lot less of the good juicy stuff about movie stars leaks out to the general public. Luckily, some still does. Will today's young stars reach the "depraved" depths of their predecessors? Judging from the following anecdotes, we think so. The real question is, who's dumber, males or females? At least some of the young stars have a clear understanding of what it really takes to make it in Hollywood. According to Christina Ricci, "I just do what I'm told."

YOUNG MALE STARS
DO THE DUMBEST THINGS

⭐ Leonardo DiCaprio ran around with a bunch of friends he called his "p***y posse." One night the gang returned to a hotel with two strippers, and called room service for a supply of condoms. Reportedly, DiCaprio got so trashed that the hotel had to call his older brother to help calm him down, while one of the strippers supposedly peed in the hallway. "I certainly don't think I'm leading a destructive life," the actor reasoned later, "at least compared to other people my age."

⭐ Leonardo refused to attend the Oscar ceremony the year of *Titanic* (1997). He left a message on director James Cameron's machine saying, "It just ain't me, bro."

📰 Leo and his "p***y posse" were having an early morning snack at a restaurant, when a girl at the next table tried to say hello to the heartthrob. "You have to have sex with me to meet Leo," one of the posse giggled. When another repeated the line, the girl dumped her plate on the guy's head. DiCaprio laughed like a loon and started a food fight.

⭐ Leonardo went strolling on a beach north of Malibu, California. He looked so bad that an elderly lady offered him a sandwich. The young star took it and said, "You know I'm actually a movie star." The woman responded, "Yeah, and I'm Raquel Welch. Enjoy."

⭐ During tryouts for the lead in *Boogie Nights* (1997), actor/model Mark Wahlberg told the director, "I've got an inch on Leo DiCaprio." At that point, the former Marky Mark displayed the inch and won the part.

⭐ Fun-loving DiCaprio jumped up on a table at a Miami Beach nightclub one night, grabbed his crotch, and danced a bump and grind. He also managed at different times to chase after model Kate Moss, actress Alicia Silverstone, actress Claire Danes, singer Mariah Carey, and Wonderbra model Eva Herzigova, among others. "I'm obsessed with girls," Leo confessed. "When you're my age your hormones are just kicking in and there's not much besides sex on your mind."

⭐ Leonardo DiCaprio attended the premiere of *Star Wars: Episode One— The Phantom Menace* (1999) in Hollywood. Before *Star Wars*, fans were treated to a trailer for DiCaprio's movie *The Beach* (1999). The movie star sat frowning while the people surrounding him chanted, "Leo sucks!"

✪ Ed Norton went to a yoga class with his actress girlfriend Courtney Love. The two were more into sex than enlightenment, so the instructor told them to leave each other alone. At lunchtime, the yoga-loving couple sought enlightenment together in the bathroom.

✪ A woman met humorist Chris Rock at the 1997 Emmy Awards, less than a year after Rock married Malaak Compton. When Rock hit on her, she asked, "Aren't you married?" Rock quipped, "What the hell does that have to do with anything?" The woman asked, "Where's your wife?" "Home," funnyman Rock replied, "where all wives belong."

✪ Funnyman Ben Stiller was doing bench presses at a gym when he got pinned under a barbell and screamed for help. A woman lifted the barbell off him with one hand and suggested to the mighty movie star, "You should use less weight."

✪ Matt Damon fell in love with actress Minnie Driver while they were filming *Good Will Hunting* (1997). Then Damon appeared on Oprah Winfrey's TV talk show and told Oprah that he no longer had a girlfriend. Understandably, Minnie was miffed.

✪ Denzel Washington took his seat on an airplane, but was annoyed to find someone sitting next to him. He complained to the stewardess, "I thought I was going to sit alone." "You are alone!" the man next to Denzel snarled. "I don't know who you are, I don't care, and I don't plan to talk to you!" The Oscar winner pouted for the rest of the flight.

✪ David Arquette once appeared on a television bike show while he was reportedly feeling no pain. "I like rode out and fell off and dislocated my finger," Arquette explained. "It's not a smart idea."

✪ Will Smith did his own underwear scenes for *Enemy of the State* (1998). "I have a special butt," Smith declared. "It has special curves, and it kinda has it's own attitude. . . . I think the audience can feel that, and if I were to try to put someone else's butt in that place, the audience would feel cheated and emotionally insulted."

✪ After he lost a chess match to a crew member of *Enemy of the State,* Will Smith went out and bought a book on chess strategy. Not satisfied that he was getting enough to help him beat his chess nemesis, Smith flew in the author to give him private lessons.

✪ Will Smith jumped off a cliff in Jamaica, even though he couldn't swim. "Even if I pass out, the [other divers] won't let me drown," he rationalized.

✪ While dating Asian model Donna Wong, Wesley Snipes commented that Asian women were "bedroom generals." Snipes also once commented to movie's "007" Sean Connery that the Scotsman was so cool and tough he must have some black blood in his veins.

✪ When Vince Vaughn graduated from high school, his guidance counselor looked at him and said, "There's nothing great about you intellectually."

✪ The first time Vaughn attended the Cannes Film Festival, the American flag at his hotel was hanging upside down. Vaughn asked the management to right the problem. When Vaughn returned to the hotel, the flag was still upside down, so he stood outside the hotel on the sidewalk and yelled, "You'd all be speaking German if it weren't for us."

✪ Before he was anybody in Hollywood, Vaughn would call hot nightspots and pretend to be an agent bringing in important clients from out of town so he and his buddies could get in the club.

✪ In between takes of a kissing scene with costar Jenna Elfman for *EdTV* (1999), leading man Matthew McConaughey chewed tobacco. "It tastes good," Matthew declared, "and I think Jenna liked it." She didn't.

✪ After receiving his first Hollywood paycheck, Ben Affleck took care of some essentials, saying, "I was sleeping on a couch at the time, so I bought a bed and a mattress . . . and a Jeep Grand Cherokee."

✪ At a press conference to promote the film *Forces of Nature* (1999), Ben Affleck claimed that his co-star Sandra Bullock "missed more periods than a third-string goalie."

✪ One of the Farrelly brothers—Peter and Bobby, the young filmmakers who created *Dumb & Dumber* (1994) and *There's Something About Mary* (1998)—posed for a nude photo with his hands over his crotch. When the photographers looked at the printed photo, they realized that Farrelly had painted a watch face on his penis and wrapped it around his wrist.

✪ Brad Pitt paid $20,000 for exotic plants at a nursery in Malibu, California, but never bothered to pick them up.

✪ In response to criticism of *Buffalo '66* (1998), Vincent Gallo, who directed and starred in the independent release, sneered, "If you don't like it, sister, why don't you go to Sundance, where all the commie films win prizes?"

✪ Comedian/actor Denis Leary once went to dinner with Dean Martin. When Dean offered Denis whiskey and Denis declined, Martin snapped, "What are you, a p***y?" "I had just gotten called a p***y by Dean Martin," Leary gushed later. "That was like one of my lifetime goals realized."

✪ Matt Stone and Trey Parker once were driving around Los Angeles in a limo with a pal. The friend suffered an attack of diarrhea, so they pulled over at an Arby's fast-food restaurant. The friend rushed in and came out sweating after twenty minutes. "He had completely destroyed Arby's," Trey reportedly recalled. "And then we just drove off—didn't even buy a burger."

✪ Matt Zone claimed that Barbra Streisand was the only celebrity he really hated. "And you can actually have nasal sex with her," the porn star observed. "Triple penetration: oral, anal, and nasal."

YOUNG FEMALE STARS
DO THE DUMBEST THINGS

✪ When actor Chris O'Donnell flubbed his lines on the set of *Bachelor* (1999), his sweet costar Renee Zellweger reportedly snarled, "Either s*** or get off the pot!"

✪ Screen star Cameron Diaz had a clause in her contract that required the producer to provide a cat-sitter to attend to her kitty while she was working on a movie.

While shooting a football film in Miami, Florida, twenty-six-year-old Cameron Diaz fell for fifty-two-year-old director Oliver Stone. However, when Diaz noticed Stone flirting with another woman in a bar, she went ballistic. "I'm not one of your groupies!" the enraged Diaz shrieked. "It looks like a harem in here." "Stop acting like white trash," Stone yelled back. Cameron allegedly jumped on Oliver's back and "love tapped" the director on the head. Stone finally threw Diaz in a corner, held her down, and yelled, "Get this crazy bitch off me!" Diaz left, but was discovered partying with Stone the next night.

✪ Cameron Diaz liked to eat six Egg McMuffins for breakfast, and wore a girdle to keep her girlish good looks on the movie set.

✪ "Everyone needs to understand one thing," declared beautiful actress Anne Heche, a self-declared lesbian. "I have a wife and I love her dearly." Heche's "wife," comedian/actress Ellen DeGeneres, ordered ten men's suits from London's Saville Row at a cost of $50,000.

✪ At Outfest, an annual gay/lesbian film festival, Anne Heche told the crowd that her mother confessed, "I've been with a woman myself, but that doesn't make it right." Heche's mom corrected her daughter, "It was just touching and kissing . . . it might have lasted twenty minutes . . . it was a very long time ago."

★ When asked what was her most painful beauty secret, Halle Berry explained, "Taping my boobs for a low-cut dress, taking the tape off is the beauty treatment that hurts the most."

★ Rose McGowan became the girlfriend and then the fiancée of shock rocker Marilyn Manson. Rose accompanied her creepy beau to the 1998 MTV Video Music Awards, wearing little more than a leopard skin thong. When asked about her non-outfit, Rose told the press, "There's not a lot of options besides nudity at this point."

★ Rising young star Christina Ricci liked to stub out cigarettes on her arm. "You get this rush," Ricci enthused. "You can actually faint from the pain. It's kind of calming."

★ Jennifer Aniston, one of TV's *Friends* (1994–present), appeared in the horror film *Leprechaun* (1993). While making the movie, she poked an attacking leprechaun in the eye with a club and cut her hand. "I still have a scar from that f***ing movie," a bitter Jennifer admitted. "Can you believe that?"

★ Aniston was proud of the lines she ad-libbed for the film *Picture Perfect* (1997). The script called for her to say, "S***, s***," but creative Jennifer came up with the line, "S***, s***, s***, s***, s***, s***, s***, s***, s***, s***, s***." "Good line, huh?" Jennifer bragged later, "Nine of them were my s***s."

★ Juliette Lewis, a self-proclaimed pothead from the age of thirteen, once stood on her head in a movie theatre and yelled, "I love you, Superman."

★ Slim Gwyneth Paltrow decided to have breast implants to improve her figure. However, she decided to only have little ones implanted.

★ On location in the Philippines for the making of *Brokedown Palace* (1999), Claire Danes tried to usurp power and dictate the movie's ending. She described her phone conversations with the executives back in Hollywood: "Nobody else was an eighteen-year-old girl, so that really gives you the upper hand."

★ One night during the making of *Brokedown Palace*, Danes was on the phone with her boyfriend when she spotted a roach. She started screaming, then her boyfriend suggested she simply turn on the lights. After discussing this option for half an hour, Claire confessed, "I went screaming into the bedroom and turned on every light and ran back panting, 'I did it.' I was going to have the hotel staff turn on the lights for me, but I braved it." Danes was proud of herself for having "survive[d] the worst."

✪ When Catherine Zeta-Jones first got to Hollywood, she was a bit intimidated. Staying at a friend's place in Malibu, she confessed, "I was so scared, I slept in the closet."

✪ After watching *Alien Resurrection* (1997), Wynona Ryder wasn't sure why she was in the flick. "I'm just this little girl who's running around," she opined.

🐶 Actress Drew Barrymore, of the famous Barrymore acting clan, wanted to get close to her pet cat—really close. She vowed, "If I die before him, I want a little of my ashes put in his food so I can live inside him."

✪ At the age of fourteen, Drew tried to kill herself. "Eckh!" she recalled, "I caught one glimpse of the blood and passed out."

✪ In 1989, three months after going through rehab, fourteen-year-old Barrymore took her mother's credit card, flew to Los Angeles, did a bunch of drugs, and went to a mall. Drew explained, "What was the point of having a credit card if you weren't going to shop?"

✪ Drew married bar owner Jeremy Thomas on March 20, 1994. "I'm so lucky to have met this person," Drew cooed. "I've never met anyone so supportive." Less than two months later, Drew filed for divorce, and referred to her ex as "the biggest schmuck I've ever met in all my years of existence." She explained that her marriage was "a green card situation."

Don Johnson

FACTS OF LIFE

ORIGIN: Born Don Wayne "Donnie Wayne" Johnson, December 15, 1949, Galena, Missouri.

FORMATIVE YEARS: Spent time in a juvenile detention center, attended the University of Kansas at Lawrence, Kansas, and the American Conservatory Theater in San Francisco, California.

FAMILY PLANNING: Married "a dancer," 1968; annulled 1968; married "a bimbo," 1973; annulled 1973; married Melanie Griffith (actress), February 1976; divorced 1977; had a child with Patti D'Arbanville (actress); married Melanie Griffith (again), June 26, 1989; divorced (again) 1995; married Kelley Phleger (debutante), April 29,1999.

ROMANTIC INTERESTS: Anita Sorrels (professor), Jodi Lyn O'Keefe (actress), Pamela Des Barres (groupie), Barbra Streisand (actress), Denise Hale (heiress).

SELECTED HITS (and Misses)

FILMS: *Zachariah* (1970), *The Magic Garden of Stanley Sweetheart* (1970), *The Harrad Experiment* (1973), *A Boy and His Dog* (1975), *Soggy Bottom U.S.A.* (1982), *Sweet Hearts Dance* (1988), *Dead Bang* (1989), *The Hot Spot* (1990), *Paradise* (1991), *Guilty as Sin* (1993), *Born Yesterday* (1993), *Tin Cup* (1996), *Goodbye, Lover* (1997—released in 1999).

TV SERIES: *Miami Vice* (1984–89), *Nash Bridges* (1996–present).

QUICKIE BIO

As the sockless, pastel-clad detective Sonny Crockett on the TV cop show *Miami Vice* (1984–89), Don Johnson became a cultural icon. However, Johnson's real vices earned him the nickname Don Juanson. Born to a farmer and his sixteen-year-old wife, Don slept his way through college and into the San Francisco theater scene. He became a 1970s Southern California bad boy, married teenage Melanie Griffith, got drunk, got divorced, got sober, got remarried, got drunk, and got divorced again. After twenty-three years of drugs, drinking, cheating, and fighting, Melanie dumped Don for actor Antonio Banderas. Don sighed, "This is a very hard world that by and large sanctions monogamy. It's murder on relationships."

DON JOHNSON
DOES THE DUMBEST THINGS

⭐ Johnson got a job as a butcher and took pride in selling bad meat. "I had one of those faces that people trusted, the poor suckers," bragged Don, who liked to describe himself as "an expert on b.s."

⭐ After he fell asleep in his high school business class, Don had to attend drama classes. "Are you kidding?" a fearful Don said. "Isn't that for guys who are a little, uh, light in their loafers?"

⭐ Years later, Don was less terrified of light-loafered men. "I mean, if there were nothing but old whores and nasty old, hard women," Don confessed, "I'd be out looking for some young, sweet, little fifteen-year-old boy."

⭐ Johnson described his sexual orientation as "sort of a desire to melt into women then out of them."

⭐ In the mid 1980s, Don Johnson had dinner at the Ronald Reagan White House. "I know there were a lot of people saying, 'What the f*** is he doing at the White House?'" Johnson recalled. "And in fact, I said the same thing myself."

Don Johnson (center) co-starred with Tippi Hedren (right) in the campus-sex film *The Harrad Experiment* (1973). Then Don started experimenting with Tippi's sixteen-year-old daughter, Melanie Griffith (left). [photo courtesy of Fotos International/Archive Photos]

⭐ At one point, Don's daily intake included a case of beer, a few martinis, several bottles of the best wine, and good Napoleon brandy. "I do not throw tantrums or stomp off or yell at people," hard-partying Johnson has claimed. "I have very enthusiastic creative discussions."

⭐ Johnson has had very enthusiastic discussions with women. Once he stopped a girl on the street in San Francisco and said, "You have beautiful hands, do you play the piano?" She said, "No." Then Don asked, "Do you f***?" She said, "Sometimes." "It started right there," he sighed.

⭐ Johnson got into drugs heavily. He was so coked out at one point that he decided to get married to a girl who was "a bimbo" and "didn't do anything. . . ." "I thought that might be fun to do for a while," Don shrugged. "A short while—we got it annulled in a matter of days."

⭐ While riding high on TV's *Miami Vice* (1984–89), Don recorded two albums, and a duet with his then girlfriend Barbra Streisand entitled "Till I Loved You." Streisand loved him for a while. Some people speculated that she dumped him because the Jewish diva couldn't stand Crockett's uncircumcised johnson.

Don started going out with Melanie Griffith when she was sixteen and he was twenty-two. He nicknamed her "Pinky." She called him "Pear" and had a pear tattooed on her butt. "It wasn't incredibly romantic," he recalled. "It was almost . . . uh, clinical."

✪ The night before Don married Griffith the first time, he spent the evening in bed with a former beauty pageant queen.

✪ Johnson's wife Melanie Griffith was surprised to learn that six million people were murdered in the Nazi holocaust. When told about it, she said, "Oh, my god, so many people." Later, Melanie defended her ignorance by saying, "I don't know why I didn't know. Maybe I missed school that day. . . . I'm not stupid." Another time, Griffith went to Congress to lobby for the National Endowment for the Arts. While the Senators debated the future of the arts, she fell asleep.

✪ For a time, Melanie Griffith broke out in red pimples whenever she snuggled with her husband Don Johnson. It turned out she was allergic to the cologne she had bought for him.

✪ Johnson fell off the wagon in 1993. When actor Gary Oldman wouldn't drink with him, Don pitched a fit. A short while later, a drunk Don called a talk radio show in Miami and slurred, "Hey Bubba . . . we'll see who gets bitch-slapped."

✪ Johnson liked the women he worked with on TV's *Nash Bridges* (1996–present). The word on the set was "bring a chastity belt to work." According to a female production assistant, Johnson reportedly came up to her, pushed her against a wall, and said, "I know you want me, I want you," and stuck his hand under her bra. Later, Johnson kissed her, thrust his hands down her pants and allegedly offered her a promotion if she had sex with him. A friend warned, "If you sleep with him, he'll fire you like all the others." Johnson's female chauffeur claimed that Don climbed in the front seat of the car with an open bottle of wine, put his hands over her eyes, told her to speed up, and stuck his hand down her dress while she was driving on the Bay Bridge. Johnson reportedly sued the women for extortion, and they later settled out of court.

✪ After divorcing Melanie Griffith for the second time, forty-eight-year-old Don started dating nineteen-year-old Jodi Lyn O'Keefe, who played his daughter on the TV series *Nash Bridges* (1996-present). While he was dating Jodi, Don started going out with sixty-six-year-old socialite Denise Hale. As it turns out, Don was going out with Hale only to get contact with twenty-nine-year-old socialite Kelley Phleger. When Don scored with Kelly, he dumped grandma Denise and his TV daughter Jodi.

✪ Don Johnson took his bride-to-be Kelley Phleger on a romantic weekend—to get plastic surgery. Don planned to have liposuction on his chin and gut, while Kelley had her eyes reworked and her lips inflated. The couple planned to spend the weeks after the operation healing together romantically.

✪ On the set of his TV show *Nash Bridges*, Johnson often took a break from filming by entertaining guest actresses in his bus-like trailer. The other folks on the set called these sessions "riding the bus."

✪ The first thing visitors used to see when they entered Don Johnson's Beverly Hills home was a larger-than-life-size photo of . . . yes, you guessed it, Don Johnson.

Grace Kelly

FACTS OF LIFE (and Death)

ORIGIN: born Grace Patricia Kelly, November 12, 1928, Philadelphia, Pennsylvania; died September 17, 1982, Monaco, as the result of a car accident.

FORMATIVE YEARS: Studied acting at the American Academy of Dramatic Arts, New York City, New York.

FAMILY PLANNING: Married His Most Serene Highness Rainier I (Rainier Louis Henri Maxence Bertrand Grimaldi), April 19, 1956.

ROMANTIC INTERESTS: Don Richardson (acting teacher), Mark Miller (actor), Clark Gable (actor), Bing Crosby (actor), Jimmy Stewart (actor), Cary Grant (actor), Prince Aly Khan (royalty), William Holden (actor), Gary Cooper (actor), David Niven (actor), Oleg Cassini (designer), Ray Milland (actor), Frank Sinatra (singer), Shah of Iran (royal despot), Spencer Tracy (actor).

SELECTED HITS (and Misses)

FILMS: *Fourteen Hours* (1951), *High Noon* (1952), *Mogambo* (1953), *The Country Girl* (Oscar for Best Actress—1954), *Dial M for Murder* (1954), *Rear Window* (1954), *Green Fire* (1954), *The Bridges at Toko-Ri* (1954), *To Catch a Thief* (1955), *The Swan* (1956), *High Society* (1956).

QUICKIE BIO

Before there was Princess Di, there was Princess Grace. Born to a self-made social climbing Philadelphia millionaire, Grace Kelly was pretty disgraceful. Dubbed "The Snow Princess" by film director Alfred Hitchcock, characterized as a "nymphomaniac" by reporters, Grace loved high society, but still knew how to get down. Grace's passion for married movie stars was actually revealed not by a nosy paparazzo, but by her own mother in a series of juicy newspaper stories. "I can't believe it!" her father exclaimed when Grace won an Oscar in 1954, "Of my four children, she's the last one I expected to support me in my old age!" He underestimated the power of Grace.

GRACE KELLY
DOES THE DUMBEST THINGS

★ Grace Kelly lost her virginity to the husband of a close friend of hers. She waited until the pal left the house one afternoon, then hopped into the sack with hubby.

★ Kelly was upset in her acting class, so her teacher took her out for tea and sympathy. When he found she didn't have any money, he took her to his apartment and started making coffee in the kitchen. When the hot drink was ready, he found Grace naked, waiting for him in bed.

★ For a time, Grace modeled lingerie professionally in New York City. During lunch breaks, she'd go to her lover's pad for a nooner. Then she'd go back to modeling lingerie. Grace said the sex helped her modeling. It put a light in her eyes.

★ While staying at the Chateau Marmont hotel in Los Angeles early in her career, Grace Kelly sharpened her man-hunting claws. Hotel staff confirmed that if she was interested in a male guest, she would always ask for his room number and call upon him. And always, always, always wearing her little white gloves.

★ "I'm not saying that Grace was a nymphomaniac," one of her lovers explained. "After, say, four times, well that was just fine for her."

★ Grace's lover Bing Crosby was married. So the two made love in a house owned by one of Crosby's buddies. When the friend came home early one day, he found the two hot and heavy on the sofa. He asked "Der Bingle" why he didn't go to a motel. Crosby, who was a notorious cheapskate, said he didn't want to lose his nice guy image.

★ When Kelly asked her dad if she could bring her lover Oleg Cassini over to the house to meet the family, her father exploded and called fashion designer Cassini a "worm," a "wop," and a "dago." He was actually a Russian Jew. Cassini eventually did visit the Kellys, but said that the experience was "like eating a chocolate éclair filled with razor blades."

★ Married actor William Holden went on a self-proclaimed crusade to "screw every girl in the country." He did it with Kelly too. Their affair

"The Prince comes up to Grace's titties," complained Grace Kelly's father (right) after he first met his future son-in-law Prince Rainier (second from left). "Royalty doesn't mean anything to us!"
(photo courtesy of Popperphoto/Archive Photos)

didn't start out rosy, however. When Grace went calling on Holden in his dressing room on the set of *The Country Girl* (1954), he yelled, "Baby, when I want somebody, I go to them!"

⭐ Grace Kelly once performed a private strip show for director Alfred Hitchcock. Hitchcock liked to watch the star of his *To Catch a Thief* (1955) get naked through a telescope. The famed director of thrillers later harrumphed about her when she declined to star in *Marnie* (1964) and called her "Princess Disgrace."

⭐ Greek shipping tycoon Aristotle Onassis and the owners of other casinos in Monte Carlo (the capital of Monaco) were losing money. So they encouraged Monaco's Prince Rainier to marry a movie star to boost business. The Prince met Grace Kelly in Monaco, then appeared at her house in Philadelphia on Christmas day with a priest and told her father that he wanted to marry her. Grace's father was not interested and yelled, "I don't want any broken-down prince who's head of a country that nobody ever heard of marrying my daughter."

⭐ Before they got married, the Prince demanded that Grace pay a dowry of two million dollars. Pa Kelly paid up, although he complained that Rainier was a "broken down prince." Then Grace took a fertility test. She passed, but thereafter tried to pretend she was a virgin, explaining that her hymen had been broken while she was playing field hockey in high school.

✪ After Grace's engagement to the Prince was announced, her mother Margaret sold the sordid details of her daughter's life to the newspapers. When Grace tearfully asked her parent why she wrote the tell-all articles that ruined her reputation and almost ruined her marriage, her mother assured her it was all right because she was "donating royalties to charity."

✪ The Kellys visited their daughter at her royal residence in Monaco. "The servants have so much braid [on their uniforms] I can't tell them from generals," Ma Kelly cracked. Pa Kelly couldn't find the bathroom in the palace, and couldn't figure out how to communicate with the servants. So he took a limousine to a nearby hotel and used a friend's bathroom.

✪ In the early 1990s, a priest in Monaco asked the Vatican to make Princess Grace a saint. Many people claim that a visit to her tomb cures diseases.

Peter Lawford

FACTS OF LIFE (and Death)

ORIGIN: Born Peter Sydney Vaughn Aylen, September 7, 1923, London, England; died December 24, 1984, Los Angeles, California.

FORMATIVE YEARS: Never went to school.

FAMILY PLANNING: Married Patricia Kennedy (President John F. Kennedy's sister), April 24, 1954; divorced 1966; married Mary Ann Rowan (daughter of comedian Dan Rowan), October 30, 1971; divorced 1975; married Deborah Gould (aspiring actress), June 25, 1976; divorced 1976; married Patricia Seaton (aspiring actress), July 5, 1984.

ROMANTIC INTERESTS: Lana Turner (actress), Judy Garland (actress), Nancy Davis (actress/future Mrs. Ronald Reagan), Dorothy Dandridge (actress), Lee Remick (actress), Rita Hayworth (actress), Acujack (sex toy).

SELECTED HITS (and Misses)

FILMS: *Poor Old Bill* (1931), *Mrs. Miniver* (1942), *The White Cliffs of Dover* (1944), *Son of Lassie* (1945), *It Happened in Brooklyn* (1947), *Easter Parade* (1948), *Little Women* (1949), *It Should Happen to You* (1954), *Ocean's Eleven* (1960), *Exodus* (1960), *Advise and Consent* (1962), *The Longest Day* (1962), *Harlow* (1965), *The Oscar* (1966), *Salt and Pepper* (1968), *The April Fools* (1969), *Skidoo* (1969), *They Only Kill Their Masters* (1972), *Rosebud* (1975), *Won Ton Ton, the Dog Who Saved Hollywood* (1976), *Body & Soul* (1981), *Where Is Parsifal?* (1983).

TV SERIES: *Dear Phoebe* (1954–55), *The Thin Man* (1957–59).

Sophisticated jet setter Peter Lawford was a cool cat with White House connections, but not much of an actor, dig? His mom dressed him up in female clothing for the first nine years of his life and got him into the movies both in England and then in Hollywood. Billed in the 1940s as a sophisticated surfer, Lawford became the Rat Pack's presidential connection, hanging out with the charlies and chicky babies until the Rat Pack turned Republican, and Peter wound up playing straight man to Jimmy Durante in Las Vegas. "I wish I could think of one great, dramatic scene with Peter Lawford," one Hollywood insider recalled. "I'm sure there is one, but I just can't think of it."

PETER LAWFORD
DOES THE DUMBEST THINGS

✪ Peter was working as an usher in a Los Angeles movie theatre. He was standing in the back of the balcony trying to have sex with Lana Turner when his parents showed up for a surprise visit. Later, Lawford's mother walked into studio boss Louis B. Mayer's office and told the movie mogul that her son was a homosexual. Lana Turner told Mayer he wasn't.

✪ Lawford was a TV game show staple in his later years. During one outing, Peter and his partner were about to win a bunch of money. All Lawford had to do was identify "A famous singer named John. City in Colorado." Peter smiled a knowing smile, rang the buzzer, and said, "Boulder! John Boulder!" Every time Lawford saw John Denver on television after that he said, "There's that Boulder chap again."

✪ At one point, Lawford's son was reportedly high on drugs and standing on the ledge of his New York City apartment threatening suicide. The police arrived, grabbed the youth, and pulled him to safety. A short time later, the law enforcers dragged Lawford's son out of the apartment along with a large marijuana plant. The movie star looked wistfully at the cops taking away his son and cried, "Oh, no, not that plant."

✪ Before landing on a flight to Australia, Lawford talked wife number four into hiding several grams of cocaine up her privates. By the time they reached their hotel, the drugs had gotten lodged inside her. A sympathetic doctor helped them retrieve their excess baggage.

✪ While waiting in line to go through customs at the Rome airport, Peter saw a Chihuahua and got paranoid that it was a drug sniffing police dog. Lawford dumped all his marijuana, cocaine, and hashish in a nearby trash can. After clearing customs, he saw the Chihuahua get into a woman's limousine. When Lawford realized the Chihuahua was a pet, he rushed back into the airport, ran through customs and grabbed the trash can. While passengers stared in amazement, Lawford shook the can and opened it. The drugs, however, had been cleaned out.

✪ Elizabeth Taylor hired old MGM buddy Lawford to appear in a TV movie. Lawford gave Liz grief about her drinking, then he showed up on the set intoxicated. He couldn't manage to mumble the line "Hello, my name is Tony," before he passed out and, consequently, was fired.

Lawford and his manager were flying on Air Force One with President Kennedy. Peter's manager pulled out three joints and dropped them on the floor in full view of the Secret Service. "What the f*** do you think you're doing here?" Peter hissed. "You just dropped grass on Air Force One, you s***." Lawford's manager ate the joints to destroy the evidence.

✪ Peter had five television sets in his home in Los Angeles. He liked to turn them all on, then walk over to them and pee on them if the entertainment was bad. He always peed on Nixon.

✪ Lawford's nicknames in the Rat Pack included: the brother-in-Lawford, and Charlie the Seal because he had a bad arm and liked to have oral sex.

✪ President John F. Kennedy asked his brother-in-law Lawford to read through and evaluate the script for the movie PT 109 (1963). Peter opened up the script, then got drunk and passed out.

✪ "I was Frank's [Sinatra] pimp and Frank was Jack's [John Kennedy]," Lawford explained. "It sounds terrible now, but then it was really a lot of fun." The night before JFK's funeral in 1963, Peter partied with a flight attendant he met on the Air Force One press plane.

When his friend drove him out to the Betty Ford drug treatment clinic near Palm Springs in California, Lawford thought it was just a social call. "Are we going to visit her?" he said. "I've always liked Betty."

✪ At the dry-out clinic, Lawford still managed to do drugs. He told the staff he was going for a walk, then met a helicopter in the desert which delivered him cocaine. Lawford charged the whole thing to his American Express card.

✪ After Lawford returned home from the Betty Ford clinic, he snorted lines of cocaine and ran the vacuum cleaner for hours. His wife called the treatment center and complained that they had turned her husband into "a f***ing maid that gets high."

Eventually, drugs and alcohol ruined Lawford's sex life. In desperation he purchased something called an Acujack. This electrical device became Lawford's "best friend and companion," according to his fourth wife. It sounded like a kitchen blender, but Peter didn't care, and kept it turned on for hours. "The new relationship was almost as disgusting as his women," recalled wife number four, "except that it looked ridiculous." She threw it into the trash, but Lawford retrieved it.

⭐ When Lawford met his fourth wife, he didn't realize that her jaw was wired shut from surgery. "I thought you were kind of British," he said, referring to the fact that she spoke through clenched teeth.

⭐ At the end of his life, Lawford suffered from heart disease, a pancreatic condition, and other serious ailments. However, he believed that as long as he had a tan, he was healthy.

"Peter was such a mistake!" declared Peter Lawford's mother (left). Lawford (right) was the illegitimate son of a British General (center) who married his mother after her husband, a Colonel, committed suicide when he found out that his wife was pregnant by the General. Lawford's mother later wrote an autobiography entitled, *Bitch!*
[photo courtesy of Archive Photos]

Pamela Anderson Lee

FACTS OF LIFE

ORIGIN: Born July 1, 1967, Ladysmith, British Columbia, Canada.

FORMATIVE YEARS: High school graduate.

FAMILY PLANNING: Married Tommy Lee (musician), February 19, 1995; divorce filed, 1996; divorce refiled, 1998; reconciled 1999.

ROMANTIC INTERESTS: Bret Michaels (musician), Jon Peters (producer), Sylvester Stallone (actor), Scott Baio (actor), Kelly Slater (surfer).

SELECTED HITS (and Misses)

FILMS: *Crimes of Passion* (1984), *Some Kind of Wonderful* (1987), *The Taking of Beverly Hills* (1992), *Raw Justice* (1994), *Naked Souls* (1995), *Barb Wire* (1996), *Pam & Tommy Lee: Stolen Honeymoon* (1998).

TV SERIES: *Home Improvement* (1991–92), *Baywatch* (1992–97), *V.I.P.* (1998–present).

QUICKIE BIO

Teenage Pamela Anderson Lee filled out a T-shirt so well that the horny cameraman at a football game in Vancouver, Canada, flashed her chest up onto the jumbotron, launching her career. Pamela became one of the Labatt's "Blue Zone Girls." After graduating from high school, she left behind her hometown in Canada for the bright lights of Hollywood. Although she wrote in her diary "I'm going to be a virgin until I'm 19," nothing could have been farther from the truth. She became *Playboy's* Miss February 1990, went on to appear on the cover of *Playboy* a record eight times, and warned her enemies "Don't call me babe" in her feature film *Barb Wire* (1996). However, Pam's most memorable appearance was in the X-rated home video she taped with her hubby rock star Tommy Lee. The video became so popular on the Internet that more than 145,000 Web sites listed her name. "I call us s*** magnets," ex-hubby Tommy sighed about his marriage to Pamela. "We go somewhere and s*** happens to us." Watch for Pamela's next X-rated release, home videos of herself and boyfriend Bret Michaels of the rock band Poison.

PAMELA ANDERSON LEE
DOES THE DUMBEST THINGS

✪ After filming a commercial in Uruguay, Pamela attended a press conference in an outfit with a super-revealing top. The Uruguayans got so heated up, they shouted obscenities and tried to grope the buxom actress. Pamela was so upset that she dropped plans to tour Argentina, and fled back to the United States, where her ex, Tommy Lee, was encouraging female fans at Mötley Crüe concerts to take off their tops altogether.

✪ Pamela confessed on Howard Stern's talk show that she had been sexually molested when she was twelve years old by a twenty-five-year-old with whom she was playing backgammon. The actress sighed, "Somehow it was a relief telling millions of people that I'd been raped."

✪ Before Tommy Lee started dating Pamela, he went out with actress/model Heather Locklear and had her first name tattooed on his arm. Pamela made Tommy change the Heather tattoo to read "eather."

✪ Statuesque Pamela was on Route 66 in Arizona doing a shoot for *Playboy* in 1992, when the police threatened to arrest her for indecent exposure. The celebrity complained, "You can't arrest me for a nipple." They didn't arrest her, but the police did make her write a letter of apology to a Baptist minister who was living on the road on which they were doing the magazine layout.

✪ Pamela enjoyed visiting strip clubs and bragged, "I'm the one who gets the lap dances." One stripper gave the actress a close-up inspection of her chest and gushed, "My stage name is Pamela because everyone says I look like you and I'm so flattered." "Well, if you're going to be me," Pamela explained to the nude dancer, "you have to part your hair on the other side and cut your bangs."

✪ Pamela liked it when her boyfriend wore her underwear, her bikinis, and her dresses. "It shows he has a sense of humor," she explained, "which is sexy." However, she didn't want Tommy Lee to wear her dresses down to the card tables in Las Vegas. "They were a little too short for him, if you know what I mean."

 Pamela's boyfriend once put his feet over his head, while she made love to him with a vibrator. Pamela confessed "that kind of freaked me out." When freaked-out Pamela told her girl pals about the adventure, they all tried it, then they broke up with their boyfriends.

 Newlywed Pam and her husband Tommy Lee liked to make home videos. Silly Pam pulled down Tommy's underwear and videotaped his wanger. Then Tommy pulled up his shorts, and Pam videotaped his wanger from below. Then Pam videotaped Tommy honking the horn of a speed boat with his wanger. Then she videotaped herself playing with Tommy's wanger and sighing, "I get this for the rest of my life. Yes! Mom is a happy camper."

✪ Pamela was pregnant and taking a bath when milk started squirting out of her breasts. The excited actress called in her rocker husband, Tommy Lee, and shouted, "They work!"

✪ Pamela Anderson Lee claimed that she met her husband Tommy Lee on New Year's Eve 1994. "He came up, grabbed me, and licked my face," she recalled. "I thought he was a nice guy and gave him my phone number."

✪ "I never thought I would get married unless it was total caveman-style," Pamela later confessed. "Someone who would come over and grab me by the hair, bat me on the head with their stick, and drive me back to their cave . . . and that's what Tommy did."

✪ Three years after the wedding, Pamela didn't think so much of the primitive mating style. Tommy kicked her on the legs and butt while she held on to her infant son. Pamela suffered a broken fingernail and filed for divorce. Tommy was later sentenced to six months in jail. After the court decision, Pamela declared, "I'm very proud of Tommy."

Gone but not forgotten. The silicone enhanced breasts of Pamela Anderson Lee. [photo courtesy of Ron Brazil/Archive Photos]

⭐ After their divorce, Pamela had her Tommy tattoo altered to read Mommy. While Tommy was in jail, Pam sent him pin-up photos of herself. After he was let out of incarceration, she took her son and her boyfriend to see Tommy perform with his rock band Mötley Crüe. When Tommy appeared escorting a well-known porn star, Pamela was so upset that she spent the entire concert sitting in the limo. "I'm not going anywhere near that whore," she fumed. "I'm sure they'll be making porn videos together—and selling them!"

⭐ Pam got her brother Gerry to manage her own Web site. The first item Pam offered was women's underwear for $19.95. "I've created the most amazing thong ever," Pam pitched. "Girls—get this to wear for your man and guys get it for your girl!"

⭐ "I've obviously evolved," Pamela observed, "but you know what? I like being a Barbie." Pamela changed her mind in 1999 and decided to have her breast implants removed. After shrinking from a 36D to a 34C, Pam revealed that one of her implants had a leak. Even so, she refused to sell them to Ripley's Believe It or Not Museum in Hollywood. Gushed the less buxom blonde, "I feel much sexier."

★ Silicone-free Pam was actualy silicone-reduced. Pam's implants had been so large that she needed smaller "shaper" implants to keep her breasts from sagging.

★ After fixing up her relationship with Tommy, Anderson was asked if she was pregnant. "Not at all! Tommy has been fixed, actually," Pamela responded. "He has been neutered or spayed. What do you call it?" She also explained that in the future Lee "could be un-neutered."

★ In April 1999, Tommy dropped out of Mötley Crüe and got back together with Pam. "We haven't worked out all our problems," Pam confided, "but the sex is better than ever!"

Spike Lee

FACTS OF LIFE

ORIGIN: Born Shelton Jackson Lee, March 20, 1957, Atlanta, Georgia.

FORMATIVE YEARS: Graduated from Morehouse College, Atlanta, Georgia; Tisch School of the Arts, New York University, New York—master's degree in filmmaking.

FAMILY PLANNING: Married Tonya Linette Lewis (lawyer), October 2, 1993.

ROMANTIC INTERESTS: Cheryl Burr (dancer), Veronica Webb (model).

SELECTED HITS (and Misses)

FILMS AS ACTOR: *She's Gotta Have It* (1986), *School Daze* (1988), *Do The Right Thing* (1989), *Mo' Better Blues* (1990), *Jungle Fever* (1991), *Lonely in America* (1991), *Malcolm X* (1992), *The Last Party* (1993), *Hoop Dreams* (1994), *Drop Squad* (1994), *Crooklyn* (1994), *Clockers* (1995), *Girl 6* (1996), *When We Were Kings* (1996), *He Got Game* (1998), *Summer of Sam* (1999), *Love and Basketball* (2000).

FILMS AS DIRECTOR: *Joe's Bed-Stuy Barbershop: We Cut Heads* (1983), *She's Gotta Have It* (1986), *School Daze* (1988), *Do The Right Thing* (1989), *Mo' Better Blues* (1990), *Jungle Fever* (1991), *Malcolm X* (1992), *Crooklyn* (1994), *Clockers* (1995), *Girl 6* (1996), *Get on the Bus* (1996), *4 Little Girls* (1997), *He Got Game* (1998), *Summer of Sam* (1999).

QUICKIE BIO

Spike Lee wanted to be an athlete, but this five-foot-six-inch multi-talented phenomenon became a pitchman, instead, for sneakers and pizza. The sharp-tongued son of a jazz musician father and a school teacher mother, Lee grew up in Brooklyn, and earned the nickname "Spike" because he was a tough baby. He got interested in the movies while earning his undergraduate degree at Morehouse College in Atlanta, Georgia, and made a name for himself in film school in New York City by directing an updated and personalized version of the Ku Klux Klan epic *Birth of a Nation* (1915). In his first feature film *She's Gotta Have It* (1986), Lee appeared as the fast talking hustler Mars Blackmon. Dubbed by French critics as the "black Woody Allen," Lee has been blabbing ever since—from the lecture podium at Harvard, from the sidelines at Knicks games, and in ads for Levi's, Taco Bell, American Express, and Diet Coke. As spokesperson for Pizza Hut, Lee posed the timely question, "Ever wonder why New Yorkers have such big mouths?" Answer: they have to put up with Spike Lee.

SPIKE LEE
DOES THE DUMBEST THINGS

✪ When he couldn't get a waiver from the Screen Actors Guild in 1984 to hire nonunion members for his film *Messenger,* Lee described the decision as "a definite case of racism."

✪ When a newspaper reporter from the *New York Post* called Spike to confirm rumors that his screen biography of *Malcolm X* (1992) was over budget, Lee yelled over the phone, "The *Post* is a motherf***ing racist rag and I hate it!"

✪ Spike was furious when his film *Do the Right Thing* (1989) did not win the grand prize at the Cannes Film Festival. Spike allegedly warned filmmaker-judge Wim Wenders that he'd be "waiting for his a**" and let it be known that "somewhere deep in my closet I have a Louisville Slugger baseball bat with Wenders' name on it."

✪ When a fan suggested that Lee stop acting in the movies he directs, Spike responded, "Do me a favor, hit this guy over the head with a baseball bat."

After an African-American official announced that it was discriminatory for schools to have scholarships for black students, Spike reportedly called the person an "Uncle Tom handkerchief-head Negro" and added "that guy should be beat with a Louisville Slugger in an alley."

"I've never seen black men with fine white women," bespectacled Spike Lee declared. "They be ugly, mugly dogs." [photo courtesy of Reuters/Jeff Christensen/Archive Photos]

⭐ In 1991, Spike Lee complained to *Playboy* magazine that all of America's wars since WWII were against people of color. When asked about the Cold War, the actor/director/producer commented, "They didn't send no troops into Lithuania and s***."

⭐ "The value system of black youth is very distorted," Lee complained. "There's too much emphasis on materialism—gold chains, cars, even sneakers." He made this statement while he was directing and starring in ads for Nike Air Jordan sneakers.

⭐ Spike has always believed in uplifting African-Americans, but not every member of this minority. In 1991, when Spike was set to release *Jungle Fever*, Matty Rich, another black filmmaker, wanted to put his debut film *Straight Out of Brooklyn* out in the marketplace. The outraged Spike growled, "If you're movie comes out at the same time as mine, I'll crush it!"

★ Lee didn't give credit to singer Tisha Campbell for her singing performance in *School Daze* (1988). Tisha sued Spike and the filmmaker had to settle out of court for what he called "$25,000 of my motherf***ing hard-earned money."

★ Spike declared that "black people can't be racist," but he proved that they could be rude, especially to others of the same race. Lee hated the esteemed black critic Stanley Crouch, and referred to him as "that ignorant motherf***er."

★ At one time Spike complained that Oscar-winning actress Whoopi Goldberg wore "motherf***ing blue contact lenses." While appearing on Arsenio Hall's TV talk show, the outspoken director called his host an "Uncle Tom" figure.

★ Spike Lee used the f-word a lot, but he got angry when director Quentin Tarantino used the n-word in his film *Jackie Brown* (1997). "What does he want to be made—an honorary black man?"

★ At the Cannes Film Festival in the spring of 1999, while complaining to reporters about actor Charlton Heston, president of the NRA, "Shoot him with a .44 Bulldog." He later explained that the comment was a joke. "He gave me a big laugh," Heston shrugged. The man who once played Moses in the movies then added, "If he wants to come and take a shot at me, go let him try it."

Jerry Lewis

FACTS OF LIFE

ORIGIN: Born Joseph Levitch, March 16, 1926, Newark, New Jersey.

FORMATIVE YEARS: Dropped out of Irving Vocational High School,
Newark, New Jersey.

FAMILY PLANNING: Married Patti Palmer (the former Esther Calonico,
singer), October 2, 1944, remarried in a Jewish ceremony April 1945;
divorced 1980; married SanDee (or Sandra, or Sam) Pitnick (flight atten-
dant/dancer) February 13, 1983.

ROMANTIC INTERESTS: Gloria De Haven (actress). Jerry claimed he went
out with many women, "but it was always like they wanted to burp me."

SELECTED HITS (and Misses)

FILMS: *My Friend Irma* (1949), *At War with the Army* (1950), *The Stooge* (1951),
Jumping Jacks (1952), *Scared Stiff* (1953), *The Caddy* (1953), *Living It Up* (1954),
Artists and Models (1955), *Hollywood or Bust* (1956), *The Delicate Delinquent*
(1956), *The Sad Sack* (1957), *The Geisha Boy* (1958), *The Bellboy* (1960),* *Cinder-
fella* (1960),* *Visit to a Small Planet* (1960), *The Errand Boy* (1961),* *The Ladies'
Man* (1962),* *The Nutty Professor* (1963),* *The Disorderly Orderly* (1964),* *The
Patsy* (1964),* *Boeing Boeing* (1965), *The Big Mouth* (1967),* *Which Way to the
Front?* (1970),* *Hardly Working* (1981),* *The King of Comedy* (1982), *Cracking Up*
(1983), *Slapstick of Another Kind* (1984), *Cookie* (1989), *Arizona Dream* (1991—
released in 1993), *Mr. Saturday Night* (1992), *Funny Bones* (1995).

TV SERIES: *The Colgate Comedy Hour* (1950–55), *The Jerry Lewis Show* (1963),
The Jerry Lewis Show (1967–69).

*Also directed by Lewis.

QUICKIE BIO

Jerry Lewis was a putz, a schlemiel, a spastic nerd ("Lady! Lady!"), a self pro-claimed "genius," and an "imbecile." Born into the world of Jewish show business, he dropped out of high school and hit the borsch circuit in New York's Catskill Mountains as a "dummy act," lip-synching to records. At dif-ferent times, he was a nightclub superstar with Dean Martin, the highest-paid performer in Hollywood, the best-rewarded talent on network television, the highest-paid actor on Broadway, the most successful charity fund-raiser in history, and the first Jewish comedian to direct himself in a movie. Despite his astounding success, Jerry never failed to shock audiences with his coarse, tasteless shtick. Looking back on his multi-faceted career, Jerry once observed, "I was as discreet as a f***ing bull taking a p*** in your living room."

JERRY LEWIS
DOES THE DUMBEST THINGS

⭐ Jerry started off in show business as "Joey Levitch and his Hollywood Friends," lip-synching Frank Sinatra and Carmen Miranda records. However, when he brought his dummy act to a strip joint in Buffalo, the small crowd yelled, "Get the f*** off! Bring on the babes!"

⭐ While performing with Dean Martin at a Chicago nightclub, Jerry got annoyed with a customer at the front table who was talking during his performance. Lewis reached down from the stage, grabbed the guy by the shoulder and squawked, "Hey, pal, the show is up here!" The man turned out to be Charlie "Trigger-Happy" Frischetti, gangster Al Capone's cousin. "If you don't move away right now," the underworld figure said to the putz, "I'll blow your f***in' head off!" After the show, Jerry apologized profusely.

⭐ On the set of the first Martin and Lewis movie, *My Friend Irma* (1949), hypersensitive Jerry went berserk. He poured water all over the place, cut people's neckties, lit handkerchiefs on fire, and rubbed black shoe polish into the director's brown shoes.

⭐ Jerry appeared in *My Friend Irma Goes West* (1950), along with an actress and a chimp. The chimp harassed the actress on the set, smacking his lips at her and fondling his crotch in her presence. Jerry, in turn, imi-tated the chimp. According to the actress, he "turned into a human monkey."

⭐ Lewis wears socks only once. After that, he throws them away.

★ Jerry spoke of his relationship to Dean Martin as "a love affair." After the two broke up in 1956, he said, "For the first time in ten years, I am rid of cancer."

★ Lewis smoked four packs of cigarettes a day and kept a bowl on his desk filled with cigarettes. "That's the secret of all my pep," he admitted. "It's my corpuscles fighting off the nicotine. Very combustible."

★ Jerry covered the walls of his office with pictures of himself, and emblazoned pencils, pens, rulers, cigarette lighters, and stationery with his logo. He designed special note paper for the bathroom with the slogan, "JL Doodling on the Throne." He bought a solid gold Nikon camera with a diamond viewfinder, and hired a photographer to follow him around all day taking photos as he, Jerry, attended meetings, walked on the street, etc.

★ To promote *The Nutty Professor* (1963), Jerry set out on a promotional tour. His baggage included ten tuxedos, six sport coat and trouser ensembles, ten pairs of white yachting sneakers, ten pairs of black loafers, thirty-six sweaters, ninety pairs of shorts monogrammed with his caricature, an oxygen tank, four suitcases of camera equipment, and a case of his newly self-published manual, *Instruction Book for Being a Person.* Jerry got fed up with the tour in Chicago and screamed, "I'm through with playing toilets!"

★ At home, Papa Jerry reportedly chased his kids around the house, slapped them, and punched them. "There are two sets of Jerry's Kids," said Jerry's son Joseph. "Those physically crippled by a dreadful disease and those emotionally crippled by a dreadful father."

★ Lewis's dumbest screen project was *The Day the Clown Cried.* In the film, Jerry played a German circus clown who led children to the gas chamber for the Nazis. Jerry shot the movie in Sweden in 1972, even though he didn't have the rights to the script. The feature was so bad, it was never released.

★ Jerry got angry after a nightclub gig in Miami in 1973. Back in his hotel suite, he poured lighter fluid around the room, set fire to it, and screamed, "Burn down the f***ing hotel! Burn down the whole f***ing town!"

★ Lewis smoked marijuana as an aphrodisiac and bragged, "Once I came from January third to mid-February. It was the longest shoot in the history of America. I mean, it sucked my skin inward and became part of my marrow."

"Hello, you bunch of frogs! Here's Zherry Loueee!" Jerry Lewis screamed to his French fans. Jerry was awarded the French Legion of Honor and the Order of Arts and Letters. Oooo La La!
[photo courtesy of Archive Photos]

⭐ When invited to a birthday party for a wealthy buddy, Jerry hired a homeless, alcoholic midget, packed him in a crate, and had him delivered to the party with a note reading, "For the man who has everything—his own human being."

⭐ History was made during the bicentennial Labor Day Telethon in 1976. Frank Sinatra appeared on the TV fund-raiser, then introduced a surprise guest, Dean Martin. It was the first time in twenty years that the legendary team of Martin and Lewis were sharing the same stage again. It was a memorable occasion, but Jerry was so messed up on Percodan and other drugs that he didn't remember it. "I didn't have any recollection the next day," Lewis confessed. "I had to run a videotape to see what happened because I was told that Dean and I were on television."

⭐ Jerry first appeared on a telethon in 1948. Fifty years later, the Jerry Lewis Muscular Dystrophy Association Labor Day Telethon was the most successful in history—and one of the most insulting. Viewers were amazed when Jerry began the broadcast by lip-synching along with a chorus of male singers, picking his nose, giving the audience the finger, pointing to the person next to him and apparently mouthing the words *He's a fag!* then pretending to strangle the guy, four times. Later in the broadcast, Jerry complained that working with the floor manager was like "working with Eva Braun," and snarled at the cameraman, "You're gonna make a Jew sandwich in a minute." The telethon raised more than $51 million.

Sophia Loren

FACTS OF LIFE

ORIGIN: Born Sofia Villani Scicolone, September 20, 1934, Rome, Italy, in a charity ward for unwed mothers.

FORMATIVE YEARS: Attended acting school in Naples, Italy.

FAMILY PLANNING: Married Carlo Ponti (producer), September 27, 1957; annulled 1962; remarried 1966.

ROMANTIC INTERESTS: Rossano Brazzi (actor), Cary Grant (actor), Gig Young (actor), Peter Sellers (actor), Omar Sharif (actor).

SELECTED HITS (and Misses)

FILMS: *Variety Lights* (1950), *It's Him! Yes, Yes!* (1951), *Aida* (1953), *The Gold of Naples* (1954), *Scandal in Sorrento* (1955), *Lucky to Be a Woman* (1956), *The Pride and the Passion* (1957), *Boy on a Dolphin* (1957), *Desire under the Elms* (1958), *Houseboat* (1958), *The Black Orchid* (1959), *Heller in Pink Tights* (1960), *Two Women* (Oscar for Best Actress—1961), *The Millionaress* (1961), *El Cid* (1961), *The Condemned of Altona* (1962), *Yesterday, Today and Tomorrow* (1963), *The Fall of the Roman Empire* (1964), *Marriage Italian-Style* (1964), *Arabesque* (1966), *Lady L* (1966), *A Countess from Hong Kong* (1967), *Sunflower* (1970), *Man of La Mancha* (1972), *The Voyage* (1973), *The Cassandra Crossing* (1977), *A Special Day* (1977), *Angela* (1978—released in 1984), *Saturday, Sunday and Monday* (1990), *Ready to Wear* (1994), *Grumpier Old Men* (1995), *Messages* (1996), *Sun* (1997), *Destination Verna* (1999).

QUICKIE BIO

Abandoned by her father, banged on the head by her mother as she practiced piano, Sophia Loren decided to get into show business, and attracted attention as a teenager by appearing topless in films and racy Italian photo books. Italian producer Carlo Ponti fell in love with the blossoming fifteen-year-old, even though he was married already. As their affair heated up, the Italian press declared that if Sophia had been born in the Middle Ages, she would have been burned at the stake. Instead, Sophia rode the wave of publicity to stardom in Italy and then to Hollywood, where she spent more than four decades driving men (and female rivals) crazy. "As the years go by, the structure holds," sixty-something Sophia proclaimed. "It's like when you build a house with a good foundation. There's no secret!"

SOPHIA LOREN
DOES THE DUMBEST THINGS

⭐ One of Sophia's early roles was as a topless harem girl in *It's Him! Yes, Yes!* (1951). When actor William Holden saw stills from the movie several decades later, he was shocked and showed them to Sophia. Loren shrugged, "They look pretty good to me."

⭐ Sophia Loren's smashing figure caused a sensation everywhere. Once, when she went shopping for brassieres in Rome, a crowd of men mobbed the shopping plaza, trapping Sophia in the dressing room. Three fire brigades had to be called to break up the near-riot.

⭐ Busty fellow-Italian actress Gina Lollobrigida turned down a chance to costar with younger, bustier, and more statuesque Sophia. The battle of the boobs was on. "I do not talk about Sophia," Lollobrigida scoffed. "I do not wish to make for her publicity." "Gina's personality is limited," Sophia countered. "She is good playing a peasant but is incapable of playing a lady." "Who's bigger, you or Lollo?" reporters asked Loren. "It is true that my measurements excel Gina's," Sophia admitted, "but is that a reason why she should be so furious with me?"

⭐ In London, Gina Lollobrigida stormed out of a press conference after reporters asked if she would participate in a bust-measuring contest with Sophia Loren. Then she told gossip columnist Hedda Hopper "Sophia's may be bigger but not better." "I never criticize my elders," Sophia countered. The feud continued until 1955, when Gina finally cried, "I don't want to hear any more about that Neapolitan giraffe!"

★ In one of her first Hollywood-financed films, *Boy on a Dolphin* (1957), Sophia appeared soaking wet on-screen which greatly improved her, um, visibility. After that, Loren complained. "I spent my first five years in the movies having people throw pails of water on me."

★ Pint-sized actor Alan Ladd was not so sure about his voluptuous costar in *Boy on a Dolphin.* "It's like being bombed by watermelons," he said.

★ When Sophia arrived at the Washington, D.C., airport in 1957, photographers climbed up on poles, and on each others' shoulders, to get shots down her cleavage. Later, at a reception in her honor, Sophia sneezed and her tight dress split wide open in back. A publicist had to sew it back up as the media watched.

★ American bosom rival Jayne Mansfield went one step further. At a Hollywood reception for Sophia, Jayne bent over. As Sophia tells it, "one of [Mansfield's] ample breasts tumbled out of her dress as photographers clicked away." Actor Clifton Webb was sitting next to Sophia when Jayne leaned in. "Please, Miss Mansfield," acerbic Webb complained, "we're wine drinkers at this table."

★ Sophia met actor Frank Sinatra on the set of *The Pride and the Passion* (1957). He taught the Italian movie star to say things like "it was a f***ing gas" and "how's your c***?" When Sophia realized what he had done, she called him a "mean little guinea son of a bitch."

★ While making *Houseboat* (1958), Sophia got fed up with child star Paul Petersen. When he couldn't cry on cue after twenty takes, she reportedly said, "You are being paid to cry, so cry." She punctuated her demand with a "love" tap. He cried.

★ Loren was considered once for the screen part of the saintly nun Mother Cabrini. However, the Mission Sisters of the Sacred Heart of Jesus, Mother Cabrini's order, made the following objections: "In the first place, there are bigamy charges against her in Italy. Secondly, she doesn't have the physique. Mother Cabrini was a small, slender woman. Miss Loren is bulky."

★ Sophia insisted that she had two faces. Her right profile was for drama. Her left profile was for comedy.

★ After the first take of a big kissing scene in *A Countess from Hong Kong* (1967), Marlon Brando whispered to his costar that she had long hairs growing out of her nose. On the retake, he bit her lip until it bled. Director Charlie Chaplin later said that "each clasped each other as if embracing a werewolf."

✪ In 1982, Sophia served a jail sentence in Italy for tax evasion. Fans thronged outside the prison and danced the tarantella whenever she looked outside. After her first few days of relative luxury in prison (with an espresso machine, a Sony Walkman, etc.) were protested, she was bunked with other inmates and became depressed. "What hell it was," she said. She served a total of seventeen days.

✪ When Loren thumbed her nose at "politically correct" standards and posed for an Italian furrier, sixty-year-old sex kitten Brigitte Bardot was furious. "[Sophia is] a killer of small animals!" the French star told Italian newspapers. Later, Sophia turned down an offer of half a million dollars from another clothing manufacturer to put her face on a line of men's boxer shorts.

✪ During the filming of *Grumpier Old Men* (1995), costar Walter Matthau entertained Sophia by arranging for kosher salamis of varying lengths to pop out of his fly.

"Now it is the power of the nipple!" Sophia Loren complained. "The nipple is always outside. It's terrible."
[photo courtesy of Archive Photos]

Shirley MacLaine

FACTS OF LIFE

ORIGIN: Born Shirley Maclean Beaty, April 24, 1934, Richmond, Virginia. She changed her surname to make it more "interesting."

FORMATIVE YEARS: Graduated from Washington and Lee High School in Arlington, Virginia. She was awarded an honorary doctorate of humane letters from New York City's Hunter College in 1984.

FAMILY PLANNING: Married Steve Parker (actor/producer), September 17, 1954; lived 6,000 miles away from him for almost thirty years; divorced 1983. According to Shirley, "It was time."

ROMANTIC INTERESTS: Pete Hamill (writer), Sander Vanocur (newsman), Andrei Mikhalkov-Konchalovsky (director), Danny Kaye (actor), Yves Montand (actor), Robert Mitchum (actor). Shirley claimed "Monogamy is not a natural human condition."

SELECTED HITS (and Misses)

FILMS: *The Trouble with Harry* (1955), *Around the World in Eighty Days* (1956), *Some Came Running* (1958), *The Sheepman* (1958), *The Matchmaker* (1958), *Ask Any Girl* (1959), *Can-Can* (1960), *The Apartment* (1960), *All in a Night's Work* (1961), *The Children's Hour* (1962), *Two for the Seesaw* (1963), *Irma la Douce*

(1963), *What a Way to Go!* (1964), *John Goldfarb, Please Come Home* (1965), *Sweet Charity* (1969), *Two Mules for Sister Sara* (1970), *The Possession of Joel Delaney* (1972), *The Turning Point* (1977), *Being There* (1979), *Loving Couples* (1980), *Terms of Endearment* (Oscar for Best Actress—1983), *Cannonball Run II* (1984), *Madame Sousatzka* (1988), *Steel Magnolias* (1989), *Postcards from the Edge* (1990), *Used People* (1992), *Guarding Tess* (1994), *The Evening Star* (1996), *Mrs. Winterbourne* (1996), *A Smile Like Yours* (1997), *Get Bruce* (1999), *Bruno* (1999).

QUICKIE BIO

A self-described tomboy and self-created Hollywood New Age guru, Shirley MacLaine grew up with her brother, Warren Beatty, in a nice Virginia neighborhood. The tall redhead was a cheerleader and a ballet dancer before hoofing it to the Broadway stage in 1954, chopping her hair off, and traveling to Hollywood. By 1960 she was on the cover of *Time* magazine as "The Ring-A-Ding Girl." Shirley was one of the few "chicks" who messed with the Rat Pack and managed to keep her clothes on. In more recent years, an older, wiser MacLaine once again became a box office draw, and managed to reclaim her title as America's favorite "kook."

SHIRLEY MacLAINE
DOES THE DUMBEST THINGS

★ One of Shirley MacLaine's first gigs was performing at trade shows. "I danced around a refrigerator for six months," she bragged.

★ In 1960 MacLaine told the press that she collected rubber bands, bubble gum, match boxes, unmatched gloves, old typewriter ribbons, and dull pencils. She also said her daily diet consisted of four hot-fudge sundaes and snails.

★ During her Rat Pack days, MacLaine played gin with gangster Sam Giancana. When the underworld figure cheated, the redhead threatened him with a water pistol. Giancana pulled out a real .38. MacLaine giggled, "It was all so theatrically dangerous and amusing to me."

★ When Soviet Premier Nikita Krushchev visited the set of the movie *Can-Can* (1960), Shirley danced for the stocky head Red and his wife. "Immoral," Krushchev later said, describing her performance. "The face of humanity is more beautiful than its backside." "If he thinks we were risqué," Shirley snapped back, "he should have seen the original can-can . . . in the nineties [1890s] French girls danced it without panties!"

- MacLaine traveled to Russia in 1962 and spent fifty-three hours talking with Russian students about everything from politics to Elizabeth Taylor. One exhausted student finally asked, "Is this lady what you call in United States a filibuster?"

- MacLaine went out one evening with a producer named Steven Parker. After four hours together, he proposed to her. "Man, I had him figured for a real nut!" MacLaine said. The next morning she agreed to wed him. Then they "forgot" to get married until a year later.

- In the 1970s, after being married for more than twenty years, Shirley became promiscuous. She started having "sex for sex's sake" because she believed that "it would be liberating for women, who had been subjected to a double standard."

- MacLaine was indignant after critics panned her films *A Change of Seasons* (1980) and *Loving Couples* (1980). "If friendly f***ing is threatening to the critics," she snarled, "then I'm in bad trouble because I made a decision to make two films on this theme."

- For the comedy *John Goldfarb, Please Come Home* (1965), Shirley dressed up in wild outfits to distract an Arab sheik before scoring a touchdown by riding on an oil gusher. "What a movie!" MacLaine recalled. "A dumb broad runs through the whole Notre Dame football team."

- While traveling in the Himalayan nation of Bhutan, Shirley got mixed up in a palace coup. She tried to smuggle her native guide out of the country by disguising him as her chauffeur. He was discovered, but escaped. She, however, was held at gunpoint until he was recaptured. After she left the country, Shirley told reporters that a good luck sash given her by a Tibetan monk was the only thing that saved her. "I'll never take it off," she said. She then explained that she couldn't take off her overcoat because the sash was the only thing she was wearing underneath it.

- On the set of *Terms of Endearment* (1983), Shirley disagreed so furiously with costar Debra Winger that, at one point, Winger reportedly lifted up her skirt and farted in the direction of the spiritual MacLaine.

- "Nobody really knows me," Shirley sighed. She also claimed that a UFO was stationed over her head, and that in previous lives she had been a Mongolian nomad, a Parisian prostitute, and a court jester beheaded by Louis XV. Shirley wrote books about her spiritual journeys and released a video entitled *Shirley MacLaine's Inner Workout*.

✪ Shirley has long been intrigued by the playboy reputation of her brother, Warren. At different times, she has said on the subject: "I'd love to do a kissing scene with him, to see what all the fuss is about." "Warren's looking for a woman like me." "It's too bad we're related. I'd like to find out what all the shouting is about." And finally, "I keep my daughter as far away from Warren as I can."

Jayne Mansfield

FACTS OF LIFE (and Death)

ORIGIN: Born Vera Jayne Palmer, April 19, 1933, Bryn Mawr, Pennsylvania; died June 29, 1967, New Orleans, Louisiana, in a car wreck.

FORMATIVE YEARS: Attended the University of Texas at Austin.

FAMILY PLANNING: Married Paul Mansfield (student), January 28, 1950; divorced 1958; married Mickey Hargitay (muscleman), January 13, 1958; divorced 1964; married Matt Cimber (director), September 22, 1964; divorced 1966.

ROMANTIC INTERESTS: Greg Bautzer (lawyer), Elvis Presley (singer/actor), Steve Cochran (actor), John F. Kennedy (President), Robert Kennedy (brother of President), Sam Brody (lawyer).

SELECTED HITS (and Misses)

FILMS: *Underwater!* (1955), *Pete Kelly's Blues* (1955), *Illegal* (1955), *Hell on Frisco Bay* (1955), *The Female Jungle* (1956), *The Girl Can't Help It* (1956), *Will Success Spoil Rock Hunter?* (1957), *It Takes a Thief* (1959), *The Loves of Hercules* (1960), *Panic Button* (1962), *Promises! Promises!* (1963), *Primitive Love* (1964), *Las Vegas Hillbillys* (1966), *Single Room Furnished* (1968).

171

QUICKIE BIO

Jayne Mansfield based her career on bosomy public relations highlights. She was always the poor man's Marilyn, one of the original *Playboy* centerfolds, who designed her own skintight clown suit and squealed, undulated, purred, popped, and wiggled her way into immortality in the 1950s. The 1960s found her va-voom image more humorous than scandalous. Still, Jayne almost always got the attention she craved. During an appearance on *The Tonight Show* in 1964, swinging guest TV host Dick Cavett introduced the former Texas co-ed by saying, "And here they are, Jayne Mansfield!"

JAYNE MANSFIELD
DOES THE DUMBEST THINGS

✪ Jayne earned the beauty titles Miss Photoflash, Miss Negligee, Queen of the Chihuahua Show, Miss Nylon Sweater, Miss Freeway, Blossom Queen, Miss Electric Switch, Miss Geiger Counter, Miss 100% Pure Maple Syrup, Miss July 4th, Miss Fire Prevention, and Miss Texas Tomato. Jayne did decline to be Miss Roquefort Cheese, saying it didn't "sound right."

✪ After divorcing her first husband, Jayne became quite the party girl in Hollywood. Whenever she crashed a social gathering, she proclaimed to the men attending that she wasn't wearing panties or a bra.

✪ Between acting parts, Jayne did odd jobs for publicity. For one assignment, she dressed in a sexy Santa outfit and delivered booze to newspaper writers. "I gazed upon a young blonde with the most beautiful pair of breasts I'd ever seen," reported one drooling columnist. She also once strolled down Sunset Boulevard in Hollywood clad only in a pink ribbon.

✪ After seeing herself on-screen for the first time in the mid-1950s in *The Female Jungle* (a.k.a. *The Hangover*), Jayne declared tearfully, "I love you, Jayne Mansfield! I'll work hard for you! Nothing or no one could ever make me let you down!" The next job she had was selling candy.

✪ Mansfield tried to convince studio boss Darryl F. Zanuck to pick her over Marilyn Monroe for the lead in *The Seven Year Itch* (1955). When she didn't get the assignment, Jayne moaned, "He probably didn't even see the chest—I mean the test!"

✪ Jayne's publicity appearances were often accompanied by "accidents." One such accident occurred when actress Jane Russell was doing a publicity shoot at a pool in Miami for her film *Underwater!* (1955). Jayne "accidentally" fell in the pool, and her swimsuit strap popped off. Mansfield bobbed right up and so did her top. *Variety* noted that Jayne was "worth her weight in cheesecake."

⭐ Jayne allegedly won her first TV acting job when she simply wrote her measurements on a piece of paper and had them delivered to the producer.

⭐ While on the set for her first Warner Bros. film, *Illegal* (1955), Jayne's studio chair simply read, "40-21-35."

⭐ Mansfield was obsessed with her own inches, even when they appeared in scandal magazines such as *Confidential*. "They treated me as if I were only a 36," she whined, in response to one article. "Marilyn's only a 38! I'm a 40!" By the time Jayne got to London in 1957, she announced to the press at the airport that she was "41-18-35 and tanned over every inch of me!" Things had apparently shifted in Jayne's favor since her *Illegal* measurements!

⭐ After 452 performances of *Will Success Spoil Rock Hunter?* on Broadway in the mid-1950s, Jayne screen-tested for the film version. She reportedly exposed her breasts to the cameraman. Director Billy Wilder said it was the first time he'd seen an actress rub "her bosom against the camera lens." Needless to say, the footage was extremely popular at Hollywood parties and bachelor fetes.

⭐ Mansfield met Queen Elizabeth in London. "Everything about her was so marvelous," Jayne burbled. "From the moment [the queen] came in and the band played 'My Country 'Tis of Thee.'" The song was actually "God Save the Queen."

💰 Jayne really did "think pink." Her Beverly Hills mansion was known as the "Pink Palace." Everything inside was pink, including the bathroom, the living room, her Cadillac, a Jaguar, and a heart-shaped tub. Mansfield claimed to bathe in pink Champagne and even used pink soap to wash with. The pool was heart-shaped and had "I love you Jaynie" written on the bottom. The star thought pink all the way down—her pubic hair was allegedly trimmed to a heart-shape and also dyed pink.

⭐ In the swinging 1960s, Jayne's platinum bombshell image was square. When the Beatles expressed interest in meeting her, she showed up at a reception for them in Los Angeles and got drunk. George Harrison tried to throw a drink in her face but missed and hit statuesque actress Mamie Van Doren instead. In *Playboy* in 1965, Paul McCartney referred to Jayne as an "old bag." Mansfield was thirty-two.

⭐ As Mansfield's boobs fell out of favor she started making appearances abroad, and once found herself stranded in South America for not paying taxes. The lawyer who saved her day was Sam Brody. Brody became her lover after he lost $20,000 gambling in Vegas on their first date.

⭐ Brody was killed with Mansfield in a car accident outside New Orleans in 1967. When fans saw pictures of her go-go-booted corpse and a mass of blond hair on the car hood, they thought that Mansfield had been beheaded in the accident. In reality, the picture only showed that her platinum wig had been knocked off.

Dean Martin

FACTS OF LIFE (and Death)

ORIGIN: Born Dino Crocetti, June 7, 1917, Steubenville, Ohio; died December 25, 1995, Beverly Hills, California.

FORMATIVE YEARS: In the tenth grade dropped out of Wells High School, Steubenville, Ohio.

FAMILY PLANNING: Married Elizabeth "Betty" MacDonald (singer), October 2, 1940; divorced 1949; married Jeanne Bieggers (Orange Bowl Queen), September 1, 1949; divorced 1973; married Catherine Hawn (receptionist), April 25, 1973; divorced 1976.

ROMANTIC INTERESTS: Dora Fjelstad (chorus girl), June Allyson (actress), Pier Angeli (actress), Miriam LeVelle (dancer), Lana Turner (actress), Gail Renshaw (Miss World—USA), Peggy Crosby (Bing Crosby's daughter-in-law), Andre Boyer (economics student), Phyllis Elizabeth Davis (actress).

SELECTED HITS (and Misses)

FILMS: *My Friend Irma* (1949), *At War with the Army* (1950), *The Stooge* (1951), *Jumping Jacks* (1952), *Scared Stiff* (1953), *The Caddy* (1953), *Hollywood or Bust* (1956), *Ten Thousand Bedrooms* (1957), *The Young Lions* (1958), *Some Came Running* (1958), *Rio Bravo* (1959), *Career* (1959), *Ocean's Eleven* (1960), *Bells Are Ringing* (1960), *All in a Night's Work* (1961), *Toys in the Attic* (1963), *Four for Texas* (1963), *What a Way to Go!* (1964), *Kiss Me, Stupid* (1964), *Robin and the Seven Hoods* (1964), *The Sons of Katie Elder* (1965), *The Silencers* (1966), *The Ambushers* (1967), *Bandolero!* (1968), *How to Save a Marriage and Ruin Your Life* (1968), *Five Card Stud* (1968), *Airport* (1970), *Showdown* (1973), *The Cannonball Run* (1980), *Cannonball Run II* (1984).

TV SERIES: *The Colgate Comedy Hour* (1950–55), *The Dean Martin Show* (1965–74), *Half Nelson* (1985).

QUICKIE BIO

Lovable lush Dean Martin grew up playing craps in the alleys of Steubenville, Ohio, and dropped out of school to become a boxer. He decided that dealing blackjack was better than taking punches and became a professional gambler. He learned how to sing from watching Bing Crosby movies, and appeared first as Dino Martini, then as Dean Martin. He hit the show business big time with his "pallie" Jerry Lewis in the late 1940s. The "guinea" and the "monkey," as Hollywood producers called them, were box-office gold until they split professionally in 1956. For the next few decades, Dean swaggered his way through best selling records, westerns, spy flicks, and romantic comedies. According to one friend "Dino used to f*** every human he could." According to another pal, "He was a good sex man, but his big interest was golf." Dino played an awful lot of golf.

DEAN MARTIN
DOES THE DUMBEST THINGS

Dean was good at cards and worked as a professional dealer. But he wasn't good at math. He promised 10 percent of his earnings to his first band leader, 10 percent to MCA, 35 percent to a guy who loaned him cash, 20 percent to another guy who loaned him funds, 20 percent to comedian Lou Costello, 10 percent to a radio programmer, and 5 percent to a New York club owner. By 1946, Dean had given away *110 percent* of his earnings. He declared himself bankrupt.

While he was filming his first movie, *My Friend Irma* (1949), nobody told Dean you were supposed to fake punches. Martin socked his costar on the jaw and knocked out his tooth.

Dean gave Jerry Lewis a golf bag bearing the inscription "To the Happy Hebrew from the Nasal Neapolitan."

Unlike his longtime performance partner Jerry Lewis, Dean hated France. When asked about French cuisine, the crooner observed, "Barney's Beanery in Los Angeles has better food." In reference to the artists in the famous museum the Louvre, Martin snorted, "I had a guy once who did my house in two days, was a better painter than those guys."

On the set of the western *Rio Bravo* (1959), Martin's costar Ricky Nelson turned eighteen. Martin and John Wayne presented Nelson with a birthday present—a three-hundred-pound sack of cow manure. The sack was emptied on the ground. Then the two older actors picked up Nelson by both arms and threw him into the pile of poop.

✪ Appearing on stage with Frank Sinatra and Sammy Davis Jr., Dean picked up Sammy and held him out to Frank, "Here," Dean said. "This award just came for you from the National Association for the Advancement of Colored People."

✪ During the 1960s, Dean led a protest march. He marched up and down on stage with a sign that read "We Want Free Broads."

✪ During the first episode of TV's *The Dean Martin Show* in 1965, Dean walked out singing his big hit, "Everybody Loves Somebody Sometime." Then he stopped. "No point in singing the whole song," Martin said, "you might not buy the record." Later, he sauntered to the onstage bar and told the audience, "This is going to be a family show. The kind of show where a man can take his wife and kids, his father and mother, and sit around in a bar and watch." The variety series was a huge hit.

✪ On his TV variety outing, Martin suggested in Italian that his guest star Bill Dana "fa 'n cul"—which, translated from the Italian, means, um, er, something not very masculine. NBC announced that from then on, all of Dean's comments in Italian would be censored. Martin's response to the network was not printed.

✪ When a businessman sitting next to Frank Sinatra and Dean Martin at a nightclub told them to keep it down, the two Rat Packers punched him out and gave him a skull fracture. Dean later told reporters that "he hadn't seen a thing."

✪ In the mid-1950s, Martin told an interviewer that rock-n-roll was "disgusting." "Thank heaven it is on the way out," he added.

✪ In 1964, Dean's song "Everybody Loves Somebody Sometime" knocked the Beatles "A Hard Day's Night" out of the number one spot on the recording industry charts. In 1968 Dean Martin sold more albums than Jimi Hendrix, but he didn't have a passion for music. Two of his favorite lines in the recording studio were "Hey, why don't we forget this f***in' tune," and "I don't care. F*** it."

✪ Martin's license plate in the 1970s read DRUNKY.

⭐ At the rehearsal for President Reagan's inauguration gala in 1981, Martin staggered onstage with a glass in his hand and gazed around in a drunken haze until Frank Sinatra led him off. Later, Martin was too drunk to perform.

⭐ In 1987, an ailing and seriously depressed Dean Martin returned to the stage in a tour with Sammy Davis Jr. and Frank Sinatra. Dean got bored after a few shows, flicked a lit cigarette at the crowd, and walked off the tour.

Bette Midler

FACTS OF LIFE

ORIGIN: Born December 1, 1945, Honolulu, Hawaii.

FORMATIVE YEARS: Studied theater at the University of Hawaii in Honolulu, but dropped out.

FAMILY PLANNING: Married Martin von Haselberg (performance artist), December 16, 1985.

ROMANTIC INTERESTS: Ben Gillespie (dancer), Aaron "Baron Bruiso" Russo (manager), Peter Riegert (actor), Benoit Gautier (manager).

SELECTED HITS (and Misses)

FILMS: *Hawaii* (1966), *The Divine Mr. J* (1974), *The Rose* (1979), *Divine Madness* (concert film, 1980), *Jinxed* (1982), *Down and Out in Beverly Hills* (1986), *Ruthless People* (1986), *Big Business* (1988), *Beaches* (1988), *Stella* (1990), *Scenes from a Mall* (1991), *For the Boys* (1991), *Hocus Pocus* (1993), *The First Wives Club* (1996), *That Old Feeling* (1997), *Get Bruce* (1999), *Isn't She Great* (1999).

QUICKIE BIO

Diminutive Bette Midler worked as a chunker in a pineapple factory near her Hawaiian home, before she turned herself into the Divine Miss M and enthralled towel-wrapped gay men at the Continental Baths in New York City. Midler made her screen debut as a seasick wife in the epic *Hawaii* (1966), and spent years as a campy singer before becoming a campy movie star. Bette moved away from Hollywood in 1977 and declared that Los Angeles was full of "morons." Midler's own personal motto? "F*** 'em if they can't take a joke."

BETTE MIDLER
DOES THE DUMBEST THINGS

⭐ Bette's mom was a star-struck movie buff who named her daughter after Bette Davis, but thought that Bette Davis pronounced her name "Bet."

⭐ In 1972 journalist Geraldo Rivera interviewed Bette in her New York City apartment. According to Geraldo, they had a passionate fling in which the Divine Miss M proved to be sexually insatiable. According to Midler, Geraldo drugged her and then groped her.

⭐ During her early tours in the 1960s, Barry Manilow played piano for Bette. Midler liked to change the song list during the show, which made Barry furious. Backstage they threw ashtrays at each other.

⭐ Bette enjoyed performing for an underclad gay crowd. "They all sit in front of me and when they love me they throw their towels at me . . ." the performer gushed. "And when they give me standing ovations, all their towels fall to the floor." Midler later announced, "I have no gay friends. I wouldn't know a homosexual if I saw one."

During a concert tour in 1973, Midler landed in Detroit. She went with her entourage to a restaurant without telling her manager Aaron Russo where she was heading. When he finally arrived at the dining establishment, he screamed at Bette. She threw a baked Alaska at him. Then Russo tossed an entire tray of baked Alaskas at Bette.

⭐ Russo claimed he and Bette were lovers for years, but she has said that their relationship was strictly business after the first few months. "What do you think he's going to say?" Bette scoffed. "That I schtupped him once and threw him out because he wasn't good enough?"

⭐ In one low-budget film *The Divine Mr. J* (1974), Bette appeared as the Virgin Mary. She sang "I've Got a Date with an Angel" before the immaculate conception. Then, after she became pregnant with Jesus, she sang, "It's Beginning to Look a Lot Like Christmas."

⭐ At a 1978 concert in London, fans unfurled a sign that read "We Love Your Tits." Bette cracked up, then pulled down her bustier.

⭐ In 1979, Midler finished a concert, left the stage, and started to take a shower. However, the fans were screaming for her so loudly that she came back onstage wrapped in a towel, then pulled off the towel and flung it over her head.

For her New Year's 1973 show, Bette decided to put a joint under every seat in the house. Since there were 1,800 seats, Bette spent most of the day rolling joints. When word leaked out about the party favors, Bette was afraid of getting busted and decided to stop rolling. Instead, she performed onstage, sat on King Kong's hand, and took off her dress.

⭐ In the late 1970s, Midler starred in an NBC-TV special. "I want an hour devoted to the twin deities of truth," she announced on the air, pointing to one of her boobs, "and beauty," she said, pointing to the other one. "Talk about your big events." However, she got into trouble with the censors when she said the phrase "you're an a**." "That's the anatomical a**," the NBC censor explained. "We can't have that."

⭐ While making the film *Jinxed* (1982), costar Ken Wahl despised Midler so much that when he had to act in love scenes with her, he thought about his dog.

⭐ On the way to an audition for *The Tonight Show* with Johnny Carson, Bette got out of a cab and ripped her dress "right on the a**." "Fortunately," Bette explained, "I was wearing underwear—one of the few times I was wearing underwear."

⭐ "I donated my tits to Cher," Bette admitted in her younger years. "And she was so glad to get 'em I can't even tell you." By 1998, Cher and Midler were bosom buddies no longer. "The woman's disgusting," Bette shrieked. "She called me a c***. I'll never speak to her again."

Liza Minnelli

FACTS OF LIFE

ORIGIN: Born March 12, 1946, Los Angeles, California.

FORMATIVE YEARS: Attended the Sorbonne in Paris, France.

FAMILY PLANNING: Married Peter Allen (entertainer), March 3, 1967; divorced 1974; married Jack Haley Jr. (producer), September 15, 1974; divorced 1979; married Mark Gero (stage manager), December 4, 1979; divorced 1992.

ROMANTIC INTERESTS: John Gary Gorton (Prime Minister of Australia), Bob Fosse (choreographer), Peter Sellers (actor), Ben Vereen (actor), Pedro Aquinaga (Brazilian playboy), Martin Scorsese (director), Mikhail Baryshnikov (dancer), Adam Ant (rock star), Joe Pesci (actor), Gene Simmons (rock star).

SELECTED HITS (and Misses)

FILMS: *In the Good Old Summertime* (1949), *Charlie Bubbles* (1967), *The Sterile Cuckoo* (1969), *Tell Me That You Love Me, Junie Moon* (1970), *Cabaret* (Oscar for Best Actress—1972), *Lucky Lady* (1975), *A Matter of Time* (1976), *New York, New York* (1977), *Arthur* (1981), *The Muppets Take Manhattan* (1984), *Arthur 2: On the Rocks* (1988), *Rent-a-Cop* (1988), *Stepping Out* (1991).

QUICKIE BIO

If ever anybody was bred to be an entertainer it was Liza. Her first visitor as a newborn infant was Frank Sinatra. "When your mother is [actress] Judy Garland and your father is [director] Vincente Minnelli, you really don't have much choice except to go into the family business," Liza capitulated. She

182

followed her mom into show business—and chemical dependency. With her designer buddy Halston, Minnelli became a fixture at New York City's disco-and-decadence ground-zero club, Studio 54. Said one partygoer of the scene, "We all took drugs openly and indulged in every type of sex act. Halston and Liza were there practically every night." Life was a cabaret, indeed.

LIZA MINNELLI
DOES THE DUMBEST THINGS

✪ Liza spent her sixth birthday with her father Vincente Minnelli at songwriter/composer George Gershwin's house in Hollywood. During her party, Liza jealously watched a little girl engage father Vincente's attention. Little Liza walked over and socked her papa in the nose in front of guests Humphrey Bogart and Lauren Bacall.

✪ Mama Judy promised daughter Liza that the two would celebrate when Liza became a woman. On the day Liza began menstruating, Judy found that her hubby, Sid Luft, had locked up all of the booze. So Judy raided the kitchen and toasted Liza with cooking wine.

✪ Liza Minnelli was unable to consummate her marriage to Peter Allen on the night of their nuptials, because the groom was out having sex with a gay lover. "There are just certain things that I don't think are right," Liza said on reflection. "Bisexuality is one of them."

✪ In Puerto Rico, Liza fell in love with a stray dog named Ocho. "Sometimes I see him looking at me and I know exactly what he's thinking," she claimed. Too bad she couldn't read the dog's mind all of the time. After Minnelli illegally brought the pooch back into the States, Ocho got feisty one night and bit the hand of Liza's wardrobe mistress. The woman sued, and the court awarded her damages. Liza then ordered someone to remove Ocho's choppers.

✪ Minnelli brought her Scottish terrier, Lilly, to Sweden in 1989. By doing so, she violated the country's animal quarantine laws. The canine was put under house arrest and customs agents were put at Minnelli's door to make sure the owner obeyed the order. To get out of the ordeal, Liza chartered a $50,000 jet and had the doggie, escorted by her bodyguard, flown to Paris. Lilly was then put up in a luxury hotel suite and dined on gourmet rabbit stew. Liza phoned twice daily to see how her pooch was handling their separation.

✪ "Halston liked bosoms when bosoms weren't in," Liza Minnelli blabbed about her bosom buddy designer Roy Halston Frowick. Liza and

Halston liked to hang out at the Studio 54 disco, where Halston once held a contest to see which man could, uh, squirt the farthest.

 In 1979 Minnelli was apparently so high that she was convinced the space station Skylab was going to fall on her head. She retreated to fashion designer Halston's Long Island compound. When the terrified Minnelli arrived, Halston took her by the hand, led her out to the porch, pointed to the lawn and said, "Look, that's where Skylab is going to fall." They sat down and waited for Skylab until it was announced that the space station had disintegrated over Australia.

⭐ One night at Studio 54 in Manhattan, Liza reportedly went up to Halston and said, "Give me every drug you've got." Halston obligingly gave her a vial of cocaine, a few Quaaludes, some marijuana, and a Valium. Liza then went off with director Martin Scorsese, who had been hiding around the corner.

⭐ Three weeks later she repeated the scene. This time, dancer Mikhail Baryshnikov did the waiting. One observer of the affair commented, "Liza and Baryshnikov were taking so much cocaine. They took so much, just shoving it in, and it was so exciting to see two really famous people right there in front of you taking drugs about to go make it with each other."

⭐ After Halston's death, Liza attended seances to contact him. She missed the days of Studio 54 so much, she wanted to make sure Halston had met up with Andy Warhol and club owner Steve Rubell and was partying with the gang in disco heaven.

💬 In *Lucky Lady* (1975), Minnelli delivered the dumbest line of her (or anyone's career): "It's so quiet you could hear a fish fart."

⭐ During the production of the stage musical *The Act* (1978), Minnelli became very friendly with director Martin Scorsese, even though she was still married to Jack Haley Jr. and Scorsese was still wed to writer Julia Cameron. At the opening night party, Haley gave Liza a gift of a fourteen-karat gold Valium.

⭐ During a performance of *The Act*, Liza spotted Marlene Dietrich in the front row. At show's end, Minnelli bent down and took Dietrich's hand in order to kiss it. As she bent down, she realized it wasn't Dietrich at all but a New York shrink who was a dead ringer for the actress. Liza became so flustered, she jammed one of the psychiatrist's fingers up her nose. Liza then became hysterical and left the stage in tears.

★ In 1998 Liza refused to participate in a two-week tribute to her mother, Judy Garland, at Carnegie Hall in New York City. Minnelli claimed she was "unable to attend . . . for reasons my mother would have understood." What was the reason? Liza was feuding with the host of the event, her half sister, Lorna Luft.

Marilyn Monroe

DUMBEST QUOTES

"Ever notice that 'What the hell' is always the right decision?"

"I never understood it—the sex symbol. I always thought symbols were things you clashed together."

FACTS OF LIFE (and Death)

ORIGIN: Born Norma Jeane Baker (Mortenson), June 1, 1926, Los Angeles, California; died August 5, 1962, Los Angeles, California, of a drug overdose.

FORMATIVE YEARS: Dropped out of high school, worked folding parachutes and spraying paint in a defense plant.

FAMILY PLANNING: Married James Dougherty (neighbor), June 19, 1942; divorced 1946; married Joe DiMaggio (baseball player), January 14, 1954; divorced 1955; married Arthur Miller (playwright/author), June 29, 1956; divorced 1961.

ROMANTIC INTERESTS: Johnny Hyde (agent), Joseph Schenck (producer), Harry P. Cohn (movie mogul), John F. Kennedy (U.S. President), Robert Kennedy (U.S. Attorney General), Frank Sinatra (singer/actor), Howard Hughes (producer), Yves Montand (singer/actor).

SELECTED HITS (and Misses)

FILMS: *Love Happy* (1949), *Ladies of the Chorus* (1949), *The Asphalt Jungle* (1950), *All About Eve* (1950), *Love Nest* (1951), *Clash by Night* (1952), *We're Not Married* (1952), *Don't Bother to Knock* (1952), *Niagara* (1953), *Gentlemen Prefer*

Blondes (1953), *How to Marry a Millionaire* (1953), *River of No Return* (1954), *There's No Business Like Show Business* (1954), *The Seven Year Itch* (1955), *Bus Stop* (1957), *The Prince and the Showgirl* (1957), *Some Like It Hot* (1959), *Let's Make Love* (1960), *The Misfits* (1961).

QUICKIE BIO

Her assets? "Blond hair and breasts," Marilyn admitted, "that's how I got started." Norma Jeane Baker never knew her father. After her mother was sent to a mental institution, she grew up with a series of foster parents who didn't know how to handle her amazing physical assets. Others had a better idea, including a local boy who married her just after her sixteenth birthday. Later, she traded sex for food until she got into movies, appeared in the first issue of *Playboy* magazine, and climbed the ladder to stardom "wrong by wrong." Marilyn's death by drug overdose at age thirty-six only added to her mystique. Was it the CIA? The mob? The Kennedys? Or was Marilyn just plain dumb? According to filmmaker Otto Preminger, who worked with her on *River of No Return* (1954), "Directing her was like directing Lassie."

MARILYN MONROE
DOES THE DUMBEST THINGS

⭐ In 1944 an Army photographer had the future Marilyn Monroe pose for cheesecake shots for *Yank* and *Stars & Stripes*. The GIs voted her the girl they would most like to examine. "Getting paid to take my clothes off was the easiest thing in the world," Marilyn gushed.

⭐ During her first marriage, Marilyn supplemented her income by working as a hooker. After her first "john" wanted her to take off her clothes for fifteen dollars, she observed, "I thought it was a pretty good deal. At the beach I was almost naked . . . for nothing." And Marilyn—in an era before AIDS— believed sex was safe, noting, "Nobody ever got cancer from sex."

⭐ Monroe was a classic casting couch potato. Twentieth Century-Fox executive Joseph Schenck took a fancy to Marilyn. "After dinner, he told me to take my clothes off and he would tell me Hollywood stories." Schenck played with her breasts. "He didn't want to do much else since he was getting old," Marilyn explained. "Sometimes he'd fall asleep." Schenck moved Marilyn into his pool house so he could call her on those rare occasions when he could perform. "Sometimes it took hours," Marilyn sighed. "I was relieved when he fell asleep."

✪ Rival studio boss Harry Cohn wanted to have sex with Marilyn because she was Schenck's mistress. Marilyn complained, "Harry just told you to go to bed without saying hello."

✪ The casting director at Twentieth Century-Fox gave Marilyn a sealed letter of introduction and told her to visit the other studio executives. After they read the letter, the executives walked around their desks and started to unzip their pants. "I spent a great deal of time on my knees," Marilyn explained. Later she added, "They weren't shooting all those sexy movies just to sell peanut butter. They wanted to sample the merchandise."

✪ One morning music director Fred Karger was making love with Monroe when his sister barged into the bedroom. "Hi," Marilyn chirped. "Can I have some juice?"

✪ When Grauman's Chinese Theatre asked Marilyn Monroe to put her hand and footprints in cement, she suggested that they use her bosom instead. Grauman's declined.

✪ Joe DiMaggio was cut out for baseball but not for marriage to Marilyn Monroe. After their honeymoon in Japan in early 1954, Marilyn flew to Korea to entertain the troops. She appeared onstage in sub-zero temperatures in a low-cut purple dress with no underwear. The troops went wild, Marilyn caught pneumonia, and Joe got extremely jealous.

✪ Joe heard rumors that Marilyn was having an affair with a woman. So he and Frank Sinatra hired detectives to follow Marilyn. One night the sleuths found out that Marilyn was having a rendezvous with a female "friend." They decided to catch Marilyn in the act. So they snuck up to the apartment and kicked in the door. Surprise! It was not Marilyn's apartment, but the apartment of a very dismayed elderly woman. The woman sued DiMaggio and collected $7,500.

✪ After divorcing DiMaggio in 1955, Monroe decided to go intellectual. She took acting classes in New York City, converted to Judaism, and married playwright Arthur Miller. Miller was less intellectual about Marilyn. "I don't approve of her or know how to talk to her," he moaned, "but I find her overwhelmingly sexually attractive."

✪ While staying overnight at Frank Sinatra's house, Marilyn wandered downstairs naked. She walked into a room where Sinatra and his pals were playing poker. Sinatra saw her and hustled her out before the others could see and told her to get her "fat a**" upstairs. She protested, "I thought they would like me more than their stupid cards."

"I am only comfortable when I'm naked," Marilyn confessed. She liked to walk around naked so much she was nude when she interviewed a housekeeper. Once she wrapped strands of spaghetti pasta around her breasts. "This is my idea of wearing a bra."

★ Marilyn converted to Judaism. After being served matzo ball soup three times in a row, she asked, "Is there any other part of the matzo you can eat?"

★ Monroe was a slob. She slept until noon, drank champagne for breakfast, and seldom bathed unless she was going out or filming. She ate lamb chops in bed, dropped the bones under the covers, and wiped her hands on the sheets.

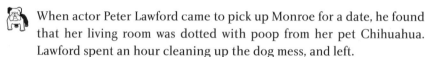 When actor Peter Lawford came to pick up Monroe for a date, he found that her living room was dotted with poop from her pet Chihuahua. Lawford spent an hour cleaning up the dog mess, and left.

★ Marilyn's maid once entered the bathroom to find America's sex symbol squatting on the toilet, bleaching her pubic hair with a toothbrush. "With my white dresses and all, it just wouldn't look nice, to be dark down there." Two days later Marilyn was forced to lie with an icepack between her legs. "It got all swollen from the bleach," she explained.

★ During the making of *Bus Stop* (1956), Marilyn met President Sukarno of Indonesia, who was a Muslim and a reported womanizer. "He kept looking down my dress," she complained. "You'd think with five wives he'd have enough." The Muslim and the sex goddess got much closer that night.

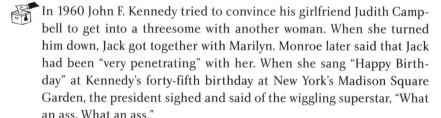 In 1960 John F. Kennedy tried to convince his girlfriend Judith Campbell to get into a threesome with another woman. When she turned him down, Jack got together with Marilyn. Monroe later said that Jack had been "very penetrating" with her. When she sang "Happy Birthday" at Kennedy's forty-fifth birthday at New York's Madison Square Garden, the president sighed and said of the wiggling superstar, "What an ass. What an ass."

Demi Moore

FACTS OF LIFE

ORIGIN: Born Demetria Guynes, November 11, 1962, Roswell, New Mexico.

FORMATIVE YEARS: Dropped out of Fairfax High School, Los Angeles, California.

FAMILY PLANNING: Married Freddy Moore (musician), February 1980; divorced 1984; married Bruce Willis (actor), November 21, 1987; separated, June 24, 1998.

ROMANTIC INTERESTS: Emilio Estevez (actor), Johnny Depp (actor), Leonardo DiCaprio (actor), Brad Pitt (actor).

SELECTED HITS (and Misses)

FILMS: *Choices* (1981), *Parasite* (1982), *No Small Affair* (1984), *Blame It on Rio* (1984), *St. Elmo's Fire* (1985), *About Last Night . . .* (1986), *The Seventh Sign* (1988), *We're No Angels* (1989), *Ghost* (1990), *Mortal Thoughts* (1991), *The Butcher's Wife* (1991), *A Few Good Men* (1992), *Indecent Proposal* (1993), *Disclosure* (1994), *The Scarlet Letter* (1995), *Now and Then* (1995), *Striptease* (1996), *The Hunchback of Notre Dame* (voice only, 1996), *The Juror* (1996), *G.I. Jane* (1997), *Deconstructing Harry* (1997), *Passion of Mind* (1999).

TV SERIES: *General Hospital* (1982–83).

QUICKIE BIO

Roswell, New Mexico, was the site of a famous alien encounter, and the birthplace of one of Hollywood's most alienating divas, Demi Moore.

Demi was a self-described "trailer park kid" whose stepfather killed himself when she was eighteen. After marrying and ditching a loser rock musician, Demi's career took off when she played a cokehead in the 1985 feature *St. Elmo's Fire*. It was a role she knew all too well at the time. Demi met and dumped Emilio Estevez, married Bruce Willis, then left him ten years later. When superstar Bruce tried to fix things up, Demi reportedly shouted, "Too late, Buster. I don't need a husband who can't keep his zipper zipped."

DEMI MOORE
DOES THE DUMBEST THINGS

✪ Demi Moore complained about the paparazzi taking pictures of her children. Then her daughter Rumer appeared in the film *Striptease* (1996), in which mom Demi appeared topless.

✪ Moore worked on her body extensively. She had surgery to uncross her eyes, had her breasts enlarged, and had fat removed from her hips, stomach, and butt. She called her boobs, butt, and legs her "goodies."

✪ While she was promoting the movie *Ghost* (1990), Demi traveled with a bodyguard, a masseuse, a hair person, a makeup person, a wardrobe person, and an assistant, who had an assistant.

✪ While filming *G.I. Jane* (1997), Demi hired a cook, three nannies, a makeup artist, hairdresser, and a personal assistant. She had such a large entourage that the producers had to hire a second jet so that her staff could accompany her during publicity appearances. Demi explained, "We're working together for a higher good."

✪ When Demi wanted to fly from Idaho to New York to attend the premiere of *A Few Good Men* (1992), Sony sent a jet to pick her up. According to sources, she decided the jet was too small because it could not carry all her luggage without putting one bag on top of another. She asked the studio to send another jet, and they did.

✪ In 1980, Demi married musician Freddy Moore. "I wanted him," Demi explained, "and there was the added adrenaline rush from the fact that he was married."

✪ When Demi showed up for wardrobe fitting for *St. Elmo's Fire* (1985), reportedly, she was staggering drunk and smelled like a sewer. She stayed at a residential treatment program during the rehearsals.

- Moore's mother Virginia blabbed to the tabloids that she did drugs with her young daughter. When Virginia got busted for drunk driving, Demi refused to bail her out.

- Demi hired three cameramen to film the birth of her first baby. As the infant's head appeared, Moore shouted, "Are you getting this?"

- Staying at a Baltimore hotel, Moore took her children down to the pool. One of them jumped into the Jacuzzi, where children were not permitted. A hotel staffer promptly asked the youngster to get out, and the child went crying to mommy. Mommy gave the hotel worker the finger and, in front of her children, began screaming four letter words. Moore supposedly then went to the management and had the hotel worker dismissed.

- Five months later, when a woman on Moore's staff was overheard cursing in front of Demi's daughter, Moore fired the employee.

- After seeing herself in a scene in *The Scarlet Letter* (1995), Moore decided her hair looked bad and demanded that they reshoot the sequence. They did—at a cost of $50,000.

- While doing voiceover work for Disney's animated feature *The Hunchback of Notre Dame* (1996) in Burbank, California, Demi told the producers that she had to attend a PTA meeting. The studio gladly agreed to provide Moore with transportation to and from the meeting. What Demi forgot to tell the studio was that her PTA meeting was in Idaho. The studio wound up paying $4,500 for a private jet.

- Moore once locked herself in the only bathroom of a swank Los Angeles restaurant and chatted away on her cell phone for over half an hour. When she emerged to a hostile crowd, the actress defended herself by claiming she was talking her daughter into going to bed.

- Demi is a serious doll collector. She brought them with her to the sets of her movies, and built a $500,000 home for them attached to her own abode in Hailey, Idaho.

- Bruce and Demi spent $85,000 on a playhouse for their daughter. The 840-square-foot "house" had two rooms and one bath. The Spanish-tiled mini-mansion even had air conditioning and its own furniture.

- One evening at a trendy Los Angeles restaurant, Demi and Bruce decided to sit under their table to eat dinner. After Bruce and Demi split, Demi agreed to keep their separation a secret until after the opening of Bruce's

1998 space epic *Armageddon*. However, when Moore discovered that Willis kept a mistress in an apartment, she spilled the beans early. Bruce got the word about Demi's "betrayal" on his cell phone while he was eating with his family at a restaurant in New Mexico. Bruce screamed at Demi, "You're determined to kick me right in the teeth!" Demi yelled back, "Happy Father's Day! You're finally getting what you deserve."

★ "I don't like to take my clothes off," demure Demi complained. Then she went topless in six movies, modeled for a revealing spread in *Oui* magazine, and posed nude for the cover of *Vanity Fair*—twice.

Eddie Murphy

FACTS OF LIFE

ORIGIN: Born April 3, 1961, Brooklyn, New York.

FORMATIVE YEARS: Enrolled at Nassau Community College (Garden City, New York), but dropped out after three weeks.

FAMILY PLANNING: Settled paternity suits with Nicolle Rader and Paulette McNeely; had a child by Tamara Hood; married Nicolle Mitchell (model), March 18, 1993, after they had two children. Eddie explained, "I wouldn't be forced into a relationship with a woman just because I had a child with her."

ROMANTIC INTERESTS: Robin Givens (Harvard student/actress), Lisa Figueroa (Adelphi University student), Jacqueline Davis (model), Britt Lorraine Pearson (singer), Maria Bayer (cocktail waitress), Musanna Overra (Howard University student).

SELECTED HITS (and Misses)

FILMS: *48 HRS.* (1982), *Trading Places* (1983), *Best Defense* (1984), *Beverly Hills Cop* (1984), *The Golden Child* (1986), *Beverly Hills Cop 2* (1987), *Eddie Murphy—Raw* (concert film, 1987), *Coming to America* (1988), *Harlem Nights* (1989),* *Another 48 HRS.* (1990), *Boomerang* (1992), *Beverly Hills Cop 3* (1994), *Vampire in Brooklyn* (1995), *The Nutty Professor* (1996), *Metro* (1997), *Dr. Dolittle* (1998), *Mulan* (voice only, 1998), *Holy Man* (1998), *Life* (1999), *Pluto Nash* (1999), *Bowfinger* (1999), *Shreck* (voice only, 2000), *The Nutty Professor II* (2000).

TV SERIES: *Saturday Night Live* (1981–84), *The P.J.s* (voice only, 1998–present).

*Also directed by Murphy.

194

QUICKIE BIO

When Eddie Murphy was a kid, all he did was watch TV. By the time he was in junior high school, he could talk like cartoon characters Dudley Do-Right and Bullwinkle, and was a huge fan of fat Elvis. At age sixteen, Eddie got together with two white guys and formed a comedy troop called "The Identical Triplets." Three years later he was starring on television on NBC's *Saturday Night Live* (1981–84). Big hit films followed for Murphy, as did a flood of bad language, and an embarrassing incident with a transsexual. However, Murphy, whose nickname was "Money," always managed to clean up his image. After all, Eddie claimed that he showered four times a day and washed his hands one hundred times a day. And this from the guy who believed that real comedy is "about d***s, farts and boogers."

EDDIE MURPHY
DOES THE DUMBEST THINGS

✪ As a young superstar, Murphy lived at home with his mother. His mom asked him to take out the garbage. Eddie handed her a one hundred dollar bill. "Okay," she said, "your little brother can throw out the garbage."

✪ After arriving in front of Rockefeller Center in New York City to work on television on NBC's *Saturday Night Live*, Eddie once stepped out of his Porsche and stepped into a pile of dog poop. He looked down, untied his shoes, and left them on the sidewalk.

✪ At one point, Bill Cosby phoned Murphy and told him to tone down his obscenity-filled act. Eddie told Cosby, "Go to Vegas and do your old man s*** there."

✪ Eddie labeled his New Jersey mansion Bubble Hill. Bubbling was Eddie's term for partying. In the rec room of his mansion, Eddie displayed a life-sized freestanding cardboard cutout of himself wearing leather.

💬 Eddie refused to do an interview with *Rolling Stone* magazine because the reporter was a woman. When they sent a male journalist, Eddie wore underwear to greet him. During the interview, some of Eddie's fifty full-time employees could only say, "You're great, Eddie." "All my old friends work for me now," Murphy later observed. "Just so's they get their paycheck, they'll say anything."

✪ The comedian once spit chewing gum on the floor of his mansion. When a guest looked at him in wonder, Eddie said, "Don't worry. Someone will pick it up."

"I can pee anywhere. I can pee outside," **Eddie Murphy bragged.** [photo courtesy of Victor Malafronte/Archive Photos]

⭐ During the taping of the HBO concert special *Eddie Murphy—Delirious* (1983), the comic performed a routine called "Faggots Revisited." "I'm afraid of gay people. Petrified. I have nightmares about gay people," Eddie joked. "I have this nightmare I go to Hollywood and find out Mr. T is a faggot." The skit was so offensive that homosexuals formed the Eddie Murphy's Disease Foundation in protest.

⭐ Later Murphy explained, "I don't have anything against homosexuals. I'm not afraid of them. I know homosexuals."

⭐ *Eddie Murphy—Raw* (1987) was even more insulting and aimed hurtful remarks at a variety of targets. A friend said that watching Eddie's performance was "like watching a public death." The movie wound up becoming the most successful concert film of all time.

⭐ When Diana Ross came off stage after a concert, Eddie told Dick Cavett, "Grab her a**, Cavett!" Cavett did, and cut his hand on the sequins.

⭐ For *Beverly Hills Cop 3* (1994), Eddie required a "personal producer" at the cost of $500,000. What is a personal producer? No one could figure it out.

⭐ Murphy claimed that he gave $1,000 to a homeless man and went to street corners to give prostitutes $5,000 and $10,000 gifts to "go home and get off the streets." Murphy stopped giving them money when he realized, "I was doing more harm than good."

 On May 2, 1997, at around four thirty in the morning, Eddie went driving in West Hollywood and picked up Atisone Seiuli, a cross-dressing prostitute. Police found Eddie and Atisone parked and talking to one another. Atisone had a warrant out for her arrest and was booked. Eddie wasn't detained. He claimed that he was looking for something to read when he came across Atisone. Murphy described picking up Atisone as "a split-second dumb decision."

Jack Nicholson

FACTS OF LIFE

ORIGIN: Born John Joseph Nicholson, April 22, 1937, Neptune City, New Jersey.

FORMATIVE YEARS: Graduated from Manasquan High School in Spring Lake, New Jersey.

FAMILY PLANNING: Married Sandra Knight (actress), June 17, 1962; divorced 1967; child born to former girlfriend Rebecca Broussard (waitress); Susan Anspach (actress) and at least three other women claim Nicholson as the father of their offspring; "I'm always going around trying to have babies," Nicholson sighed.

ROMANTIC INTERESTS: Mimi Machu (actress), Michelle Phillips (musician/actress), Margaret Trudeau (wife of Canadian Prime Minister Pierre Trudeau), Candice Bergen (actress), Faye Dunaway (actress), Meryl Streep (actress), Anjelica Huston (photographer/actress), Lisa Lyons (female bodybuilder), Amanda de Cadenet (model/actress), Karen Mayo-Chandler (model). According to Nicholson, "I've balled everybody."

SELECTED HITS (and Misses)

FiLMS: *The Cry Baby Killer* (1958), *The Wild Ride* (1960), *The Little Shop of Horrors* (1960), *The Terror* (1963), *Ensign Pulver* (1965), *Ride in the Whirlwind* (1966), *The Shooting* (1967), *The Trip* (1967—screenplay only), *The St. Valentine's Day Massacre* (1967), *Easy Rider* (1969), *Five Easy Pieces* (1970), *Carnal Knowledge* (1971), *The King of Marvin Gardens* (1972), *Drive, He Said* (1972),* *The Last Detail* (1974), *Chinatown* (1974), *The Fortune* (1975), *One Flew Over the Cuckoo's Nest* (Oscar for Best Actor—1975), *The Missouri Breaks* (1976), *Goin' South* (1978), *The Shining* (1980), *The Postman Always Rings Twice* (1981), *Reds* (1981), *Terms of Endearment* (1985), *Prizzi's Honor* (1985), *The Witches of Eastwick* (1987), *Ironweed* (1987), *Batman* (1989), *The Two Jakes* (1990), *Hoffa* (1992), *A Few Good Men* (1993), *Wolf* (1994), *The Crossing Guard* (1994), *Mars Attacks!* (1996), *The Evening Star* (1996), *Blood & Wine* (1996), *As Good As It Gets* (Oscar for Best Actor—1997).

*As director only.

QUICKIE BIO

Jack Nicholson grew up in a confused New Jersey household, where he was raised by his grandmother and told that his mother was really his sister. The seventeen-year-old Nicholson wisely left home, and sought his fortune in Hollywood. Nicholson started out answering fan mail for the cartoon cat-and-mouse team *Tom and Jerry* and broke into films with the help of B-movie mogul Roger Corman. Over the next four decades, fans, lovers, and drug buddies grew to love Jack's fiendish grin as he puffed, dropped, snorted, and leered his way to the top. Nicholson earned a reputation among the critics as an actor's actor, and a reputation among his girlfriends as "Spanking Jack."

JACK NICHOLSON
DOES THE DUMBEST THINGS

✪ As a struggling actor in the late 1950s and early 1960s, Nicholson bought half-gallon bottles of wine and used them to induce people to have group sex sessions. "They never really came together," Nicholson confessed. "I've never been in an orgy of more than three people."

✪ While filming *Easy Rider* (1969) in New Mexico, Nicholson dropped acid with costar Dennis Hopper. They found themselves running down a road in the headlights of a truck. Jack panted to Hopper, "We're geniuses, you know that? We're both geniuses. Isn't it great to be a genius?" The next morning, Nicholson woke up in a tree. He had no idea how he got there.

Nicholson claimed that he smoked 155 joints while filming the camp-fire scene in *Easy Rider.*

During the shooting of a bedroom scene for *Five Easy Pieces* (1970), Jack reportedly took a snort of coke after every six takes. They did thirty takes on this scene alone.

Nicholson co-wrote and co-produced *Head* (1968). Jack titled the movie after a slang term for pothead and claimed that the script was a verbalization of philosopher Marshal McLuhan's cultural theories. One scene featured members of the rock band The Monkees dancing around as flakes of dandruff in the hair of veteran movie star Victor Mature.

Jack was never much involved in politics, but he did support Colorado Democrat Gary Hart's campaign for President. "I'm a Hart supporter because he f***s," confessed Nicholson. "Do you know what I mean?"

Nicholson made more than one hundred women strip for him as part of the audition for the X-rated *Drive, He Said* (1972), his directorial debut. After feasting his eyes, he gave the part to an old friend.

During the making of *Chinatown* (1974), Nicholson got into a fight with director Roman Polanski. Polanski chased Jack into his dressing room, picked up his TV set, and smashed it on the floor. Nicholson then took off all his clothes and stormed off the set.

Later, Nicholson and Polanski got into an even bigger mess when Polanski was arrested in Nicholson's house for allegedly raping a thir-teen-year-old "aspiring actress" named Sandra.

"He's into fun and games in bed, all the really horny things I get off on, like spankings, handcuffs, whips and Polaroid pictures," Nicholson's girlfriend Karen Mayo-Chandler once blabbed. "His idea of being sexy is dressing in blue-satin boxer shorts and fluorescent orange socks and chasing me around the room with a Ping-Pong paddle." Mayo-Chandler also noted that Nicholson liked to eat peanut-butter-and-jelly sand-wiches in bed to maintain his strength. "But the strangest thing about him in bed is his ability to make his hair stand on end to the point of no return," the model confessed. "I never could understand how he did that."

Nicholson wanted to add realism to a hot sex scene in the 1981 film *The Postman Always Rings Twice.* "I wanted to have a full stinger," explained Nicholson, "because they'd never seen that in movies." Nicholson went

"Yes, I smoke marijuana! Do you want to see me do it?" Jack Nicholson yelled defensively.
[photo courtesy of Popperfoto/Archive Photos]

upstairs and worked on his "stinger" for forty-five minutes, but nothing popped up. "Somebody else might have said I was a pervert," sighed Nicholson, "but in my terms, this would've been extremely artful."

⭐ Jack claimed that he never used a condom. Explained the actor who fathered as many as seven illegitimate children, "I'd as soon cohabitate with a warm garbage bag."

⭐ During the 1984 NBA playoffs between the Boston Celtics and the Los Angeles Lakers, Lakers' mega-fan Nicholson began taunting the Celtic enthusiasts in Boston Garden. Sitting in his private box, he first made a choke sign, holding his throat with his hand. Then as the Celtics were about to win the game, Jack pulled down his pants and mooned the crowd. "I've seen a lot of fans in my day," the Celtics coach said, "and to me there's a difference between being an a** and being a fan."

⭐ In 1994, Jack Nicholson pulled up next to a car at a stop light, jumped out of his car, yelled "You cut me off" to the driver, pulled out a two iron golf club and reportedly started hitting the roof and windshield of the car. "I use graphite clubs," Nicholson later explained, "and I expected the club to break."

⭐ The year following the golf club episode, Jack was honored by the Los Angeles Police Historical Society for "significant contributions to the Los Angeles Police Department."

Ryan O'Neal

FACTS OF LIFE

ORIGIN: Born Patrick Ryan O'Neal, April 20, 1941, Los Angeles, California.

FORMATIVE YEARS: U.S. Army High School, Munich, Germany.

FAMILY PLANNING: Married Joanna Moore (actress), April 3, 1963; divorced 1967; married Leigh Taylor-Young (actress), February 28, 1967; divorced 1974; fathered a child by Farrah Fawcett (actress).

ROMANTIC INTERESTS: Ursula Andress (actress), Jacqueline Bisset (actress), Oona O'Neill Chaplin (wife of actor Charlie Chaplin), Joan Collins (actress), Britt Ekland (actress), Mia Farrow (actress), Anjelica Huston (actress), Bianca Jagger (wife of singer Mick Jagger), Carole King (musician), Ali MacGraw (actress), Liza Minnelli (actress), Joni Mitchell (musician), Diana Ross (singer/actress), Barbra Streisand (singer/actress), Margaret Trudeau (wife of Canadian politician Pierre Trudeau), Farrah Fawcett (actress).

SELECTED HITS (and Misses)

FILMS: *The Games* (1968), *The Big Bounce* (1969), *Love Story* (1970), *Wild Rovers* (1971), *What's Up, Doc?* (1972), *The Thief Who Came to Dinner* (1973), *Paper Moon* (1973), *Barry Lyndon* (1975), *Nickelodeon* (1976), *A Bridge Too Far* (1977), *Oliver's Story* (1979), *The Main Event* (1979), *So Fine* (1981), *Partners* (1982), *Irreconcilable Differences* (1984), *Tough Guys Don't Dance* (1987), *Chances Are* (1989), *Faithful* (1996), *Hacks* (1997), *Zero Effect* (1998), *An Alan Smithee Film: Burn, Hollywood Burn* (1998), *Coming Soon* (1999).

TV SERIES: *Empire* (1962–64), *Peyton Place* (1964–69), *Good Sports* (1991).

QUICKIE BIO

One longtime Hollywood observer described Ryan O'Neal as "the greatest roger of all time," roger being a term for promiscuous rogue. O'Neal was born in Los Angeles, reared in several European countries, and made a name for himself as a Golden Gloves boxer before going into acting. As star of TV's *Peyton Place* (1964–69), the nighttime soap opera, O'Neal bragged, "My principle function in the script was to get everybody pregnant." This seemed to be Ryan's principle function in Hollywood as well. Though his fame as a popular actor peaked with his performance in *Love Story* (1970), his performance as a lover piqued everyone's interest, including Farrah Fawcett. After their breakup, Ryan returned once again to being a jolly "roger."

RYAN O'NEAL
DOES THE DUMBEST THINGS

✪ Young Ryan the boxer was once sentenced to fifty-one days in jail on charges of assault and battery.

✪ Ryan liked to jog on the beach in California—nude.

✪ When O'Neal's daughter, actress Tatum, announced to her classmates she was leaving the school, they stood up and cheered. Tatum was upset. "But Tatum," father Ryan told her,"that's what actors live for—applause."

✪ Tatum was tolerant of her father's sexual hi-jinks, but even she thought his affair with Oona O'Neill Chaplin was a bit much. "Someone's gotta put a stop to this," Tatum said. "She's too old."

✪ Ryan and his teenage son Griffin got into a fight in 1983 over the boy's lifestyle. During the conflict, Ryan punched out two of Griffin's teeth. Pop explained, "I punched him and his teeth exploded."

💬 O'Neal's marriage to actress Leigh Taylor-Young fell apart when he started seeing his *What's Up, Doc?* (1972) costar Barbra Streisand. When O'Neal and Babs were in bed, they entertained themselves by reading the book *It Pays to Increase Your Word Power,* then quizzing each other on spelling and definition.

✪ Ryan wanted to costar in the film *The Bodyguard* with his then girlfriend diva Diana Ross, but the screen project fizzled. "She didn't want to play a woman guarded by a white bodyguard because Diana Ross doesn't want to show her body, doesn't want to do sex scenes on the screen, doesn't want to sing, and doesn't want to be black," Ryan whined. "As

"Man's got the whitest damn teeth I ever seen in my life," was how Motown record producer Berry Gordy described **Ryan O'Neal (right).** [photo courtesy of Fotos International/Archive Photos]

you can see, we are no longer an item." Kevin Costner and Whitney Houston later made the movie.

⭐ Diana Ross was not amused when Ryan teased her by once answering her hotel room door and saying, "Well, look who's here! Come in, come in! Diana, it's Tatum! . . . Just joking."

⭐ Ryan dated former Mrs. Canadian Prime Minister Margaret Trudeau. The liaison fizzled quickly, then got ugly. O'Neal banned her from his property. Margaret climbed the wall around his house and tried to talk to him, but it was all over. Finally Margaret gave up. "I've had enough of Ryan's conceit, his self-obsession." Later, in a Japanese restaurant, she threw a bowl of noodles at a poster of him on the wall.

⭐ Ryan got so tired of snoops picking through his garbage that he began planting rat traps in his refuse.

★ O'Neal brought his dog to a Malibu party. The canine propped his paws up on a table and started eating thirty-eight-dollar-an-ounce caviar right out of one of the bowls.

★ For son Redmond's fifth birthday party, O'Neal rented a theatre to screen movies for the kids. When he saw his main squeeze Farrah Fawcett, the 1970s *Charlie's Angels* TV star, flirting with a theatre employee, Ryan went nuts. Farrah stormed out and the couple had to have a second party for Redmond to atone for ruining the first one.

★ Farrah and Ryan hired an African-American named Calvin Watkins to teach their son Redmond soccer. Calvin wound up moving into their home, and reportedly introduced himself as Farrah and Ryan's adopted son. Some people believed him.

★ O'Neal once said, "I ask Farrah to marry me every day." In February 1998, Ryan O'Neal stopped asking Fawcett to marry him and started dating actress Leslie Stefanson who was thirty years his junior. Farrah left him after fifteen years of unwed bliss. Asked if the couple might reunite, Farrah chirped, "Oh, golly, I honestly can't answer that."

★ During her celebrity heyday hair days in the 1970s, Farrah Fawcett promoted a line of cosmetics and hair products. She found the work limiting, explaining, "I've been so tied up with promoting the Farrah cosmetic range that I don't feel I've any time for world affairs." Later Farrah introduced other products including Farrah dolls, Farrah wigs, and the Farrah Faucet plumbing fixture.

★ Twenty years after bombing out in cosmetics and shampoos, Farrah was promoting her nude layout in *Playboy*, which celebrated her fiftieth birthday. A video special she filmed for *Playboy*'s pay-per-view audiences had her creating a painting with her naked body. She went on David Letterman's late night TV talk show in June 1998, where she sat on camera slack-jawed and speechless, staring into space, saying "wow." Later denying charges of being on drugs, she explained, "I was being vague and playful." After the Letterman "incident," Farrah's publicist denied anything was wrong with the aging poster girl. After that, Ryan's ex-playmate, with whom he costarred in the short-lived TV sitcom *Good Sports* in the early 1990s, went to the south of France to take cooking lessons.

Sean Penn

FACTS OF LIFE

ORIGIN: Born Sean Penn, August 17, 1960, Santa Monica, California.

FORMATIVE YEARS: Graduated from Santa Monica High School, Santa Monica, California.

FAMILY PLANNING: Married Madonna Louise Ciccone (singer), August 16, 1985; divorced 1989; married Robin Wright (actress), April 26, 1996.

ROMANTIC INTERESTS: Naomi Campbell (model), Elle MacPherson (model), Mary Stuart Masterson (actress).

SELECTED HITS (and Misses)

FILMS: *Taps* (1981), *Fast Times at Ridgemont High* (1982), *Bad Boys* (1983), *Racing with the Moon* (1983), *The Falcon and the Snowman* (1984), *At Close Range* (1985), *Shanghai Surprise* (1986), *Colors* (1988), *Casualties of War* (1989), *State of Grace* (1990), *The Indian Runner* (1991),* *Carlito's Way* (1993), *The Crossing Guard* (1995),* *Dead Man Walking* (1995), *U-Turn* (1997), *Hugo Pool* (1997), *She's So Lovely* (1997), *The Game* (1997), *The Thin Red Line* (1998), *Hurlyburly* (1998), *Up at the Villa* (1999), *As I Lay Dying* (1999), *Autumn of the Patriarch* (2000).*

*As director, but not actor.

QUICKIE BIO

The son of TV and film producer Leo Penn and actress Eileen Ryan, Sean Penn was a California kid who spent the 1970s surfing. When he completed high school, he realized his sub-par grades wouldn't get him into college, let alone law school, so he used his family connections to get into acting. After doing theater work, he hit a high note with his screen debut performance in *Taps* (1981). Press-shy and terribly jealous, Penn didn't do himself any favors by marrying media magnet Madonna. The couple became known as the Poison Penns or S & M. The union crumbled after Penn became known as Mr. Madonna and had a series of high-profile run-ins with nosy picture takers that eventually led to jail time. After making the move from actor to director, Penn earned a reputation as a solid filmmaker, though members of the press considered him to be one of "the most offensive people on the planet."

SEAN PENN
DOES THE DUMBEST THINGS

⭐ During a trip to Nashville in 1985, Penn threw a rock at one photographer, then punched out another one. Later, Sean told a female photographer that he had a water pistol and if she didn't leave he would go "into the men's room, fill the pistol with urine, and come out and squirt [her]."

⭐ When Penn noticed photographers in helicopters buzzing his Malibu home prior to his 1985 wedding to Madonna, he walked out onto the beach and scratched out twenty-foot-tall letters that spelled the words "F*** OFF." Then he reportedly fired a gun at the helicopters and told his guests, "I would have been very excited to see one of those helicopters burn and the bodies inside melt."

⭐ When Penn saw a guy give his wife Madonna a friendly smooch, he flew into a rage and smashed the guy in the head with a chair. For his "chivalry," Penn paid a $1,700 fine and was given a year's probation.

⭐ Penn's probation wasn't much of a deterrent. In the summer of 1986, he got in a shoving match with two photographers who approached him as he was leaving his wife's New York apartment. One of Penn's bodyguards supposedly said to the photo people, "If you take one picture, we'll kill you."

⭐ Madonna and Penn came home one evening after shopping and found a prowler on their property. Sean allegedly attacked the intruder and bashed him on the head with a bottle of salad dressing.

⭐ An extra on the set of Penn's cop movie *Colors* (1988) made the mistake of taking a snapshot of Sean. Penn chased the extra, smashed the camera, and then reportedly went after the extra. Penn served thirty-four days in jail for his photo attack. When a reporter asked if Madonna was glad to see him after his prison stay, Penn shrugged, "Not particularly."

⭐ On Christmas Day 1988, Madonna told Penn she wanted out of their three-and-a-half-year marriage. Sean responded by holding her captive for four days inside their Malibu home. The low point came when a drunk Penn supposedly physically abused Madonna for nine hours and tied her up. Madonna eventually escaped and Penn was charged with battery. Twelve days later Madonna dropped the charges, but went ahead with the divorce.

⭐ With his divorce from Madonna pending, Penn went into a Santa Monica (California) disco and heard one of her songs. He stormed into the deejay's booth, pulled the record off the turntable, and stomped on it.

⭐ Not long after their split, Penn ran into Madonna at a small dinner party in France. The singer, who still carried a torch for her ex, went over, sat on his lap, and started flirting. Sean told her to get lost. She responded with a barrage of obscenities. Penn told a reporter afterward, "I've never met that woman before." Penn later said about his Madonna marriage, "I was drunk most of the time."

⭐ At his wedding to actress Robin Wright in 1996, Penn's idol Marlon Brando got drunk, fell asleep, woke up, lurched to his feet, rambled an incoherent toast, and then began to sing. When Jack Nicholson tried to get Brando to sit down, Marlon pulled down Nicholson's pants.

⭐ In 1998 Sean was walking with his father, when a cameraman approached him. The paparazzi claimed that Penn picked up a rock and threw it at him. Not so, according to the movie star. Penn claimed that he only picked up a stone to defend himself, and that the paparazzi injured himself by lunging head first into the rock as Penn held it.

⭐ Penn's friends often were as badly behaved as he was. At a New York City nightclub, a Penn pal went to the deejay booth, stripped, mooned the dance floor, and peed over the edge of the railing. Asked why Sean would allow someone to act this way, a spokesman for the grumpy actor said, "He's an assistant."

⭐ Penn was hanging out with a couple of pals when one friend's beeper went off. At that point, Penn went off himself. He grabbed the beeper and smashed it to bits. He handed his buddy three hundred dollars to cover the damages and noted, "Those things drive me up the wall."

✪ Penn acted with Nicolas Cage in *Fast Times at Ridgemont High* (1982) and *Racing with the Moon* (1984). But he later looked down on his buddy and sneered, "Nic Cage is no longer an actor." Cage shot back, "He kept calling us his family and then the next day he stabs me in the back." Penn's publicist later covered for her big-mouthed boss by explaining that Penn "thinks that Nic's a nice guy and he respects his talent."

✪ After having his driver's license revoked, Penn was reduced to riding the bus for the time being. One day a stranger approached him and asked, "Anyone ever tell you that you look like Sean Penn?" The actor played along. When the passenger confided that he had been an extra in a movie starring Penn, Sean asked what the stranger thought of the movie star. "Oh," the guy said, "he's a complete a**hole."

✪ On another occasion Sean was in a phone booth when a woman approached and asked him if he was really as big an a**hole as people said. Penn claimed that yes, he was indeed a big a**hole. Later Penn explained, "It's a longer conversation if you say, 'No.'"

✪ Penn demanded a private jet to fly to a screening of *The Thin Red Line* (1998) in Houston. When the studio refused to pay the estimated $40,000 cost for the flight, Penn published an angry letter in which he compared the cost of the flight to "the fair market price of one hair on Rupert Murdoch's formidable a**." Penn addressed the letter to many people, including God.

✪ On a cable TV show, Penn confessed that his idea of heaven was "an eight ball and two hookers." An eight ball is one-eighth of an ounce of cocaine.

River Phoenix

FACTS OF LIFE (and Death)

ORIGIN: Born River Jude Bottom, August 23, 1970, Madras, Oregon; died November 1, 1993, Hollywood, California, of drug-induced heart failure.

FORMATIVE YEARS: Grew up with hippie parents, never spent more than a semester at any one school.

FAMILY PLANNING: Initiated into the world of sex at age four by leaders of the Children of God cult.

ROMANTIC INTERESTS: Martha Plimpton (actress), Suzanne "Suzy Q" Solgot (musician), Samantha Mathis (actress).

SELECTED HITS (and Misses)

FILMS: *Explorers* (1985), *Stand by Me* (1986), *The Mosquito Coast* (1986), *Running on Empty* (1988), *Little Nikita* (1988), *Indiana Jones and the Last Crusade* (1989), *I Love You to Death* (1990), *Dogfight* (1991), *My Own Private Idaho* (1991), *Sneakers* (1992), *The Thing Called Love* (1993), *Silent Tongue* (1993).

TV SERIES: *Seven Brides for Seven Brothers* (1982–83).

QUICKIE BIO

As a child, River Phoenix begged on street corners in Venezuela and Los Angeles with his siblings Leaf (later Joaquin), Summer, Rain, and Liberty, before his hippie stage mom pushed him into show biz to save the world—and help the family's bank account. Brought up to be a strict vegetarian, Phoenix liked to live his acting parts fully, which got him into trouble when he played a narcoleptic, drug addicted male prostitute for the film *My Own Private Idaho* (1991). A heavy drinker and a druggie before his twenty-first birthday, Phoenix's last party was on Halloween night 1993, at the Viper Room in Los Angeles. The twenty-three-year-old movie star died out on the street, just a few blocks from where John Belushi passed away. River's last words were "no paparazzi. I want anonymity." He got it.

RIVER PHOENIX
DOES THE DUMBEST THINGS

✪ In 1972 River's parents stopped being hippies and joined the Children of God. The cult was founded by a dude who called himself Moses David, and urged his followers to pound wooden sticks against the ground and chant "Woe." David preached that America would soon be destroyed by the Comet Kohoutec and described himself as a "toilet" to catch the "damned hippies." He also believed that kids should learn about sex by having sex with their own parents.

✪ Phoenix had sex at age four according to the rituals of the Children of God cult. He stopped having sex at age ten when the family left the group. When River announced five years later that he wanted to have sex again, his parents built a love tent for him in the backyard. River described it as "a very strange experience." Director Rob Reiner described it as, "the greatest story of lost virginity I've ever heard."

Once Phoenix went out to dinner with his girlfriend actress Martha Plimpton. She ordered soft-shell crabs. Vegetarian River left the restaurant crying because his girlfriend ate seafood. Martha said, "I loved him for that."

✪ River tried to read Herman Hesse's classic novel *Siddhartha* (1922) upside down, just to see if he could do it.

River started a band and called it Aleka's Attic. According to Phoenix, Aleka was a poet philosopher who made music "in a fairy-tale setting." The name of the song which told the story of the band? "Aleka Dozy Encircles."

- When a bunch of skinheads taunted him at a party, River said, "If you really wanted to kick my a**, go ahead, just explain to me why you're doing it." One said, "Ah, you wouldn't be worth it." River said, "We're all worth it, man, we're all worth millions of planets and stars and galaxies and universes."

- At one point Phoenix got angry with a journalist for leaving half a page blank in her notebook, and lectured her about the terrible waste of paper in American offices. "I mean if they can make a plutonium generator which will orbit Jupiter and stay there for forty-three years," he observed, "surely they can make a receipt that will save paper."

- Phoenix told reporters that when he turned twenty-one, he went into a bar and ordered herb tea. In reality, he went into a bar and drank several beers.

- To research his role as a male hooker in *My Own Private Idaho* (1991), River and a friend jumped into a person's car, agreed to have sex, then jumped out of the vehicle.

- After finishing *My Own Private Idaho*, River did an interview in Los Angeles. When a reporter asked, "Oh, how are you today, Mr. Phoenix?" He replied, "Not too bad except for the crotch rot." Then he began to scratch his groin for the cameras.

- Phoenix became obsessed with UFOs and often repeated the phrase, "Thanks be to UFO Godmother."

- On the set of *Sneakers* (1992), a friend described River as "so high he was like an alien."

- During the making of *The Thing Called Love* (1993), Phoenix also was high a lot of the time and fell in love with his costar, Samantha Mathis. "In the lovemaking scene, can we really do it?" he asked director Peter Bogdanovich. "Can you just put us in there and close the door and let us go?"

- River showed up at the Dallas Film Festival awards so whacked out, he almost fell into his plate. Then he dropped a piece of cake on the floor, picked it up, and ate it.

- While filming *Dark Blood* (unfinished and unreleased) in 1993, River's costar Judy Davis asked him why he was so out of it. Phoenix said it was because he had eaten too much sodium the night before.

★ At the memorial service following River's death by drug overdose, one director got fed up with the eulogies and asked, "Is there anybody here who can tell us why River took all those drugs?" Phoenix's girlfriend explained, "River was so sensitive. . . . When he wanted to eat artichokes he would eat ten at a time. He did everything to that degree." Months later, Phoenix's mom explained, "River knew the earth was dying and he wanted to give his passing as a sign." Don't think so . . .

Elvis Presley

DUMBEST QUOTES

"My mouth feels like Bob Dylan's been sleeping in it."

"Caucasian? It was on my army draft card.
I thought it meant circumcised."

"If you like things like *The French Connection*,
the Chinese connection, the British connection,
the knee bone connected to the jawbone,
the jawbone is connected to the hambone . . ."

"Man, if I could get people to talk about me
the way they talked about Liberace,
I would really have made it."

FACTS OF LIFE (and Death)

ORIGIN: Born Elvis Aron Presley, January 8, 1935, Tupelo, Mississippi; died August 16, 1977, Memphis, Tennessee. The coroner's report listed the cause of death as "cardiac arrhythmia"—a heart attack. Others have claimed that the cause of death was a drug overdose.

FORMATIVE YEARS: Graduated from L. C. Humes High School, Memphis, Tennessee.

FAMILY PLANNING: Married Priscilla Beaulieu Presley, May 1, 1967; divorced 1973.

ROMANTIC INTERESTS: June Juanico (receptionist), Natalie Wood (actress), Mamie Van Doren (actress), Tempest Storm (stripper), Patti Parry (hairdresser), Ann-Margret (actress), Linda Thompson (beauty queen), Ginger Allen (beauty queen).

SELECTED HITS (and Misses)

FiLMS: *Love Me Tender* (1956), *Jailhouse Rock* (1957), *King Creole* (1958), *G.I. Blues* (1960), *Blue Hawaii* (1961), *Kid Galahad* (1962), *Follow That Dream* (1962), *Girls! Girls! Girls!* (1962), *It Happened at the World's Fair* (1963), *Viva Las Vegas* (1964), *Roustabout* (1964), *Girl Happy* (1965), *Tickle Me* (1965), *Harum Scarum* (1965), *Paradise, Hawaiian Style* (1966), *Spinout* (1966), *Easy Come, Easy Go* (1967), *Double Trouble* (1967), *Clambake* (1967), *Speedway* (1968), *Live a Little, Love a Little* (1968), *Charro!* (1969), *The Trouble with Girls (and How to Get into It)* (1969), *Change of Habit* (1969), *Elvis: That's the Way It Is* (documentary, 1970), *Elvis on Tour* (documentary, 1972).

QUICKIE BIO

Thin Elvis and fat Elvis were both movie stars. The King made his first feature film, *Love Me Tender,* in 1956, just two years after he took time off from his truck driving job in Memphis, made a record for his mama, and got into the music biz. The man once called "The Prince from Another Planet" cared for his mom, but didn't really care much about his nearly three dozen films. "Who is that fast-talking, hillbilly son-of-a-bitch that nobody can understand?" Elvis commented on his screen persona. "One day he's singing to a dog, then to a car, then to a cow. They are all the damn same movie with that southerner just singing to something different."

ELVIS PRESLEY
DOES THE DUMBEST THINGS

✪ In April 1952, Elvis got his first job in the movie business—as an usher at a movie theatre in Memphis, Tennessee. Elvis was fired after he knocked down another usher who squealed on Elvis for taking candy from the refreshment counter.

✪ Elvis sang the entire theme song for *Follow That Dream* (1962) with his back to the camera.

💬 In the film *Easy Come, Easy Go* (1967), a spiritual Elvis performed "Yoga Is As Yoga Does" in a duet with Elsa Lanchester, the star of the horror classic *Bride of Frankenstein* (1935). The dumbest tune from *Harum Scarum* (1965) was "Harem Holiday." In *Girls! Girls! Girls!* (1962), it was "Song of the Shrimp." In *Paradise, Hawaiian Style* (1966), Elvis performed "Queenie Wahine's Papaya," and in *Girl Happy* (1965), he sang "Do the

Clam," which was written by Dolores Fuller, the former girlfriend of junk film director Ed Wood Jr.

✪ Presley's favorite movies were the ones he made of his wife Priscilla and other women wrestling in pure white bras and panties.

✪ On TV's *The Steve Allen Show* in 1956, Elvis wore a tux and crooned the tune "Hound Dog" to a basset hound sitting on a stool. Presley later recalled that the dog was "peeing, and I didn't know it."

✪ During his concerts in the 1970s, Presley wore a two-shot pistol strapped to his ankle. The gun-toting movie star shot at cars that wouldn't start, at restaurant ceilings, at hotel chandeliers, at television sets, and at his daughter's swing set.

✪ Presley wrote to President Nixon that he had done "an in depth study of drug abuse and communist brainwashing techniques" and agreed to help the President "just so long as it is kept very private." The President agreed to meet Elvis, and gave the King a Bureau of Narcotics badge. Elvis hugged Nixon. "Well," Nixon said, "I appreciate your willingness to help, Mr. Presley."

✪ Elvis helped Nixon with his war on drugs by gobbling them up as fast as he could. While on the road Presley's drug diet was roughly as follows: When he woke up at 3:00 P.M. he took laxatives, appetite suppressants, and testosterone (the sex hormone) supplements; before he hit the stage he munched codeine, amphetamines, and occasionally synthetic heroin; after the show he downed tranquilizers and Demerol; and before bed he ingested Quaaludes, a laxative, and three sedatives. Elvis's favorite bed-time reading? *The Physician's Desk Reference.*

✪ In the film *Change of Habit* (1969), the drug-addicted Presley played a doctor opposite Mary Tyler Moore, who was cast as a nun.

✪ During his last years, the King was so constipated from drug use that he spent many of his waking hours on the toilet.

✪ In the summer of 1973, Elvis appeared onstage riding on a friend's back with a toy monkey on his neck. "Good evening, ladies and gentlemen and animal lovers," Elvis proclaimed. "I brought one of my relatives with me. I'm in trouble if he has to go to the bathroom!" Elvis later ad-libbed lyrics to "Love Me Tender" and sang, "Adios, you motherf***er, bye bye, Papa, too/To Hell with the whole Hilton Hotel, and screw the showroom too."

✪ Presley gained so much weight that he split his pants onstage. Then he made it a regular part of his act, changing his pants backstage while he sang the song, "Memories."

⭐ On vacation in Palm Springs, Elvis liked to stand on a coffee table and preach. "Whoa, all ye Pharisees and motherf***ers," he shouted, and also observed that a rich man's chance of getting into heaven was "like a camel's a** trying to get through the eye of a needle."

⭐ On a visit to Hollywood, Elvis outfitted all of his buddies in sunglasses and dark clothing, and made them carry briefcases so they would look like they had jobs. One of Elvis's buddies carried a hairbrush and a doorknob in his briefcase.

⭐ When Presley met Barbra Streisand in her dressing room, Elvis said, "Hi," then he got down on one knee and painted her fingernails.

⭐ On other occasions, Elvis was not so gracious. In 1974 Christina Crawford, the daughter of Joan Crawford and a featured player in Presley's film *Wild in the Country* (1961), visited Elvis at Graceland. At one point during their conversation, the King got angry, grabbed Crawford by the hair, dragged her across a marble coffee table, pushed her into another room, kicked her in the butt, and showed her the door.

⭐ Presley wanted to have a nose job, but he was apprehensive. So he asked an old buddy to go with him. "If you can do it, then it's okay for me to do it." They both had their noses done.

⭐ In 1967 Elvis decided to give his manager, Colonel Tom Parker, half of everything he made. Parker was actually Andeas Cornelius van Kujik, an illegal alien from Holland, who broke into show business with his dancing chickens act. The chickens danced when Parker put them on a sawdust covered hot plate.

⭐ Like Barbra Streisand, Elvis looked to his stylist for more than a good haircut. Elvis called his hairdresser Larry Geller "Guru" and consulted him about the spiritual world. Elvis asked Geller, "What is your purpose?" Geller responded, "If there is a purpose . . . then my purpose is to discover my purpose." "Whoa, whoa, man," Elvis said. "Larry, I don't believe it. I mean, what you're talking about is what I secretly think about all the time . . . I mean, there has to be a purpose . . . why I was chosen to be Elvis Presley."

⭐ After his meeting with Larry, Presley really got into spirituality. He claimed that he was going off in a spaceship, that he could turn a neighboring country club's sprinkler system on and off with his mind, that he could cure all his friends of diseases, and that a bird's call was actually the voice of Christ.

Elvis believed his name had religious significance. He believed that "el" was a contraction of Elohim, the god of the ancient Hebrews, and "vis" was an oriental word for force or power. At one point, Presley raised his hand through the roof of his car and addressed a thunderstorm, saying, "I order you to move to the side and leave us alone!" Elvis didn't get rained on.

At the end of his life, Presley's diet was as follows: breakfast—six large eggs, a pound of bacon, half a pound of sausage, and twelve buttermilk biscuits; lunch—two "Fool's Gold" sandwiches (a jar of peanut butter, a jar of strawberry jelly, and a pound of bacon); dinner—a few peanut butter and banana sandwiches and five double cheeseburgers. He ate so much and took so many pills that he often passed out with his mouth full. One time he passed out face first into a bowl of soup, and almost drowned before his girlfriend Linda Thompson saved him from a soggy death. No one was there to save Elvis Presley when he died on the toilet, reading the book *The Scientific Search for the Face of Jesus*.

Keanu Reeves

FACTS OF LIFE

ORIGIN: Born September 2, 1964, Beirut, Lebanon.

FORMATIVE YEARS: Dropped out of high school.

FAMILY PLANNING: "The fact is I've never had a male sexual experience in my life."

ROMANTIC INTERESTS: Sharon Stone (actress), Sofia Coppola (daughter of director Francis Ford Coppola), Autumn Mackintosh (actress), Amanda de Cadenet (actress).

SELECTED HITS (and Misses)

FILMS: *Dream to Believe* (1985), *Youngblood* (1986), *River's Edge* (1986), *Permanent Record* (1988), *Dangerous Liaisons* (1988), *Bill & Ted's Excellent Adventure* (1989), *I Love You to Death* (1990), *Tune in Tomorrow* (1990), *Point Break* (1991), *My Own Private Idaho* (1991), *Bill & Ted's Bogus Journey* (1991), *Bram Stoker's Dracula* (1992), *Much Ado About Nothing* (1993), *Little Buddha* (1993), *Speed* (1994), *A Walk in the Clouds* (1995), *Johnny Mnemonic* (1995), *Chain Reaction* (1996), *Feeling Minnesota* (1996), *The Devil's Advocate* (1997), *The Last Time I Committed Suicide* (1997), *Me and Will* (1998), *The Matrix* (1999), *The Replacements* (2000).

QUICKIE BIO

K eanu Reeves began his excellent adventure when he was born to a partying showgirl mother and a Chinese-Hawaiian father in Beirut, Lebanon. Keanu (whose name means "cool breeze over the mountains" in Hawaiian) bounced through three different stepdads and several high schools in Toronto, Ontario, Canada, before heading out for Hollywood and landing a role in *River's Edge* (1986). Keanu has played everything from a dumb teenager [*Bill & Ted's Excellent Adventure* (1989)] to a deity [*Little Buddha* (1993)], to a stud muffin cop [*Speed* (1994)]. Through it all, critics have wondered whether this guy is really talented, or just a lucky moron. "I'm a meathead," Keanu sighed. "I can't help it, man. You've got smart people and you've got dumb people." Whoa!

KEANU REEVES
DOES THE DUMBEST THINGS

⭐ Reeves played goalie for ice hockey teams as a kid. He used to deliver spontaneous snippets of Shakespeare to his teammates while in the locker room and even during games while on the ice.

⭐ Keanu's mother, Patricia, occasionally worked in the music biz, so Keanu had the chance to meet rock stars, among them Alice Cooper. "I remember [Cooper] brought fake vomit and dog poop to terrorize the housekeeper," he recalled. "He'd hang out, a regular dude. A friend of mine and I, you know, wrestled with him once."

⭐ After learning that *Just Seventeen* magazine had put his likeness on a natty neon-green key ring, Keanu inquired, "What's a key ring?"

⭐ Keanu failed his twelfth grade exams . . . twice. "I even flunked gym," Reeves admitted.

⭐ Reeves said he wanted to score with Meryl Streep because "even if it wasn't good, she could fake it the best."

⭐ When speaking of his sexually ambiguous role in the feature *My Own Private Idaho* (1991), Reeves waxed analytic. "I though it was an amazing script. Just in terms of narrative, man, there's cows, bang! bang! bang!, porno shops, salmon swimming, blow jobs, money-exchanging, and then I burst out in Idaho, smash! And then Shakespeare . . ."

⭐ During a press blitz for *Bill & Ted's Bogus Journey* (1991), Keanu started asking his own bogus questions. "Is there anyone I can talk to?" he shouted. "Anyone from *US* or *People* perhaps? Any animal periodicals I can do? Oh, I had an operation. Perhaps I can be in a medical guide."

✪ On another occasion, after almost an hour with a reporter from the *Los Angeles Times,* Reeves got up, walked out to his hotel room balcony, and began windmilling his arms while screaming and swearing at himself. He walked back into the suite, sat back down, rewound the tape recorder, then continued with the interview. His explanation? "I'm a basket case, man. Look at me, man. I'm a basket case."

For *Little Buddha* (1993), Reeves went on a water-and-oranges-only diet. The regimen affected more than his physique. "I felt like sticking my finger into an electrical socket," said Reeves. "I dreamed about bread and cheese and had fantasies of pouring wine on my head while I rolled naked in the dirt."

✪ Keanu turned down twelve million dollars to costar in *Speed 2* (1997) so that he could tour with his rock band Dogstar. And what did Keanu think of Dogstar? "We're really bad."

✪ While he was in Winnipeg, Manitoba, Canada, working on a stage production of *Hamlet,* a rumor got started in Europe that Reeves "married" media mogul David Geffen in a secret ceremony on a Mexican beach. Another version had the whole thing going down in Hollywood, with a rabbi officiating. Keanu told the press that the gossip was false, then said of the entire experience, "It taught me that you have to share."

Burt Reynolds

DUMBEST QUOTES

"Because of past relationships, people don't think of me as a leg man. But I love great muscular calves."

"Very often I say outrageous things to women because it's sometimes the only way to get out of a situation that could get sticky."

FACTS OF LIFE

ORIGIN: Born Burton Leon "Buddy" Reynolds, February 11, 1936, Waycross, Georgia.

FORMATIVE YEARS: Dropped out of Florida State University (FSU) in Tallahassee, but received an honorary doctorate of humane letters from FSU in 1981, after donating more than half a million dollars to the university.

FAMILY PLANNING: Married Judy Carne (actress), June 28, 1963; divorced 1968; married Loni Anderson (actress), April 29, 1988; divorced 1994.

ROMANTIC INTERESTS: Inger Stevens (actress), Miko Mayama (actress), Tammy Wynette (country singer), Sally Field (actress), Dinah Shore (singer/actress), Candice Bergen (actress), Tawny Little (former Miss America/newscaster), Cookie Knomblach (nurse), Pam Seals (cocktail waitress).

SELECTED HITS (and Misses)

FILMS: *Angel Baby* (1961), *Navajo Joe* (1966), *Shark!* (1969), *Deliverance* (1972), *Shamus* (1972), *The Man Who Loved Cat Dancing* (1973), *The Longest Yard* (1974), *W. W. and the Dixie Dancekings* (1975), *Gator* (1976),* *Nickelodeon* (1976), *Smokey*

and the Bandit (1977), *Semi-Tough* (1977), *Hooper* (1978), *The End* (1978),* *Starting Over* (1979), *Smokey and the Bandit II* (1980), *Rough Cut* (1980), *Sharkey's Machine* (1981),* *The Cannonball Run* (1981), *The Best Little Whorehouse in Texas* (1982), *The Man Who Loved Women* (1983), *City Heat* (1984), *Stick* (1985),* *Malone* (1987), *Physical Evidence* (1989), *Rent-a-Cop* (1988), *Breaking In* (1989), *Cop & ½* (1993), *Striptease* (1996), *Citizen Ruth* (1996), *Bean* (1997), *Meet Wally Sparks* (1997), *Boogie Nights* (1997), *Crazy Six* (1998), *Big City Blues* (1999), *Mystery, Alaska* (1999), *Hunter's Moon* (1999), *Pups* (1999), *The Crew* (2000).

TV SERIES: *Riverboat* (1959–60), *Gunsmoke* (1962–65), *Hawk* (1966), *Dan August* (1970–71), *B. L. Stryker* (1989–90), *Evening Shade* (1990–94).

*Also directed by Reynolds.

QUICKIE BIO

The son of a Florida police chief, young Burt Reynolds was part Cherokee Indian, and later admitted "I'm dumb." A college football star until he crashed a car and wrecked his knees, Reynolds began acting on television before making movies in Italy. After appearing as the first male centerfold in *Cosmopolitan* magazine in 1972, and starring in *Deliverance* that same year, Reynolds parlayed his good-ol' boy charm into a series of southern car chase movies that made him one of the world's most popular movie stars. In the 1990s, a sputtering career and a nasty divorce from actress Loni Anderson left Reynolds broke and ignored, until his role as a porno producer in *Boogie Nights* (1997) put him back in the spotlight. "I just knew there was a poet inside of me," Reynolds once observed, "maybe not a very good one. . . ."

BURT REYNOLDS
DOES THE DUMBEST THINGS

 As a kid in Florida, Reynolds liked to jump off airboats onto the backs of running deer, a trick he referred to later as "a stupid stunt."

✪ When a girlfriend sent him a Dear John letter while at college, Burt walked down a dormitory hall and put his fist straight through a door. Unfortunately, his arm got stuck.

✪ Burt went to a party at Gore Vidal's house. A male guest wearing a fringed leather jacket came up to Burt and said, "I love you." Reynolds snarled, "Are you crazy?" His admirer responded, "You can have the jacket." The star picked up the guy and threw him into another room.

- On the set of the TV series *M Squad* in the late 1950s, his costar began to improvise. Burt grabbed his shirt, tore it off, lifted him up and threw him out the door.

- While shooting the TV show *Riverboat* (1959–60), Burt threw an assistant director into a fake lake because the guy made a pass at a girl that interested Reynolds.

- Burt griped about his work on *Riverboat*, "I was nothing but a dum-dum riverboat pilot." To take out his frustrations, he went down to Skid Row and sat in a bar. "I'd wait for someone to make the inevitable crack, belt the guy in the teeth, and go home feeling much better."

"My hair will probably outlive the human race," bragged Burt Reynolds, who later spent $8,000 on hair transplants that didn't work.
[photo courtesy of Archive Photos]

- One night, Burt met the legendary Greta Garbo. "All I saw were boobs that pointed straight at me." When Garbo asked him to talk to her, Burt looked at his watch and ran away. He later called the incident, "one of the dumbest things I've ever done in my life."

- Reynolds was astounded when he first saw his future girlfriend Miko Mayama in Tokyo. "Amazingly, while you usually think of Asian women as small-busted, she had gorgeous, gigantic breasts," Burt recalled. The only phrase Miko could say in English was "What's up doc?"

- When Burt first met British actress Judy Carne, someone warned him she was amoral. "I knew moral was good," Burt recalled, "and A was better than B. So it sounded good to me."

- Burt was introduced to singer Dinah Shore when he appeared as a surprise guest on her TV talk show. He jumped out of a closet, then he threatened to kill himself if Dinah didn't go out with him. When Dinah said, "No," Burt took a nosedive into a breakaway table. She later went out with him.

When director John Boorman wanted to send a dummy over a waterfall for a scene in *Deliverance* (1972), Burt insisted on doing the stunt himself. The force of the water ripped his clothes off, and he cracked his tailbone on a rock. After the stunt, the injured Reynolds asked the filmmaker "How'd it look?" Boorman answered, "Like a dummy going over a waterfall."

★ At a fancy restaurant in Hollywood, Reynolds lay down on the floor and asked, "Does anyone happen to have a Valium?" He was showered with pills.

★ Burt dumped actress wife Loni Anderson, then asked her to be nice and not get any lawyers involved. After a bitter divorce, Burt wound up paying Loni ten million dollars. He sighed, "It was obvious how stupid I'd been."

★ Reynolds invested in the Po' Folks restaurant chain. When the enterprise went bust, Burt became one of the poor folks and filed for bankruptcy. His unpaid debts included $121,796 for custom hairpieces.

★ After a fire on the set of TV's *Evening Shade* (1990–94) set his head carpets ablaze, Burt ordered new toupees treated with fire-retardant chemicals.

★ When Burt Reynolds made his footprints at Mann's Chinese Theatre in Hollywood, he misspelled his own name.

Mickey Rooney

FACTS OF LIFE

ORIGIN: Born Joe Yule Jr., September 23, 1920, Brooklyn, New York.

FORMATIVE YEARS: Attended MGM studio's school for child actors.

FAMILY PLANNING: Married Ava Gardner (actress), January 10, 1942; divorced 1943; married Betty Jane Rase (student), September 30, 1944; divorced 1949; married Martha Vickers (actress), July 3, 1949; divorced 1951; married Elaine Mahnken (beauty queen), November 18, 1952; divorced 1958; married Barbara Thomason (actress), December 1, 1958; widowed 1966; married Marge Lane (Barbara Thomason's best friend), September 10, 1966; divorced 1967; married Jan Chamberlin (singer), July 28, 1978. "I loved every one of them," Mickey claimed.

ROMANTIC INTERESTS: Betty Grable (actress), Tempest Storm (stripper), Lana Turner (actress), Nembutal (barbiturate), Seconal (barbiturate), Tuinal (barbiturate).

SELECTED HITS (and Misses)

FILMS: *Not to Be Trusted* (1926), *My Pal, the King* (1932), *Manhattan Melodrama* (1934), *A Midsummer Night's Dream* (1935), *Ah, Wilderness!* (1935), *Little Lord Fauntleroy* (1936), *Captains Courageous* (1937), *Love Finds Andy Hardy* (1938), *Boys Town* (special Oscar for "significant contribution"—1938), *Babes in Arms* (1939), *Young Tom Edison* (1940), *Strike Up the Band* (1940), *Life Begins for Andy*

225

Hardy (1941), *Babes on Broadway* (1941), *The Human Comedy* (1943), *Girl Crazy* (1943), *National Velvet* (1944), *Words and Music* (1948), *The Fireball* (1950), *The Bold and the Brave* (1956), *Baby Face Nelson* (1958), *The Private Lives of Adam and Eve* (1961),* *Requiem for a Heavyweight* (1962), *It's a Mad, Mad, Mad, Mad World* (1963), *How to Stuff a Wild Bikini* (1965), *Ambush Bay* (1966), *The Comic* (1969), *Cockeyed Cowboys of Calico County* (1970), *Pulp* (1972), *Find the Lady* (1976), *Pete's Dragon* (voice only, 1977), *The Magic of Lassie* (1978), *The Black Stallion* (1979), *Erik the Viking* (1989), *Sweet Justice* (1992), *That's Entertainment III* (1994), *Boys Will Be Boys* (1997), *Animals* (and the Tollkeeper) (1998), *Babe: Pig in the City* (voice only, 1998), *The First of May* (1999).

TV SERIES: *The Mickey Rooney Show* (a.k.a. *Hey Mulligan*) (1954–55), *Mickey* (1964–65), *One of the Boys* (1982).

*Also co-directed by Rooney.

QUICKIE BIO

Mickey Rooney grew up as a child actor in the MGM studios, a breeding ground for dysfunctional humans. This was after Rooney's vaudeville mom put him onstage when he was two and reportedly supported her son's career by working part-time as a prostitute. On-screen, randy Rooney became America's favorite doe-eyed kid. By the time he was eighteen, he was Hollywood's biggest draw. At age forty-eight, he was playing bit parts in beach movies. He turned to pills for a while, but managed to stay in show business long enough to make money as his own cliché. Perhaps what enabled Rooney to last was the fact that he never took himself too seriously. The title of one of his autobiographies? *Life Is Too Short* (1991).

MICKEY ROONEY
DOES THE DUMBEST THINGS

✪ In the mid-1930s Mickey played in a stage version of Shakespeare's *A Midsummer Night's Dream* as Puck. During dress rehearsal, he was supposed to drop out of a tree when he heard the line "My gentle Puck, come hither." He heard the line three times, but was too hung up to make his entrance. The jock strap he wore as part of his costume had gotten caught on a branch of the tree.

✪ Among Mickey's early sexual conquests was a girl he claimed had extraordinarily developed sex muscles. "She could snap carrots . . . no hands."

✪ Rooney starred with pal Judy Garland in many MGM movies. When the young screen teens played romantic scenes together, each would try to make the other laugh by whispering lines like, "I hear the doctor says you have the clap."

★ Mickey wooed and won the lovely Ava Gardner. She was a virgin on their wedding night, and stayed a virgin. Rooney was too drunk to perform his marital duties. Rooney later managed to perform, and described their honeymoon as "sex and golf and sex and golf."

★ Ava Gardner claimed that husband Mickey "had big brown nipples which, when aroused, stood out like some double-long, golden California raisins." Ava quickly grew bored of raisin-breasted Rooney and left him saying, "I'm godd***ed tired of living with a midget."

★ While married to wife number four but romancing soon-to-be spouse number five, Rooney bought his new girlfriend an expensive fur coat. He felt so guilty, he went out and bought the same coat for wife number four.

★ The media loved to joke about the star's multiple marriages. The best headline appeared after the star's fifth wedding. The headline blared, "Half Pint Takes a Fifth."

★ Rooney earned a reputation as one of Hollywood's dumbest entrepreneurs. He started a cosmetics company called Lovely Lady Cosmetics with a cologne called "Me." Its campaign slogan? "Put Me next to him."

★ When his cologne business dried up, Mickey invested in spray-on hair pieces for bald men. Rooney said that the stuff was great until it got wet and turned into "something like cotton candy."

💰 Mickey Rooney then decided to build a better hot dog. He invented a round frankfurter that could be put on a hamburger bun. It was called a Weenie Whirl. To celebrate his genius, he opened Mickey Rooney's Weenie World franchises on the East Coast. They quickly closed.

★ Rooney pitched to the Fruit of the Loom underwear firm the idea of selling disposable underwear and bras, called Rip Offs and Tip Offs respectively. Then he went to Ralston Purina with the idea of pet drinks like "doggy drink, puppy pop, [and] kitty cola." Finally he suggested to the Franklin Mint that they print commemorative Mickey Rooney coins. They had already done it. It didn't work.

★ Mickey claimed that an angel dressed as a busboy visited him while he was in a Lake Tahoe casino coffee shop and told him, "Mr. Rooney, Jesus Christ loves you very much." Rooney was also hooked on

barbiturates at the time. He took so many that he was knocked out cold for fourteen hours.

★ After his seventh marriage, Mickey and his wife moved to Florida. They were essentially broke. Rooney earned extra cash by showing up at cocktail parties and pretending to be an old friend of the host. An appearance by "my good friend" Mickey Rooney cost a mere five hundred dollars.

★ After missing a putt on a golf course, Rooney was so angry that he proceeded to destroy the water fountain on the next tee. A new water fountain was installed and dubbed the Mickey Rooney Memorial Drinking Fountain.

★ When asked if Rooney was a long distance man in the bedroom, a call girl responded, "Are you kidding? Four minutes of f***ing and sixteen minutes of imitations."

Arnold Schwarzenegger

FACTS OF LIFE

ORIGIN: Born July 30, 1947, Graz, Austria.

FORMATIVE YEARS: University of Wisconsin, B.A. in business by correspondence.

FAMILY PLANNING: Married Maria Shriver (niece of John F. Kennedy), April 26, 1986.

ROMANTIC INTERESTS: One of young Arnold's favorite pickup lines was "Do you want to go to bed with me?"

SELECTED HITS (and Misses)

FILMS: *Hercules Goes to New York* (1970), *Stay Hungry* (1976), *Pumping Iron* (1977), *Conan the Barbarian* (1982), *The Terminator* (1984), *Red Sonja* (1985), *Predator* (1987), *Twins* (1988), *Total Recall* (1990), *Kindergarten Cop* (1990), *Terminator 2: Judgment Day* (1991), *Last Action Hero* (1993), *True Lies* (1994), *Junior* (1994), *Jingle All the Way* (1996), *Eraser* (1996), *Batman & Robin* (1997), *End of Days* (1999), *Terminator 3* (2000).

QUICKIE BIO

Born in a tiny Austrian village to a former Nazi, the "Austrian Oak" arrived in the United States in 1968 to compete in the Mr. Universe competition and decided to stay. The four-time Mr. Universe and six-time Mr. Olympia, who was once described as a "condom stuffed with walnuts," had business savvy to match his muscular physique. He parlayed training seminars and personal appearances into Southern California real estate investments, and was a millionaire by his early twenties. With an eye on the bottom line and a Colonel Klink accent, Arnold soon became the world's biggest box-office star. Lots of action. Few words. Conan the Republican became an American citizen, married into the Kennedy clan, and served as the Chairman of the President's Council on Sports and Fitness under President George Bush. Still, Arnold was a bit insecure. He complained, "Why do people treat me with fun just because I am the biggest, strongest and most beautiful man in the world?"

ARNOLD SCHWARZENEGGER
DOES THE DUMBEST THINGS

⭐ Arnold went AWOL from the Austrian Army to compete in the Mr. Junior Europe body building championship. He won the title—and spent a year in the brig.

⭐ One of Schwarzenegger's first Hollywood jobs was modeling underwear for Frederick's of Hollywood.

⭐ The stern Austrian lectured, "What I want to do is make every American aware that they are f***ed up when they equate everything a person does with some sexual trip." But in *Pumping Iron* (1977) a not-so-uptight Arnold compared lifting barbells to great sex. "I'm coming day and night," the sexy muscle man told an interviewer. "I mean it's terrific, right?"

🗄 Arnold admitted to a friend, "If you told me I'd put on muscles if I ate a kilo of s***, I'd eat it."

⭐ Young Arnold was big, strong, rich, and distracted. "Many times while I was getting laid," Arnold admitted, "in my head I was doing a business deal."

⭐ Once, Schwarzenegger was accosted at a restaurant by a female fan wanting an autograph. Arnold made her a deal. "I'll sign you an autograph if you let me touch your breast." The woman grabbed his hand, placed it on her chest, then gave him a piece of paper.

⭐ At an Ohio bodybuilding seminar, the Austrian muscleman charged people fifty dollars to have their pictures taken with him. And he laid down the rules: no autographs, no shaking his hand, no talking, no eye contact, and no lingering after the pic was snapped.

⭐ After an interview at the Los Angeles Sports Arena, a security guard offered to escort Arnold to his limo. During the walk Schwarzenegger found out that the young man was studying business. Arnold then offered the star-struck student some advice. "You should sell dildoes," he said. "People buy them for presents, they like to be funny at parties. They really sell."

⭐ When an interviewer asked if his character the Terminator could have sex, Arnold got furious. "You shame your magazine," he fumed. Later, Arnold added, "I'm a funny guy, and I can take a joke, but you waste fifteen minutes on the Terminator's rod!"

⭐ Other folks wasted lots of time staring at Arnold's rod when, as a young body builder, he posed for full-frontal nude flexing portraits.

⭐ One of the first things Schwarzenegger said to Eunice Kennedy, the mother of Maria Shriver, was that her daughter had "a great a**." Later, Arnold proposed to Maria Shriver and invited the Pope to his wedding in 1986.

⭐ Arnold has shown himself to be a sensitive guy. "I don't like to dictate to Maria," he explains, "but I don't allow her to wear pants. I only like dresses and skirts."

⭐ Arnold liked a good joke. He passed out exploding cigars, poured ice water on the crotch of a co-worker, and forced a non-drinking female friend to drink tequila until she vomited.

⭐ En route to a Cannes Film Festival party on a yacht, a pregnant Maria complained that she felt queasy. Unsympathetic hubby Arnold told her, "Darling, for God's sake, be a grown-up. What's a little rough sea?" Once on the party vessel, Schwarzenegger turned green in front of about eighty guests. The seasick star then had to be helped off the ship and rushed ashore.

⭐ Arnold claimed to be a hands-on manager for Planet Hollywood, the restaurant chain he co-owned with Bruce Willis and other celebrities. Bragged Arnold, "I'm involved in everything from finding sites, choosing what memorabilia will be inside and how much money we'll spend." But he wasn't much involved with the food. Instead of eating at the Planet Hollywood in Aspen, Colorado, Arnold preferred to eat at Boogie's Diner. Aspen's Planet Hollywood closed after four years of huge losses.

⭐ Schwarzenegger hired a chef at a salary of $1,500 a week just to prepare gourmet baby food for his one-year-old daughter.

- On a flight from New York to London, Arnold pulled out a stack of magazines and started reading them—out loud.

- When wife Maria Shriver took a flight from New York to Los Angeles, she naturally flew first class. However, she put her baby daughter and the child's nanny in coach for the flight. When the infant started crying, the employee took her to Mommy for comforting. Mommy informed the nanny, "She's your problem." Maria then went to sleep while passengers in coach had to listen to the wailing toddler.

"My body is like breakfast, lunch, and dinner. I don't think about it, I just have it," explained Arnold Schwarzenegger, pictured here next to tasty Raquel Welch. [photo courtesy of Frank Edwards/Fotos International/Archive Photos]

Charlie Sheen

FACTS OF LIFE

ORIGIN: Born Carlos Irwin Estevez, September 3, 1965, Los Angeles, California.

FORMATIVE YEARS: Dropped out of Santa Monica High School, Santa Monica, California.

FAMILY PLANNING: Fathered a child when he was nineteen; married Donna Peele (model), September 3, 1995; divorced 1996.

ROMANTIC INTERESTS: Kerri Green (actress), Dolly Fox (actress), Charlotte Lewis (model/actress), Ginger Lynn Allen (ex-porn queen), Kelly Preston (actress).

SELECTED HITS (and Misses)

FILMS: *Apocalypse Now* (1979), *Red Dawn* (1984), *The Boys Next Door* (1985), *Lucas* (1986), *Platoon* (1986), *Wall Street* (1987), *Eight Men Out* (1988), *Young Guns* (1988), *Major League* (1989), *Navy SEALS* (1990), *The Rookie* (1990), *Men at Work* (1990), *Hot Shots!* (1991), *The Three Musketeers* (1993), *Hot Shots! Part Deux* (1993), *Deadface* (1993), *The Chase* (1994), *Terminal Velocity* (1994), *All Dogs Go to Heaven 2* (voice only, 1996), *The Arrival* (1996), *Money Talks* (1997), *The Shadow Conspiracy* (1997), *Postmortem* (1998), *Free Money* (1998), *A Letter from Death Row* (1998), *No Code of Conduct* (1999).

TV SERIES: *Sugar Hill* (1999-present).

233

QUICKIE BIO

When Carlos Estevez was a kid, he appeared with his dad, Martin Sheen, in *Apocalypse Now* (1979). After Carlos (now Charlie) grew up, he created an apocalypse of his own. He took the Sheen name, and found success quickly as one of the Hollywood movie brat pack—along with movie-star brother Emilio Estevez—until booze, hookers, drugs, and brawls landed him in rehab and in the tabloid headlines. Charlie eventually straightened up, sort of. At least he demanded to be billed as Charles instead of Charlie.

CHARLIE SHEEN
DOES THE DUMBEST THINGS

✪ On his sixteenth birthday, Charlie's parents presented him with a brand new BMW automobile. Shortly thereafter, a Malibu, California, sheriff found Charlie passed out behind the wheel of his beamer in the middle of a Pacific Coast Highway intersection. The cop also found him in possession of marijuana. Charlie avoided being prosecuted, and then admitted "The judge was a friend of my mom's." Martin Sheen, his dad, commented, "If he'd been black, he'd still be in jail."

✪ Sheen and a high school buddy found credit card receipts in a wastepaper basket. Charlie recalled, "It made perfect sense to both of us to call up and order a couple of portable TVs." He was arrested for credit card fraud, but the charge was dismissed. He later confessed to his high-priced lawyer, "I don't regret it . . . besides, now, as an actor, I can relate to the criminal mind."

✪ On the very last day of his high school career, Charlie showed up to take his English final, but the teacher wouldn't admit him to class because Sheen didn't have the proper admittance slip for an unexcused absence the previous day. Charlie crumpled up the test paper and threw it in the instructor's face. Then he threw a desk and a trash can across the room. The teacher filed a complaint with the police, and Charlie never graduated.

✪ "I killed a neighbor's peacock a few years ago," Charlie Sheen reportedly confessed. "It kept s***ting all over my basketball courts, so I beat it to death with a broomstick."

✪ When someone warned Oliver Stone about Sheen's bad behavior, the *Platoon* (1986) director made Charlie promise he would only drink one beer a day. After Sheen found out who tipped off Stone, Sheen took a baseball bat to the guy's hotel room and did $3,000 worth of damage.

Charlie explained, "It was do the hotel room or do this guy, and I didn't want to go to jail because I probably would have killed him."

✪ When some producers asked Charlie to take a drug test, Sheen was insulted. "Read my shoulder, pal," Sheen sneered. "I've got a new tattoo. It says EMA. It stands for 'Eat My A**.'"

✪ Charlie picked up a girl at his hairdresser's. "If you live with me, I'll give you $25,000," Sheen told her. She responded, "That sounds fair." She moved in. Then she got a phone call saying, "We need you out—he [Charlie] is coming back with his wife." She moved out, and only collected $5,000.

✪ Charlie commented about his girlfriend porn star Ginger Lynn Allen, "Why settle for hamburger when you can have prime rib?" Allen sighed, "He is spiritual." She said she had sex with "spiritual" Charlie ten times a day.

💰 During his videotaped deposition in the 1995 tax evasion trial of famed Hollywood Madam Heidi Fleiss, Charlie admitted to paying over $53,000 for "sexual services" to Fleiss's employees over a fifteen-month period, but made sure to point out that the payments were for "heterosexual services." When the prosecutor questioned him about six checks he had written for sex, Charlie quipped, "It's starting to add up." Fleiss was convicted. Sheen went back to the movies.

✪ While on location in London, Charlie tried to pick up a hooker, who turned him down. When he finally found one that would ride with him, he allegedly paid her $2,000 for cocaine which turned out to be mostly sugar. Charlie didn't seem to know the difference. He reportedly marched into a convenience store and started eating a package of cookies. When the owner asked him to pay, Charlie screamed, "Who the f*** do you think you are?" and threw $200 on the counter. The shopkeeper said he only took British currency, and Charlie exploded, "Don't you think my money's good enough?"

✪ Charlie had a tattoo of a zipper that was pulled open with a female finger holding the zipper from the inside and an eyeball looking out. "It's so deep," Sheen said, "I don't even know what it means."

✪ In June of 1997 Charlie pleaded no contest to supposedly smashing his girlfriend's face into the floor of his home. Porn star Brittany Ashland claimed the actor grabbed her by the hair and threw her to the floor, rendering her unconscious and splitting her lip. When she regained consciousness, Sheen hid her bloodied dress and allegedly threatened to kill her if she "told anyone what had happened." Sheen was fined $2,800, given two years probation, and ordered to attend counseling and perform three hundred hours of community service. At the hearing, Charlie vowed to mend his ways and proclaimed to the judge, "You will not see me back in this courtroom."

★ Less than a year later, the media reported that Charlie was dead. But no, he wasn't. He had just overdosed on drugs and wound up in the hospital.

★ After the overdose episode, Sheen checked himself into a rehab center. A mere few hours later, Charlie called for a limo and left in his pajamas. The police caught up with Sheen, and reported that he smelled of alcohol.

★ In the spring of 1998, Charlie reportedly walked out of a substance abuse treatment center twice in five days, and wound up at his dad's house. Charlie was so messed up that papa Sheen called the cops to turn his son in for violating his probation. Ten days before the incident, Charlie had complained on TV, "They don't send you anywhere to go on drugs, so why go somewhere to get off 'em?"

★ Sheen used to wrap his fingers together with tape before going out in order to avoid having to sign autographs.

★ Charlie Sheen wrote a book of poetry called *Peace of My Mind* and toured New York City publishing houses in a limo trying to convince publishers to buy it. One publisher said he might consider it if Charlie changed the title of the book to *The Rantings of Charlie Sheen.*

"I couldn't leave the house unless I smoked three joints, taken tranquilizers, and drunk a bottle of bourbon." Sometimes, Charlie Sheen couldn't leave the house at all. [photo courtesy of Riko Nose/Fotos International/Archive Photos]

Frank Sinatra

FACTS OF LIFE (and Death)

ORIGIN: Born Francis Albert Sinatra, December 12, 1915, Hoboken, New Jersey; died May 14, 1998, Los Angeles, California.

FORMATIVE YEARS: Frank was expelled from high school in Hoboken after only forty-seven days.

FAMILY PLANNING: Married Nancy Barbato (family friend), February 4, 1939; divorced 1951; married Ava Gardner (actress), November 7, 1951; divorced 1957; married Mia Farrow (actress), July 19, 1966; divorced 1968; married Barbara Marx (entertainer), July 11, 1976.

ROMANTIC INTERESTS: Lana Turner (actress), Natalie Wood (actress), Lauren Bacall (actress), Marilyn Monroe (actress), Marlene Dietrich (actress), Juliet Prowse (actress), Gloria Vanderbilt (designer), Victoria Principal (actress).

SELECTED HITS (and Misses)

FILMS: *Las Vegas Nights* (1941), *Higher and Higher* (1944), *Step Lively* (1944), *Anchors Aweigh* (1945), *It Happened in Brooklyn* (1947), *The Kissing Bandit* (1948), *The Miracle of the Bells* (1948), *Take Me Out to the Ball Game* (1949), *On the Town* (1949), *Meet Danny Wilson* (1952), *From Here to Eternity* (Oscar for Best Supporting Actor—1953), *Suddenly* (1954), *The Tender Trap* (1955), *Not as a Stranger* (1955), *The Man With the Golden Arm* (1955), *Guys and Dolls* (1955), *High Society* (1956), *Pal Joey* (1957), *The Joker Is Wild* (1957), *Some Came Running* (1958), *A Hole in the Head* (1959), *Can-Can* (1960), *Ocean's Eleven* (1960), *The Devil at Four O'Clock* (1961), *The Manchurian Candidate* (1962), *Come Blow Your*

Horn (1963), *Robin and the Seven Hoods* (1964), *Von Ryan's Express* (1965), *None But the Brave* (1965),* *Cast a Giant Shadow* (1966), *Tony Rome* (1967), *The Detective* (1968), *Lady in Cement* (1968), *The First Deadly Sin* (1980), *Cannonball Run 2* (1984).

*Also directed by Sinatra.

QUICKIE BIO

The skinny kid with the golden throat was the son of a woman who ran a part-time abortion service in their New Jersey neighborhood. After stints as a singing waiter and a frontman for Tommy Dorsey's band in the early 1940s, Frank went solo and knocked a nation of bobby-soxers off their feet. After World War II, his career went down the toilet. However, after snagging an Oscar for his supporting role in *From Here to Eternity* (1953), Ol' Blue Eyes never blinked again. Sinatra's crowd inherited the Rat Pack name from Humphrey Bogart, and headed for Las Vegas. Frank not only made appearances in nearly sixty movies, he also experienced the joy of a congressional investigation, five grand jury subpoenas, two IRS investigations, a congressional summons, and a subpoena from the New Jersey State Crime Commission. All because he did it his way.

FRANK SINATRA
DOES THE DUMBEST THINGS

✪ For one of the first Sinatra solo gigs, Frank's men paid a dozen girls five dollars each to scream and swoon at certain points during the show. The behavior caught on. Soon Frank was "much more hated than Hitler" by boys in uniform because he was at home singing to packed houses of fainting women, while they were getting shot at in the battlefields.

✪ Frank routinely abused the "help." On one occasion, Sinatra walked into his office at the Sands Hotel in Las Vegas only to find that the color of his phone clashed with the new orange sweater he was wearing. Sinatra screamed obscenities, tore the existing phone out of the wall, broke windows, and set fire to the office.

💰 After walking into his suite at a San Francisco hotel, the singer went straight to the phone, ordered eighty-eight Manhattans from the bar, and had the waiters set them in the hallway. Two days later, Frank left San Francisco without having touched a single one of the specially ordered drinks.

⭐ Frank was thrilled to be married to actress Mia Farrow. He proudly told a Las Vegas audience, "I finally found a broad I can cheat on." They were divorced two years later.

⭐ Sinatra was a big fan . . . of himself. According to one-time fling Ronnie Cowan, Sinatra liked to make love while listening to his own records. And when he wed Mia Farrow in 1966, his version of "Strangers in the Night" was playing in the background.

🗳 Frank sang the national anthem at the 1956 Democratic Convention. Afterward, Speaker of the House Sam Rayburn put his arms around the crooner and said, "Aren't you going to sing 'The Yellow Rose of Texas' for us, Frank?" Sinatra turned to Rayburn and replied, "Take your hands off the suit, creep."

⭐ When a fan ran up to him in Miami, Frank said, "Get away from me, creep." He then dispatched two of his goons to take care of the intrusive guy. One thug held up his sport jacket so the bystanders couldn't see the other thug bash in the fan's face.

⭐ At a Palm Springs party, Frank reportedly got so mad at one female that he threw her through a plate glass window, which nearly severed her arm.

⭐ After a 1958 New Year's dinner, Sinatra wanted to take his guests, which included close friend actor Peter Lawford, out to Palm Springs. When his pals, even Lawford, declined his invitation, Frank slammed his drink on the floor, charged out of the restaurant, and headed straight for the desert resort. Once there, he removed all of Lawford's clothes from the guest room closet, shredded them, and threw them in the pool.

⭐ When comedian Jackie Mason began making Sinatra jokes in his act, he started receiving death threats. A week later someone fired three bullets into the comic's hotel room. Months later someone pulled Mason out of a car and smashed his face in, saying all the while, "We warned you to stop using Sinatra material in your act."

⭐ Frank Sinatra said that Elvis Presley's music was "deplorable, a rancid smelling aphrodisiac." Later, Frank hosted the TV special *Frank Sinatra's Welcome Home Party for Elvis Presley* (1960).

⭐ Frank Sinatra changed his underwear at least ten times a day because he felt "unclean."

⭐ During the making of the detective caper *Lady in Cement* (1968), Frank spent the night with a hooker. In the morning, Sinatra invited the woman to breakfast. He ordered ham and eggs from room service, then ate the food off of the woman's chest. The call girl threatened to sue, but settled out of court.

✪ Ol' Blue Eyes hated reporters. He called them "bums, parasites, hookers and pimps." When he saw a columnist he detested at a Los Angeles restaurant, the star had his thugs pin the writer down while he punched the journalist a few times.

✪ When Frank spotted a female reporter who annoyed him, he screamed that she was nothing but a cheap tart and said, "You've been laying down for two dollars all of your life." Sinatra then reached into his pocket, took out two dollar bills, and shoved them into his victim's drink. When Frank's mom heard of the incident, she reacted by saying that her son had overpaid.

Sinatra was so excited about a visit from his buddy President John F. Kennedy, that he built a heli-pad in back of his Palm Springs spread just for the visit. When Kennedy stayed at Bing Crosby's instead, Sinatra attacked the heli-pad with a sledgehammer.

✪ In the mid-1960s, Sinatra had a paid personal entourage of eight people, including a hairpiece handler.

✪ Frank once got mad at casino manager Carl Cohen and spilled a pot of hot coffee on him. Cohen punched Sinatra, knocking out his two front teeth. Later Frank said to actor Kirk Douglas, "Never fight a Jew in the desert."

Sharon Stone

FACTS OF LIFE

ORIGIN: Born March 10, 1957, Meadville, Pennsylvania.

FORMATIVE YEARS: Dropped out of Edinboro State University (Edinboro, Pennsylvania), where she failed acting . . .

FAMILY PLANNING: Married Michael Greenburg (producer), 1984; divorced 1987; married Phil Bronstein (newspaper editor), February 14, 1998.

ROMANTIC INTERESTS: Michael Bensara (Guess Jeans CEO), Dweezil Zappa (musician), Bob Wagner (production assistant), Bill MacDonald (producer), Dwight Yoakum (country musician).

SELECTED HITS (and Misses)

FILMS: *Stardust Memories* (1980), *Deadly Blessing* (1981), *Irreconcilable Differences* (1984), *King Solomon's Mines* (1985), *Allan Quartermain and the Lost City of Gold* (1986), *Police Academy 4: Citizens on Patrol* (1987), *Action Jackson* (1988), *Above the Law* (1988), *Blood and Sand* (1989), *Total Recall* (1990), *Scissors* (1991), *He Said, She Said* (1991), *Basic Instinct* (1992), *Sliver* (1993), *The Specialist* (1994), *The Quick and the Dead* (1995), *Casino* (1995), *Diabolique* (1996), *Last Dance* (1996), *Sphere* (1997), *The Mighty* (1998), *Antz* (voice only, 1998), *Gloria* (1999), *The Muse* (1999), *Picking Up the Pieces* (2000), *Beautiful Joe* (2000).

TV SERIES: *Bay City Blues* (1983).

QUICKIE BIO

B orn to a pair of high school dropouts in rural Pennsylvania, Sharon Stone was a brainy kid who couldn't wait to leave town. She departed for New York to become a model, relocated to Italy, returned to Manhattan, and got her big break as "the good looking blonde" in Woody Allen's *Stardust Memories* (1980). After a series of generally bad (but sometimes fun) movies in the 1980s, Stone posed for *Playboy* and wowed the world when she crossed her legs in the mega hit *Basic Instinct* (1992). After becoming a Hollywood star, Stone revealed her basic instincts as a difficult diva. When asked what institution she'd like to found, the actress said, "The Sharon Stone Institute for Pretentious Behavior, Sexual Provocation, and Overall Disregard for Acceptable Behavior."

SHARON STONE
DOES THE DUMBEST THINGS

⭐ Sharon Stone declared that she didn't know her natural hair color. The colorful actress claimed, "I haven't seen it since I was fourteen."

⭐ In the Indiana Jones rip-off *King's Solomon's Mines* (1985), Stone played a drug-crazed model, which she described as "not unlike my natural self at the time." She was so nasty to some of the crew members that they peed into a pond just before Stone performed a racy bathing scene in it.

⭐ According to *Total Recall* (1990) costar Arnold Schwarzenegger, between takes tough girl Stone would complain to him, "Don't touch my hair."

⭐ After the release of *Total Recall*, Sharon was involved in a bad car accident. However, it wasn't just her body that was injured. Said Sharon, "I sat on the street for three hours. Nobody recognized me." Even though she had a major concussion, Stone went home to bed instead of to a hospital. Stone awoke the next morning and found herself paralyzed. She finally called a doctor . . . three days later.

⭐ After the huge success of *Total Recall*, Stone posed for *Playboy*. "I had just remodeled my house," she explained. "I needed the bread."

⭐ Sharon complained that she was "fed up to the teeth with years of mediocre crap and directors ogling my tits." Then she appeared nude in *Basic Instinct* (1992).

⭐ While filming the physiologically impossible sex scenes for *Basic Instinct*, Stone's gal pal lay on the floor out of sight of the camera and held Stone's hand in order to help her relax.

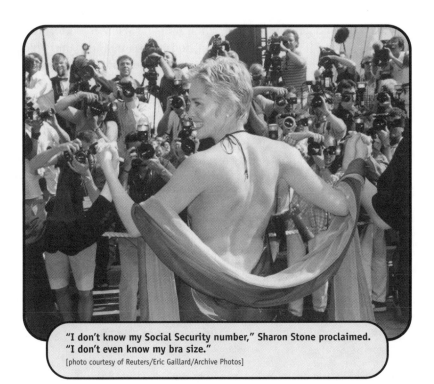

"I don't know my Social Security number," Sharon Stone proclaimed. "I don't even know my bra size."
[photo courtesy of Reuters/Eric Gaillard/Archive Photos]

✪ As Stone described the sex scenes in *Basic Instinct* to friends at a West Hollywood restaurant, her voice was so loud that people at the adjacent booths turned around and stared. Of course, when she detailed it to the press, she was less dramatic. "How can it be the 'f*** of the century' when a woman has to pretend to have three orgasms in four minutes from anatomically incorrect positions? I mean, that's a total male fantasy."

✪ Stone arrived on the set of *Basic Instinct* packing heat. As she waved the gun in the cinematographer's face, she gave him a friendly tip on how to do his job: "If I see one ounce of cellulite on the screen," she warned, "you're a dead man."

✪ In the most famous scene from *Basic Instinct,* Sharon parted her legs on-camera to reveal that she was not wearing underwear. She first said that she'd been tricked into doing the sequence, claiming that the director told her to take off her panties because they reflected too much light. After the footage made Stone a star, the actress claimed that taking off her underwear was her idea.

✪ Harry Winston, a posh Beverly Hills jeweler, loaned Stone a $400,000 diamond necklace for the *Sliver* (1993) publicity tour. Sharon thought the necklace was payment in exchange for the free exposure Winston's rocks would get on the tour. When the gem seller asked for his beads back, Stone filed a twelve-million-dollar lawsuit. The claim, which the jeweler labeled "mind-boggling," was settled out of court with Stone giving back the necklace. Winston, however, had to pay cash to Stone's favorite charity. When Winston's son ponied up the dough he quipped, "I really wanted to sue the pants off her, but she doesn't wear any."

★ Stone has claimed to hear voices and speak to the dead. After auditioning for the lead in Martin Scorsese's *Casino* (1995), she allegedly carried on a lengthy conversation with dead showgirl Geri McKee, on whom the part was based.

★ Sharon credited kicking the coffee habit with curing cancer. "When I stopped drinking coffee," she declared, "ten days later I had no more tumors in any of my lymph glands."

★ When Stone exited the premiere of *Forrest Gump* (1994), the paparazzi didn't notice her. So she went back into the theatre and left again. They still didn't notice her. So she went back into the theatre to repeat the routine. Finally, on her third departure, the reporters started pestering Stone.

★ While eating at the Polo Lounge in Beverly Hills, Sharon complained to hubby Phil Bronstein that two businessmen were staring at her. Bronstein lumbered over to their table and threatened, "I'll punch out both of you!" A waiter came to the rescue, moved the businessmen to another table, and paid for their lunch. When Phil sat back down next to Sharon, she squeezed his biceps.

★ When Sharon Stone wanted to get pregnant, she sprinkled her bed with red clover flowers, raspberry leaves, and unicorn powder root and performed an African fertility dance. In addition, she forced her hubby to drink a foul-tasting love potion made of herbs from the South American rain forest. Her husband, who was given the nickname El Macho, confided to friends, "I go back to work after one of these Olympic sessions weak at the knees and praying she's pregnant."

Barbra Streisand

DUMBEST QUOTE

"There's nothing better than to know
I can be taking a bath at home and at the
same time someone is watching me in Brazil."

FACTS OF LIFE

ORIGIN: Born Barbara Joan Streisand, April 24, 1942, Brooklyn, New York. Changed spelling of her name to Barbra in 1959.

FORMATIVE YEARS: Attended Yeshiva University, New York City, New York.

FAMILY PLANNING: Married Elliott Gould (actor), September 13, 1963; divorced 1971; married James Brolin (actor), July 1, 1998.

ROMANTIC INTERESTS: Barry Dennen (actor), Jon Peters (hairdresser), Ryan O'Neal (actor), Warren Beatty (actor), Pierre Trudeau (Canadian politician/Prime Minister), Peter Jennings (newsman), Robert Redford (actor), Richard Burton (actor), George Lucas (producer), Clint Eastwood (actor), Richard Gere (actor), Tommy Smothers (actor), Sam Elliott (actor), Kris Kristofferson (actor), Don Johnson (actor), Andre Agassi (tennis player).

SELECTED HITS (and Misses)

FILMS: *Funny Girl* (Oscar for Best Actress—1968), *Hello, Dolly!* (1969), *On a Clear Day You Can See Forever* (1970), *The Owl and the Pussycat* (1970), *What's Up, Doc?* (1972), *Up the Sandbox* (1972), *The Way We Were* (1973), *For Pete's Sake* (1974), *Funny Lady* (1975), *A Star Is Born* (Oscar for Best Song—1976), *The*

Main Event (1979), *All Night Long* (1981), *Yentl* (1983),* *Nuts* (1987),* *The Prince of Tides* (1991),* *The Mirror Has Two Faces* (1996).*

*Also directed by Streisand.

QUICKIE BIO

Born into a dysfunctional Jewish family, Barbra Streisand described her Brooklyn neighborhood as "boredom, baseball, and bad breath." She started out in show business chirping in Manhattan cabarets, worked her way up through Off-Broadway to Broadway, and smashed the entertainment world on all fronts with the play, the movie, and the album *Funny Girl* in the mid- to late 1960s. Over the next three decades, Barbra recorded more gold albums than any other performer, starred in hit TV specials, and invaded Hollywood as an actor, a director, and a producer. For a time, it seemed that America was seeing all Barbra, all the time. However, by the 1990s her star had lost some of its lustre. In 1998, "Hello Gorgeous," a San Francisco shrine to La Streisand, was forced to shut its doors. The reason? Lack of interest. Time for another world tour, Babs.

BARBRA STREISAND
DOES THE DUMBEST THINGS

✪ Streisand's mother had a simple explanation for why her daughter Barbra would never be famous. "Movie stars are pretty," mother opined. She claimed that her second husband was "allergic" to Barbra.

✪ Babs dismissed her mom by saying, "She's mainly interested in basic things, like eating and breathing. She's a very secure person, sort of like, uh, normal." When Barbra herself became a mother, she told friends that son Jason could "play with a walnut or explore the carpet."

✪ Unhappy with her Jewish family, young Barbra sought solace with a neighboring Asian family who owned a Chinese restaurant. It was from the matriarch of this family that Barbra developed her passion for having long, painted fingernails. She later said she had grown them to "ward off typing lessons."

✪ The acclaimed vocalist broke one of her fingernails just prior to a dinner in Malibu, so she did what any ordinary person would. She chartered a helicopter and flew to her favorite Beverly Hills nail specialist for emergency repairs. Total cost was $900.

✪ Someone once complimented Barbra on her unique eye makeup style, saying it looked something like the makeup Elizabeth Taylor used in

Cleopatra (1963). "It's *my* look," Barbra snapped. "I don't copy *fake* Jews." Like Sammy Davis Jr., Taylor was a convert to Judaism.

✪ Streisand's reputation for being difficult started early on. On the set of *Hello, Dolly!* (1969), she asked the director to have costar Walter Matthau say his lines differently. "I was acting before you were born," Matthau said, "so please don't tell me how to act." Babs shrieked, "Is this guy crazy or something?" Eventually, Matthau got so fed up with Barbra he yelped, "You haven't got the talent of a butterfly fart!"

✪ The cover for Barbra's 1984 album *ButterFly* featured a housefly sitting on a stick of butter.

✪ When hairdresser/producer Jon Peters first met Barbra he visited her home and she led him up the stairs. "My god!" Peters exclaimed. "What are you looking at?" Barbra demanded. "I'm looking at your butt," Peters sighed. "You've got a great a**."

✪ Barbra told Peters that she had never seen an uncircumcised penis. Peters had been clipped, so he called over a friend who dropped his trousers. Streisand stared at the natural organ in fascination.

✪ Streisand got into a fight with Peters one day while he was driving. Peters reached over and ripped off her blouse. Then Barbra reportedly swung her leg up and pressed a stiletto heal into her boyfriend's neck. No injuries were reported.

✪ Barbra has always been a perfectionist about her recording sessions. She spent hours trying to decide which of two vocal tracks to use for a song on her album *Emotion* (1984). The engineer finally pointed out to Barbra that the two tracks were identical.

✪ On the set of *The Prince of Tides* (1991), director/star Babs had an air-conditioned walkway built from her Winnebago dressing room to the set so that her makeup would not melt en route.

✪ Babs's boobs made an appearance in *The Prince of Tides*. She decided to delete the scene after showing it in previews. "It was like, all of a sudden, there's Barbra Streisand's breasts, instead of the emotion of the scene," the forty-nine-year-old actress explained. "So, I cut it differently."

Streisand flew to Washington, D.C., to attend Bill Clinton's inauguration in 1993. When she arrived at her hotel, she asked if her suite was the largest. The staff told her that there was one other suite which was slightly larger. The star demanded the larger suite, but was told that it was occupied by Hillary Clinton's parents. "I don't care," Streisand screeched. "Get them out or I will stay in another hotel!" Barbra stayed at another hotel.

⭐ Before Streisand's mid-1998 wedding day. reports suggested that her new husband, actor James Brolin, signed a prenuptial agreement that awarded him a ten million dollar bonus if he stayed married to Babs for ten years.

⭐ To deter the horde of reporters that descended on her Malibu home to cover the wedding to Brolin, Barbra's people parked a van near the media encampment and played the song "Thunder Kiss '65" for four hours. "Hopefully," said Rob Zombie who recorded the song, "the Funny Lady will use a track of my new album, 'Hellbilly Deluxe,' to ward off meddling paparazzi at her divorce hearing."

⭐ Barbra Streisand visited hubby James Brolin on the set of his TV series *Pensacola: Wings of Gold* (1997–present). Streisand wore nothing but a raincoat and high heels. She flashed her husband and the two retreated to his trailer. Streisand sang him a love song every morning and chartered a jet so the two could fly around L.A. and screw in the air. Brolin told Barbra that he didn't want to go to sleep when he was in bed with her because, "then I'll miss you."

⭐ Streisand paid one hundred dollars to buy a colorful dress off a homeless woman's back. Ever the humanitarian, Streisand also escorted the woman to a shop and bought her a new dress for seventy-five dollars.

⭐ After a dinner in Greece, Babs followed local custom and smashed her empty dinner plate against a wall. A razor sharp piece of plate came flying back at her and cut a seven-inch gash in her foot. Streisand ended up on crutches.

⭐ On the set of her debut movie, *Funny Girl* (1968), the crew referred to her as a "full-fledged monster" for the way she treated veteran director William Wyler. "She's a monster," observed her costar Omar Sharif, "but she's a fascinating monster. She wants to be a woman and she wants to be beautiful and she is neither." Thirty years later, Streisand reappeared as the voice of an animated monster on the TV comedy series *South Park*.

Quentin Tarantino

FACTS OF LIFE

ORIGIN: Born March 27, 1963, Knoxville, Tennessee.

FORMATIVE YEARS: Dropped out of high school. Once held a $1,200-a-month job as a headhunter for a firm whose clients were in the aerospace engineering industry. He left the job to work for four hundred dollars a month at a video store.

FAMILY PLANNING: None to date.

ROMANTIC INTERESTS: Grace Lovelace (actress), Mira Sorvino (actress).

SELECTED HITS (and Misses)

FILMS AS ACTOR: *Reservoir Dogs* (1992), *Sleep with Me* (1994), *Somebody to Love* (1994), *Pulp Fiction* (1994), *Four Rooms* (1995), *Destiny Turns on the Radio* (1995), *Desperado* (1995), *From Dusk Till Dawn* (1996), *Girl 6* (1996), *Full Tilt Boogie* (1998), *God Said, Ha!* (1999).

FILMS AS DIRECTOR: *Reservoir Dogs* (1992), *Pulp Fiction* (1994), *Four Rooms* (1995), *Jackie Brown* (1997), *40 Lashes* (2000).

QUICKIE BIO

Paraphrasing Hollywood producer Don Murphy, the story of Quentin Tarantino is the tale of a video store geek who watched too many movies, borrowed scenes and story lines, exaggerated the facts to get his foot in the door, thought he could act, then started to believe his own hype. Tarantino later slugged Murphy over the latter's comments. However, there is something to be said about Tarantino's hype—after all, he once worked at the Pussycat Theatre (which showed porno flicks) and was the first person in Hollywood to make a romantic comedy about heroin addiction: 1994's *Pulp Fiction*. Describing his hit to the world, Quentin rhapsodized, "The thing about this movie is that it's a great f***ing movie." Anything you say, Quenty.

QUENTIN TARANTINO
DOES THE DUMBEST THINGS

- ✪ Tarantino believed that "nobody really liked sports." He said that men actually pretended to enjoy sports only because they felt they were supposed to.

- ✪ As a budding young actor, Quentin took classes at the James Best Acting School located above a honey baked ham store in Los Angeles. And what master thespian was the school named for? None other than the man who played Sheriff Roscoe Tanner in TV's *The Dukes of Hazzard* (1979–85).

- ✪ Tarantino bragged, "I'm the patron saint of video clerks." One week, Saint Quentin and his video store followers designed a display of Charles Manson-based movies to coincide with the anniversary of Manson's murder of Sharon Tate.

- ✪ To try to gain industry contacts, Tarantino posed as a journalist who was interviewing directors for the definitive anthology of B-movies. What's even wilder is that many movie makers believed him and agreed to interviews, including Brian de Palma.

- ✪ On his resume, Tarantino reportedly claimed to have acted in the horror classic *Dawn of the Dead* (1978). He thought he'd get away with it because he looked a little like one of the guys in the movie.

- ✪ Frustrated with his video store post, Quentin cold-called Hollywood big shots and asked for work. He got a gig for twenty dollars a day working as a production assistant on a workout video. Once on location, Tarantino got his assignment: clean up the dog poop on the front lawn of the house where the video was being shot.

⭐ In the fall of 1989, Tarantino was escorted out of his apartment and arrested. The charge? Reportedly, Quentin had racked up $7,000 in unpaid parking fines. His mother refused to bail him out.

⭐ Despite his very un-dashing looks, Quentin eventually started getting calls for bit acting parts on TV shows. The biggest was as an Elvis impersonator on a segment of *The Golden Girls* (1985–92). Tarantino said of his performance, "I was the real Elvis."

⭐ After a screening of the violent *Reservoir Dogs* (1992), a reporter asked the new film director if he would let his own daughter watch it. Tarantino replied, "If she reacts harshly and has nightmares, so what? Part of being a kid is having nightmares." Fortunately, Tarantino did not have a daughter.

⭐ With a big paycheck for *Pulp Fiction* (1994), Quentin headed to Europe. He took a liking to European women because they gave him "a lot of leeway when it came to personal hygiene."

⭐ Quentin was eating at a trendy West Hollywood restaurant, when he spotted producer Don Murphy. Murphy was eating with his girlfriend who had just written a book slamming Tarantino. While Murphy's girlfriend was in the bathroom, Tarantino reportedly pushed Murphy against a wall and punched him out. Tarantino's buddy, producer Harvey Weinstein, convinced Murphy not to file charges. Weinstein was an investor in the restaurant.

⭐ Tarantino later bragged about the incident on a TV talk show. The new-breed director said he "bitch slapped" Murphy three times. Quentin then went on to say that "bitch slapping" was a good way to get respect from someone. After the "bitch slapping" comment, Murphy filed a hefty lawsuit against Quentin.

⭐ In 1998, Tarantino costarred on Broadway in a revival of the thriller *Wait Until Dark*. The critics described Tarantino's performance as a "real disaster" and "terrible." About a month after the show opened, "terrible" Quentin got into an argument at a Manhattan restaurant, swung at a photographer, missed, and hit the photographer's girlfriend.

⭐ When Spike Lee and others criticized the use of the word "nigger" in *Jackie Brown* (1997), Tarantino fumed, "This is me we're talking about! You're f***ing wrong! I have a great affinity for black people and black culture. Ricki Lake and I are the most admired white celebrities in the black community."

✪ Quentin later guested on the Howard Stern radio show to explain violent actions, but wound up dissing African-American filmmaker Spike Lee. Quentin sneered that Lee "would have to stand on a chair to kiss my a**."

✪ At the same time he was bombing on Broadway, Tarantino also was bombing with his Oscar-winning girlfriend Mira Sorvino. "Quentin is a wonderful man and a genius," Mira sighed. "He just can't keep his fly zipped." Sorvino later denied that she ever dissed Tarantino. She also denied that she said Quentin was "more interested in playmates than soulmates."

Elizabeth Taylor

DUMBEST QUOTE

"Give me the f***ing roast beef."

FACTS OF LIFE

ORIGIN: Born Elizabeth Rosemond Taylor, February 27, 1932, London, England, to American parents.

FORMATIVE YEARS: Attended MGM studio's school for child actors, but spent much of her class time admiring herself in a hand held mirror.

FAMILY PLANNING: Married Conrad "Nicky" Hilton Jr. (hotel heir), May 6, 1950; divorced 1952; married Michael Wilding (actor), February 21, 1952; divorced 1957; married Mike Todd (producer), February 2, 1957; widowed 1958; married Eddie Fisher (singer), May 12, 1959; divorced 1964; married Richard Burton (actor), March 15, 1964; divorced 1974; married Richard Burton (again), October 10, 1975; divorced (again) 1976; married John Warner (politician), December 4, 1976; divorced 1982; married Larry Fortensky (truck driver), October 6, 1991; divorced February 1996.

ROMANTIC INTERESTS: Rock Hudson (actor), Carl Bernstein (journalist), George Hamilton (actor), Montgomery Clift (actor), Malcolm Forbes (businessman), Michael Jackson (singer), Victor Luna (lawyer).

SELECTED HITS (and Misses)

FILMS: *There's One Born Every Minute* (1942), *Lassie Come Home* (1943), *National Velvet* (1944), *Jane Eyre* (1944), *Courage of Lassie* (1946), *Life with Father* (1947), *A Date with Judy* (1948), *Little Women* (1949), *Father of the Bride* (1950),

A Place in the Sun (1951), *Father's Little Dividend* (1951), *Ivanhoe* (1952), *Rhapsody* (1954), *The Last Time I Saw Paris* (1954), *Elephant Walk* (1954), *Giant* (1956), *Raintree County* (1957), *Cat on a Hot Tin Roof* (1958), *Suddenly, Last Summer* (1959), *Butterfield 8* (Oscar for Best Actress—1960), *The V.I.P.s* (1963), *Cleopatra* (1963), *The Sandpiper* (1965), *Who's Afraid of Virginia Woolf?* (Oscar for Best Actress—1966), *The Taming of the Shrew* (1967), *Reflections in a Golden Eye* (1967), *The Comedians* (1967), *Secret Ceremony* (1969), *Hammersmith Is Out* (1972), *Ash Wednesday* (1973), *A Little Night Music* (1978), *The Mirror Crack'd* (1980), *The Flintstones* (1994).

QUICKIE BIO

Oh my God, it's Liz! The beautiful, buxom, bull-headed twelve-year-old Liz Taylor took the reins as the leading lady in MGM's *National Velvet* (1944) and never let go. The first actress to demand one million dollars for a film, Taylor also demanded that she be treated like a princess—by her Hollywood co-workers and by each of her seven husbands. Liz has had a voracious appetite for, well, everything—food, sex, and especially jewelry. Hubby Eddie Fisher once noted, "To keep her happy you had to give her a diamond before breakfast every morning." After heroically surviving cancer in 1997, Liz devoted her energy to perfume merchandising, AIDS fundraising, and defending Michael Jackson. However, as a secret admirer once said, Liz's greatest contribution to humanity may have been "her breasts. Oh, Jesus her breasts."

ELIZABETH TAYLOR
DOES THE DUMBEST THINGS

⭐ Taylor was originally not considered for the lead in *National Velvet* (1944) because she was not curvaceous enough. Determined to land the plum part, she used "fast grow" creams and did daily exercises to enhance her bust.

⭐ During the filming of *A Place in the Sun* (1951) Taylor forged a deep friendship with costar Montgomery Clift. He called her "Bessie Mae," and she wrote Clift letters proclaiming her passionate love for him. Many of Liz's ardent letters ended up in the hands of the gay Clift's boyfriends.

⭐ After a party at Taylor's house, Clift was seriously injured in a car accident. She arrived at the Los Angeles intensive care unit to visit Clift, but found another woman there who was also in love with the actor. The other woman screamed, "What the f*** is she doing here?" "Screw off!" yelled Liz, while Monty lay next to them battered and bandaged.

According to a two-year investigation by the California State Attorney General, over a ten-year period, doctors wrote Liz "thousands of prescriptions" for drugs, including Ativan, Dalmane, Darvocet-N, Demerol, Dilaudid, Doriden, Empirin, Halcion, Hycodan, Lomotil, Methadone, morphine sulfate, paregoric, Percocet, Percodan, Placidyl, Prelu-2, Ritalin, Seconal, Sublimaze, Tuinal, Tylenol with codeine, Valium, and Xanax. Over one seventeen-day period in 1982, Taylor reportedly was prescribed over six hundred pills.

✪ Taylor and her third husband, producer Mike Todd, used to record their lovemaking sessions and give the tapes to friends as gifts.

✪ While dining with his best friend Eddie Fisher and Fisher's wife Debbie Reynolds, Mike Todd began arguing with Liz. Mike smacked Taylor, and they ended up tussling on the floor. Horrified, their hosts tried to referee but were spurned by the scrapping couple. "Don't be such a Girl Scout," Liz snapped. "Really, Debbie, you're so square." Todd admitted later, "We had more fun fighting than most couples do making love."

✪ Mike and Liz were not afraid to show affection in public either. At a New York luncheon, friends tried not to gape as Mike reached into Liz's cleavage and fondled her breasts.

✪ During one of her weddings, the presiding official asked Liz to name her previous husbands. "What is this, a memory test?" the star squawked.

✪ Eddie Fisher claimed that during sex Taylor would crawl around the floor on her hands and knees purring like a kitten. The hotter she got, the louder she purred. When checking into hotels, Taylor told the desk not to send the maids until the afternoon because "Eddie's favorite time to f*** is in the morning."

✪ Marriage to Eddie flew out the window for Liz when she got a look at husband number five, her *Cleopatra* (1963) costar Richard Burton. Just weeks into shooting, the also-married Welsh actor announced to the crew of the epic film that he had "nailed" Liz in the back seat of his Cadillac the night before.

✪ The first time Taylor attended a screening of *Cleopatra*, she jumped out of her seat after twenty minutes, raced to the bathroom, and threw up.

✪ Like all of Liz's husbands, Burton bought her diamonds. One of the biggest, in fact—the 33.19-carat Krupp diamond is considered one of the finest stones in the world. At a wedding, Liz offered to let England's Princess Margaret try it on. "How very vulgar!" the Princess exclaimed. "Yeah, ain't it grand," said Liz.

- After divorcing Dick in 1974, Taylor announced, "There will be no more bloody marriages or divorces." Then she married hubby number six— Richard Burton. Again. And divorced him. Again. Pianist Oscar Levant observed, "Always the bride, never a bridesmaid."

- Taylor always insisted on doing her own makeup. The director of *Ash Wednesday* (1973) walked into Liz's dressing room one day and found her powdering the roof of her mouth. When he asked what she was doing, she replied, "Well they'll see the inside of my mouth when I speak my lines. I want to look perfect."

- Liz had a prodigious appetite and once consumed mounds of mashed potatoes and gravy, five desserts, and several bottles of champagne at one sitting.

- Friend Michael Jackson wanted to dress up his three giraffes (named Kareem, Abdul, and Jabbar) in tuxedos designed by Valentino and have them serve as Liz Taylor's bridesmaids for her 1991 nuptials to Larry Fortensky. Taylor nixed the idea, but said of Michael, "He's the least weird man I've ever known."

- Liz's eighth husband, Larry Fortensky, was more interested in TV than Taylor. Lonely Liz left post-it notes around the house for Larry saying, "Please spend time with me today," "Did you shave today?" and "Are you going to get up this morning?" Later, after they divorced, Fortensky injured himself critically in a bad fall and Liz was among the first to rush to his support.

"I don't pretend to be an ordinary housewife," pronounced Elizabeth Taylor, pictured here next to Aristotle Onassis.
[photo courtesy of Archive Photos]

Mae West

FACTS OF LIFE (and Death)

ORIGIN: Born Mary Jane West, August 17, 1893 (or 1892, or 1887), Brooklyn, New York; died November 22, 1980, Hollywood, California.

FORMATIVE YEARS: Dropped out of elementary school.

FAMILY PLANNING: Married Frank Wallace (actor), April 11, 1911; divorced 1943.

ROMANTIC INTERESTS: Harry Houdini (magician), Cary Grant (actor), Max Baer (boxer), Gary Cooper (actor), Duke Ellington (musician), Joseph M. Schenck (producer), Jim Timony (lawyer), William "Gorilla" Jones (boxer), Chalky White (chauffeur), Vincent Lopez (bodyguard), Chester Ribonsky (wrestler), Paul Novak (muscleman).

SELECTED HITS (and Misses)

FILMS: *Night After Night* (1932), *She Done Him Wrong* (1933), *I'm No Angel* (1933), *Belle of the Nineties* (1934), *Goin' to Town* (1935), *Klondike Annie* (1936), *Go West, Young Man* (1936), *Every Day's a Holiday* (1938), *My Little Chickadee* (1940), *The Heat's On* (1943), *Myra Breckinridge* (1970), *Sextette* (1978).

QUICKIE BIO

If Mae West had been born as a man, she would have been Warren Beatty. A non-smoker who only drank an occasional beer, Mae grew up in Brooklyn, New York, and worked as a child actress before becoming an acrobat, a male impersonator, a playwright, a movie star, a rock and roll singer, and a sexual fixation for millions. Above all else, Mae West believed in one thing and one thing only—sex. She demanded it—sex, that is—from movie stars, chauffeurs, and whomever else struck her fancy. *Sex* was the title of her scandalous 1926 play, which landed Mae in jail for "corrupting the morals of youth." Sex was the subject of every one of her Hollywood films. Sex was also her daily exercise. "Goodness! What beautiful diamonds!" said a check girl to Mae in *Night After Night* (1932). Mae's debut line in the movies? "Goodness had nothing to do with it, dearie."

MAE WEST
DOES THE DUMBEST THINGS

✪ Among the best Mae West rumors are the following: she underwent the first sex change operation, she was frigid, she possessed both male and female organs, and she was actually a he. Edith Head put an end to the latter by saying, "I've seen Mae West without a stitch and she's all woman. No hermaphrodite could have bosoms . . . well, like two large melons."

✪ Mae West claimed that her first erotic dream was of a bear with a reddish brown organ about four inches in length. "I was modest in my demands," Mae recalled.

✪ West was married at age sixteen to one Frank Wallace. She later denied the union, but had to fess up when Frank later produced a marriage certificate. "Sex with love is the greatest thing in life. But sex without love—that's not so bad either," Mae quipped.

✪ When Mae's film *It Ain't No Sin* opened in 1934, Catholic priests marched in protest and carried signs that said, "It is!" The name of the picture was changed to *Belle of the Nineties*. Too bad for the movie's publicity crew. They were stuck with fifty live parrots who were trained to screech nothing but "It ain't no sin!"

✪ Marlene Dietrich, another Paramount studio star, kept offering to wash Mae's hair, but West wouldn't let her. Mae explained that the hair Marlene wanted to soap up "wasn't all on my head."

✪ Mae enjoyed receiving dirty fan mail, especially pictures of naked male bodies. The larger the organ in the photo, the more it tickled her. She'd say, "Look at that f***er!"

✪ West became a devotee of Sri Deva Ram Sukul, the self-styled "President and Director of the Yoga Institute of America." After she met the *sri*, Mae sighed, "I felt I had touched the hemline of the unknown."

✪ Mae liked to touch the "hemline" a lot. "Oh it's so mah-velous," she said to one of her costars, "you can reach an orgasm in thirty seconds." "Christ," the costar said, "I don't want to turn into a damned jack rabbit." "Not you, dear," Mae corrected, "the woman. ME!"

✪ One Christmas, Mae West designed a special greeting card. It was a portrait of herself nude with the caption, "Come Up and See Me Sometime. Merry Christmas, Mae West." Her publicist objected to the hot card and substituted a design of his own. The card featured a picture of an exhausted Santa Claus with the caption, "Santa Comes But Once a Year—Too Bad!"

✪ In 1956, Mae West performed onstage with Miklosi "Mickey" Hargitay, the Arnold Schwarzenegger of the 1950s, the Hungarian born Mr. Universe. However, Mickey didn't hit it off with Mae and instead started dating bosomy Jayne Mansfield. Mae flew into a jealous rage and called a press conference to explain that Hargitay was hers. Hargitay barged into the media melee and began praising Jayne Mansfield, until Mae West's bodyguard decked him. In the fight, Mae West was knocked down. "Yuh can't do this to me," Mae screamed from the floor. "I'm an institution."

Mae preserved her good looks by following a strict regimen. "I take two colonics every day 'n' I'm careful about what I eat, too," Mae explained. "So when I go to the bathroom, there's no odor. Oh, maybe like hot soup—at the very worst, beef stew."

✪ One day, boxer Max Baer phoned Mae West. It turned out that he was downstairs at her Los Angeles apartment building. West invited him to come up and see her. Baer did just that, and wound up in bed with her. After they finished making love, the athlete walked to the window, pulled up the shade, and stood naked waving to someone in the street. That someone was his agent. Baer had won a five-hundred-dollar bet that he could bed the buxom movie star. Mae liked to tell the story on herself.

✪ One room in West's home was completely furnished with dollhouse-scale furniture. When asked about the room, she explained that every year an Oriental shrank her down to twelve inches tall, and she inhabited the doll house room for a month.

✪ Mae got around the Hollywood censors with her va-voom delivery of sex drenched one-liners. Some classic Mae West observations: "I used to be Snow White, but I drifted." "I feel like a million tonight—but one at a time, please." "I've been on more laps than a table napkin." "Come on up and see me sometime. Come up Wednesday. That's amateur night." And "Is that a gun in your pocket or are you just glad to see me?" Toward the end of her life, Mae bragged, "My measurements are still the same as Venus de Milo's, only I got my arms. My teeth are my own, too."

Bruce Willis

DUMBEST QUOTES

"There are people who are starving and they could solve it by pushing one button—and they don't do it. I don't know why."

"I change diapers. I clean up dog doo."

FACTS OF LIFE

ORIGIN: Born Walter Bruce "Bruno" Willison, March 19, 1955, in West Germany.

FORMATIVE YEARS: Studied drama at Montclair State College, Upper Montclair, New Jersey.

FAMILY PLANNING: Married Demi Moore (actress), November 21, 1987; separated, June 24, 1998.

ROMANTIC INTERESTS: Sheri Rivera (former wife of Geraldo Rivera), Michele Hoyt (restaurant manager). According to Willis, "No woman is going to satisfy a man's natural impulse to procreate, procreate, procreate."

SELECTED HITS (and Misses)

FILMS: *In Search of the Guru* (1980), *Blind Date* (1987), *Sunset* (1988), *Die Hard* (1988), *In Country* (1989), *Look Who's Talking* (voice only, 1989), *Die Hard 2: Die Harder* (1990), *The Bonfire of the Vanities* (1990), *The Last Boy Scout* (1991), *Hudson Hawk* (1991), *Death Becomes Her* (1992), *Striking Distance* (1993), *Pulp Fiction* (1994), *Nobody's Fool* (1994), *Twelve Monkeys* (1995), *Die Hard: With a Vengeance* (1995), *Last Man Standing* (1996), *The Jackal* (1997), *The Fifth Element* (1997), *Mercury Rising* (1998), *Armageddon* (1998), *The Siege* (1998), *Breakfast of Champions* (1999), *The Story of Us* (1999), *The Sixth Sense* (1999), *The Whole Nine Yards* (2000).

TV SERIES: *Moonlighting* (1985–89).

QUICKIE BIO

Many years ago, when movie stars started taking over production power in Hollywood, one studio wag commented, "The lunatics are taking over the asylum." Willis became one of tinseltown's greatest lunatics. Teenage Willis took up acting to overcome his stammer. He worked as a security guard at a nuclear power plant, and played his harmonica over the loudspeaker. He moved to New York City, tended bar for stars like Richard Gere, and picked up bit parts in plays and TV shows that led to his costarring role in the TV detective comedy series *Moonlighting* (1985–89). Willis's screen career took off with the action thriller *Die Hard* (1988), then died hard with *Hudson Hawk* (1991), and bounced back. Loudmouthed and arrogant, Willis often has said, "Hollywood is like a beautiful woman with the clap." Let's all clap for Bruno!

BRUCE WILLIS
DOES THE DUMBEST THINGS

✪ While in high school, Bruce showed up at a party wearing nothing but a diaper.

✪ Willis walked down the street in Montclair, New Jersey, in the mid-1970s drinking a beer. A cop told him to stop drinking in public. The law enforcer noticed something behind Willis's ear and asked, "What's this?" "Oooops," Willis said. "A joint." Willis was arrested for possession of marijuana.

✪ After the first few seasons of the TV series *Moonlighting* in the mid-1980s, Bruce started fighting with costar Cybill Shepherd. He picked on her when she got pregnant. "Widen the doors," Bruce shouted, "Bring in a crane. Cybill's coming." Later, he sneered to Shepherd, "Your hairstyle's old fashioned." She shot back, "Well at least I've got some."

✪ On the set of *Moonlighting,* Bruce upset costar Cybill Shepherd by dropping his pants continually and mooning the cast and crew with his hairy butt. Years later Shepherd said he "could probably use some of that hair now on his head."

✪ Willis was obsessed by his bald spot, and had a personal hairdresser on the set of *The Bonfire of the Vanities* (1990). Whenever the light hit his scalp and it showed through his hair, the hairdresser yelled, "Back lights, take out!!"

✪ After viewing *Striking Distance* (1993), Willis was unhappy because it was too obvious that he was wearing a toupee. He ordered the movie's final scenes re-shot at a cost of over $750,000.

⭐ On Memorial Day weekend in 1987, Willis threw a party at his Los Angeles home. The neighbors complained about the noise and two police officers arrived on the scene. A reportedly drunk Willis screamed, "What the f*** are you doing in my house? Have you got a search warrant?" When the cops explained about the complaints, Bruce yelled, "Then get the f*** outta here." The officer asked, "Why are you saying 'f***' so much?" Willis retorted, "What is this, courtesy class?" This interchange led to Willis being handcuffed and taken down to the police station.

⭐ Willis appeared on the set of his film *Hudson Hawk* (1991) in Budapest, Hungary, in a foul mood. "Let's get this f***ing show on the road," he snarled. "I don't want to spend the rest of my life eating goulash."

🐶 During the making of *Hudson Hawk,* Bruce's scene called for him to run from a building and fall onto a flock of chickens. Willis did multiple takes of the sequence. During each take, he landed on, and killed, a chicken.

⭐ Bruce and his wife Demi Moore moved to Hailey, Idaho, in 1992, where they invested a total of thirteen million dollars in the town. Then they decided to move from Hailey, and allegedly left neighboring merchants with a stack of unpaid bills. A local resident sighed, "He's the only person I know who could spend millions of dollars in a ghost town—and turn it right back into a ghost town."

💰 Willis returned to his home town of Penn's Grove, New Jersey, in 1993 and announced plans to spend fifty million dollars to build a marina, a hotel, an open-air market, a theatre, an amphitheatre, a restaurant, and a fifty-home development. Then Bruce abandoned the ambitious project. The name of his development company? Screwball Properties, Inc.

⭐ In mid-1997, Bruce and wife Demi Moore sued a tabloid for reporting that their marriage was on the rocks. A year later, the couple announced that they were splitting up.

⭐ In the summer of 1998, Willis said that organized religions were "dying forms" and described Republican Presidential candidate Robert Dole as "a nitwit." However, Willis praised religious leader Louis Farrakhan. The movie star explained, "Anyone who stands up against injustice is a hero of mine." After Jewish groups complained to Willis about Farrakhan's anti-Semitism, Bruce said, "Louis Farrakhan is not my hero." *Daily Variety* columnist Army Archerd advised, "Hey, Bruce, stick to acting."

★ At a tribute dinner for basketballer Kareem Abdul-Jabbar, Willis fell asleep and plopped face-first into his bowl of ice cream.

★ When a reporter asked Willis, "Are you trying to tell me that you're not really a big pompous a**hole?" Willis replied, "No . . ."

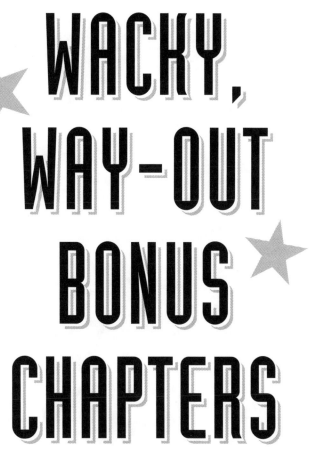

WACKY,
WAY-OUT
BONUS
CHAPTERS

Directors

DUMBEST JOB DESCRIPTION

The director, the auteur, the genius behind the camera, the wizard of cinematography who transforms dreams into theatrical wonder. . . . Yeah, sure. Long before film scholars made directors into cult heroes, they were the foremen of Hollywood, contractors who made sure pictures got completed on time and on budget. Sure, they helped with the scripts, chose the camera angles, and sometimes told the actors what to do. However, they didn't consider it magic. It was a job. "Say the f***ing words," yelled

267

Roman Polanski (*Repulsion* [1965], *Rosemary's Baby* [1968], *Chinatown* [Oscar—1974]) to his actors. "Your salary is your motivation." But what was the director's motivation? "All I was interested in doing was getting laid," moviemaker William Friedkin explained. "That's all Francis [Coppola] ever cared about, and [Peter] Bogdanovich—his muse was his cock." Quiet on the set! Action!

DIRECTORS
DO THE DUMBEST THINGS

PETER BOGDANOVICH (b. 1939)
(*The Last Picture Show* [1971], *Paper Moon* [1973], *Mask* [1985], *The Thing Called Love* [1993])

✪ When Peter Bogdanovich's girlfriend model Dorothy Stratten went missing one morning, his daughter tried to calm him, saying, "At least she's not dead." Actually, she was dead. Stratten had been killed by a shotgun blast from her possessive ex-boyfriend, who then coupled with her corpse and shot himself in the head. Bogdanovich soon began dating Stratten's younger sister.

✪ After Peter Bogdanovich declared bankruptcy, attorneys questioned his claim stating that he still paid $250 to have his hair cut. The filmmaker's attorneys defended the hairy fees, claiming "a certain standard of living is necessary to be taken seriously as a player in Hollywood."

FRANCIS FORD COPPOLA (b. 1939)
(*Dementia 13* [1963], *The Godfather* [shared Oscar for Best Screenplay with Mario Puzo—1972], *Apocalypse Now* [1979], *The Godfather Part III* [1990], *John Grisham's The Rainmaker* [1997])

✪ Before leaving for the Philippines to shoot *Apocalypse Now*, director Francis Ford Coppola approached producer/director Roger Corman for words of wisdom. Corman's advice? Don't go there. "You're going right into the rainy season—May through November. Nobody shoots there that time of year." Coppola went anyway. After he got there, a crew member warned him that typhoons would destroy his set. "What are you a f***in' weatherman?" Coppola swore. A few weeks later, a fierce storm did indeed level his constructed scenery.

✪ Coppola made himself comfortable on the set of *Apocalypse Now* by shipping in the finest wines, crystal, and stereo equipment. He had pasta flown in every week from Italy for his Italian camera crew. Then he spent more than $10,000 to throw himself a birthday party. At the same time, Coppola stopped paying many of the crew their daily allowance for food.

JOHN FORD (1899–1980)

(*The Informer* [Oscar for Best Director—1935], *Stagecoach* [1939], *The Grapes of Wrath* [Oscar for Best Director—1940], *How Green Was My Valley* [Oscar for Best Director—1941], *Fort Apache* [1948], *The Quiet Man* [Oscar for Best Director—1952], *The Searchers* [1956], *Cheyenne Autumn* [1964], *7 Women* [1966])

✪ During the production of *Fort Apache,* an Indian medicine man gave John Ford a daily weather forecast. Ford was amazed at the accuracy of the predictions, and began to plan his shooting around them. One day, the medicine man failed to make a forecast. Ford asked another Native American on the set what had happened. The man responded, "His radio broke down."

ALFRED HITCHCOCK (1899–1980)

(*The Lodger* [1926], *Rebecca* [1940], *Rear Window* [1954], *To Catch a Thief* [1955], *North by Northwest* [1959], *Psycho* [1960], *Frenzy* [1972])

✪ Hitchcock was furious when he was quoted in the press as saying, "Actors are cattle." The Britisher fumed, "I have been misquoted. What I really said is: 'Actors should be treated as cattle.'"

HERSCHELL GORDON LEWIS (b. 1926)

(*Blood Feast* [1963], *Color Me Blood Red* [1965], *Gore-Gore Girls* [1972])

✪ For one scene in *Blood Feast* director Lewis needed to film a man ripping out a woman's tongue, so he stuck a sheep's heart in an actress's mouth along with stage blood, gelatin, and cranberry juice. Then he had the hero reach into the heroine's mouth and rip out her tongue. Unfortunately for the actress, the heart had been refrigerated badly for a few days before the shooting and stunk so bad it had to be coated with Pine-Sol before it was used. Lewis eventually gave up films, got into the used car business, opened an abortion referral service, and went bankrupt.

GEORGE LUCAS (b. 1944)

(*THX-1138* [1971], *American Graffiti* [1973], *Star Wars* [1977], *The Empire Strikes Back* [1980], *Return of the Jedi* [1983], *Star Wars: Episode One—The Phantom Menace* [1999])

- Lucas spent years working on the script for *Star Wars*. When he finished it, he showed it to actor Harrison Ford, who commented, "You can type this s***, but you sure can't say it."

- Lucas pictured Princess Leia in *Star Wars* as a teenage virgin. To realize his vision, he insisted that actress Carrie Fisher flatten her breasts with electrical tape. "No breast bounce in space," Fisher joked, "no jiggling in the Empire."

MARTIN SCORSESE (b. 1942)
(*Boxcar Bertha* [1972], *Taxi Driver* [1976], *The Last Waltz* [1978], *The Last Temptation of Christ* [1988], *Casino* [1995], *Kundun* [1997], *Bringing Out the Dead* [1999])

- Scorsese once complained, "I can't deal with a woman who doesn't know who I am."

STEVEN SPIELBERG (b. 1947)
(*Jaws* [1975], *Close Encounters of the Third Kind* [1977], *E. T.: The Extra-Terrestrial* [1982], *Schindler's List* [1993], *Jurassic Park* [Oscar for Best Picture—1993], *Amistad* [1997], *Saving Private Ryan* [1998])

- On the set of the telefeature *Rod Serling's Night Gallery* (1969), Joan Crawford challenged the twenty-one-year-old director Spielberg to a burping contest, and coached him on the set on the finer points of belching.

- Spielberg brought over his friends, directors Martin Scorsese, John Milius, and George Lucas, to show off the mechanical shark that he was using for *Jaws* (1975). The moviemaker manned the controls and began manipulating the shark's mouth. When it opened, Lucas shoved his head inside. Spielberg then closed the shark's jaws on Lucas, and the shark promptly broke. By the time Lucas managed to free himself from the shark's mouth, Spielberg and his buddies had fled the scene.

- While making *Close Encounters of the Third Kind* (1977), Spielberg's relationship with his then actress wife Amy Irving became strained. Irving broke down and started crying. He apologized and explained, "Don't you understand? I'm f***ing my movie."

OLIVER STONE (b. 1946)
(*Midnight Express* [Oscar for Best Screenplay—1978], *Platoon* [Oscar for Best Picture—1986], *The Doors* [1991], *Natural Born Killers* [1994], *U-Turn* [1997], *Any Given Sunday* [1999])

⭐ After fighting as a soldier in Vietnam, Oliver Stone was reportedly arrested for possession of marijuana. The incident led to an argument between Stone and his father. "I just wanted to destroy him," Stone admitted. So Oliver supposedly dropped some LSD into his dad's drink. Stone's father wound up hanging on to a tree limb and fantasizing about African women. The filmmaker recalled later, "He was cool about it."

⭐ At a party in Los Angeles, the guests heard pounding coming from the bathroom. The hostess was shocked to see Oliver Stone bust through the bathroom door. "What kind of dump is this," complained Stone. "Don't you have a door that works?" Stone was so mellow that he couldn't figure out how to open the door.

🚬 One afternoon, Oliver and a friend decided to take a "smart drug." However, Stone was too "dumb" to take the proper amount. Instead of taking a two-teaspoon dosage, he slurped down two tablespoons, and passed out. After paramedics arrived on the scene, Stone regained consciousness, and started screaming "I gotta pee, I gotta pee."

RAOUL WALSH (1887–1980)
(*The Thief of Bagdad* [1924], *The Big Trail* [1930], *High Sierra* [1941], *Battle Cry* [1955], *Distant Trumpet* [1964])

⭐ After hard-partying actor John Barrymore died in 1942, Raoul Walsh decided to play a prank on Barrymore's equally hard-living friend Errol Flynn. Raoul, actor Peter Lorre, and other Hollywood types dragged Barrymore's corpse into Flynn's living room, and sat it in an easy chair. When Flynn returned home, he took off his coat, nodded to Barrymore, took three steps toward the bar, and froze. Then he yelled, "Oh, my God!" The movie star approached Barrymore cautiously and poked him. Flynn's buddies cracked up. Errol forgave his friends, and offered them a drink. However, he refused to help haul Barrymore back to the mortuary.

ORSON WELLES (1915–1985)
(*Citizen Kane* [1941], *The Magnificent Ambersons* [1942], *The Lady From Shanghai* [1948], *A Touch of Evil* [1958], *Chimes at Midnight* [1966])

⭐ During a scene in *Jane Eyre* (1944) in which Welles was about to be burned to death, Orson yelled to his costar Joan Fontaine, "I now know what Joan of Arc endured!" "Keep your spirits up," she snapped back. "We'll let you know if we get the odor of burning ham."

⭐ Welles once spent an entire day making alterations to a garbage dump to shoot one line of dialogue there. "Move that ketchup bottle over here, turn it on its side, move this tin can over there, take the label off the beans. . . ."

ED WOOD (1922–1978)
(*Glen or Glenda* [1953], *Bride of the Atom* [1955], *Plan 9 from Outer Space* [1956], *Night of the Ghouls* [1959], *The Sinister Urge* [1960])

⭐ Director Ed Wood was thrilled to hire Dracula specialist Bela Lugosi to star in his film *Plan 9 from Outer Space* (1956). But Bela was not thrilled when Ed took him out to a restaurant one evening. "F*** this place!" Hollywood's Dracula screamed. "I don't like this place. . . . It is stupid this place." The head waiter came over to calm the ruckus. "Mr. Lugosi, it's a great pleasure to have you here. May I shake your hand?" Bela took the head waiter's hand and yelled, "F*** you." When asked why Lugosi was so rude, Ed Wood explained, "No reason! That's the beauty of the man!"

⭐ Bela Lugosi was supposed to have a much larger role in *Plan 9 from Outer Space*, but destiny stepped in. As Ed Wood explained, "I had to kill Bela off much earlier than I had planned when he actually died."

Oscar

FACTS OF LIFE

ORIGIN: The statuette was created by Cedric Gibbons and George Stanley in 1929, stands 13½ inches high, and weighs 8½ pounds. According to tradition,

Oscar was named by Margaret Herrick, librarian at the Academy of Motion Pictures Arts and Sciences, who reportedly said that the statue looked like her Uncle Oscar.

FORMATIVE YEARS: Oscar made his first appearance in 1929 at an awards ceremony hosted by the Academy of Motion Picture Arts and Sciences. In the first years, Oscars were awarded in more than a dozen categories. In 1999 Oscars were bestowed in nearly twice that number of categories. Oscar was first made of bronze, then plaster. Today Oscar is made of gold-plated britannium by R. S. Owens and Company.

FAMILY PLANNING: Oscar spawned the Grammys, the Tonys, the Emmys, and all the other trophy shows that clog the media today.

ROMANTIC INTERESTS: Shirley MacLaine once announced to an audience, "I'd like to introduce someone who has just come into my life. I've admired him for thirty-five years. He's someone who represents integrity, honesty, art, and on top of that stuff I'm actually sleeping with him." Shirley then reached behind her piano and pulled out . . . Oscar.

QUICKIE BIO

Nothing means more to movie stars than the five words "And the Oscar goes to . . . " What began in the late 1920s as a poorly attended promotional stunt, grew over the years into one of the greatest entertainment spectacles on earth—the Oscars is now Hollywood's Super Bowl. Determined by a vote of the members of the Academy of Motion Pictures Arts and Sciences, the Oscars is an annual display of egos, greed, fashion, and especially dumb things that everyone loves to hate. "Me sit in trees seventeen years," perennial Oscar wannabe Johnny "Tarzan" Weissmuller grunted. "Me watch 'em come and go." So do we, Tarzan. So do we.

OSCAR DOES (or causes to be done) THE DUMBEST THINGS

⭐ Director Frank Capra thought his film *Lady for a Day* (1933) was a shoo-in for the Oscar. He rented a mansion in Beverly Hills, wrote many thank-you speeches, and rented a tuxedo for the big evening. On awards night, Will Rogers announced the winner for Best Director. "Come on up and get it, Frank!" Capra stood triumphantly. Oops! Wrong Frank! Rogers was calling director Frank Lloyd (for *Cavalcade*) to the stage!

⭐ Alice Brady won the Best Supporting Actress prize for *In Old Chicago* (1938). Brady was not in attendance, so a gentleman accepted the tribute for her. The only problem was, Brady had no idea who the man was. The gentleman, and the Oscar, were never seen again.

★ Joan Crawford was nominated as Best Actress for *Mildred Pierce* (1945). She was so nervous before the big night that she developed a "fever" and was ordered to bed. Photographers and press agents "happened to be" present at her home when Joan's victory was announced. She accepted her Oscar in bed while photographers snapped poses of her in a filmy nightgown, cuddling Oscar.

★ For the 1947 Oscars, held in March, there was a terrible technical problem, and the film clips of the best picture nominees were shown backward, upside down, and on the ceiling. The Screen Actors Guild president never looked up from his cue cards on the podium, and declared that the footage represented "the glories of our past, the memories of our present, and the inspiration of our future." The man behind the podium was Ronald Reagan.

★ When double-amputee World War II veteran Harold Russell (who had lost both of his arms in military duty) claimed the Oscar for Best Supporting Actor for *The Best Years of Our Lives* (1946), Cary Grant, not a nominee that year, sniped, "Where can I get a stick of dynamite?"

★ *The Three Faces of Eve* (1957) star Joanne Woodward attended the Academy Awards in a homemade dress. When she realized she would have to walk onstage wearing the frumpy outfit to accept her Oscar, she cried. Joan Crawford fumed that Woodward's outfit "set Hollywood glamour back twenty-five years."

★ When Jerry Lewis hosted the Oscars on April 6, 1958, the show was running short. "Another twenty minutes!" Lewis yelled to John Wayne, Doris Day, Cary Grant, and other stars who were dancing onstage. Then Jerry got desperate. "We're showing Three Stooges shorts to cheer up the losers," he screeched. Then he grabbed a baton, started conducting the orchestra, and shouted, "We may get a bar mitzvah out of this!" When the comedian grabbed a trumpet and started playing off-key, NBC finally ended the program and aired a sports documentary about competitive pistol shooting.

★ When Marlon Brando was voted Best Actor for his role in *The Godfather* (1972), he didn't show up. Instead a woman in a Native American outfit accepted the Oscar for him and read a long political statement. The woman identified herself as Sacheen Littlefeather, president of the

National Native American Affirmative Image Committee. She was actually Maria Cruz, the former Miss American Vampire of 1970. Eventually, Marlon Brando asked for his Oscar back.

⭐ The day after Eileen Heckart received the Oscar for Best Supporting Actress in *Butterflies Are Free* (1972), she went to the unemployment office to collect her check.

⭐ Robert Opel surprised presenters David Niven and Elizabeth Taylor by streaking the Academy Awards stage in April 1974, and flashing the peace symbol. Niven dryly commented, "The only laugh that man will ever get is by stripping off his clothes and showing his shortcomings."

⭐ The Jewish Defense League as well as neo-Nazis protested Vanessa Redgrave's appearance at the Oscars in 1978. She was burned in effigy and forty policemen were called to restore peace. When she won for *Julia* (1977), she used the moment to pontificate about politics. Playwright Paddy Chayefsky followed her onstage and commented that, "A simple thank you would have been sufficient."

⭐ Meryl Streep accidentally left her just-claimed Oscar on the back of the toilet at the 1980 festivities.

⭐ When it comes to campaigning for Oscar, no ploy seems too demeaning. Hoping to be voted Best Supporting Actress for *The Color Purple* (1985), actress Margaret Avery published a "letter to God" in the Hollywood trade papers. It ended: *"Well God, I guess the time has come fo' the Academy voters to decide whether I is one of the Best Supporting Actresses this year or not! Either way, thank you Lord, for the opportunity. Your little daughter, Margaret."*

⭐ When seventy-two-year-old character actor Jack Palance was named Best Supporting Actor for *City Slickers* (1991), he walked onstage then dropped to the floor and did one-handed push-ups.

⭐ After attending the Academy Awards ceremony in the 1990s, Kevin Costner confessed, "The Oscars made my pits wet."

⭐ After grabbing his Oscar in 1998, director James Cameron grabbed his estranged third wife Linda Hamilton and began yelling at her. Later that evening, a reporter asked Hamilton how winning eleven Oscars for *Titanic* (1997) would change director Cameron. "He was always a jerk," Hamilton responded. "So there's no way to really measure."

Producers

DUMBEST JOB DESCRIPTION

Producers are the suits, the executives, the money men, the guys/gals who make pictures happen, get it? You see, the movies are a lot like retail. You make a quality product, and you sell it. Bingo! That's why a lot of the biggies who got the Hollywood racket rolling started out in the clothing business. Hey, they had to get their costumes from somewhere? Some folks described a movie producer as "a man who knows exactly what he wants but can't spell it." Not Samuel Goldwyn. He saw his artistic role as something much, much bigger. "This will start with a bang in Hollywood and degenerate throughout the world!" An' how.

PRODUCERS
DO THE DUMBEST THINGS

⭐ While starring in the silent film production of *The King of Kings* (1927), fan dancer Sally Rand, who played a slave, started dating H. B. Warner, who was portraying Jesus. One day when the lovers arrived late on the set, angry producer/director Cecil B. DeMille shouted out through his megaphone, "Miss Rand, leave my Jesus Christ alone! If you must screw someone, screw Pontius Pilot!"

⭐ While staying in New York in the early 1970s, director Peter Bogdanovich fell deathly ill. He called Paramount president Frank Yablans. "How sick are you?" Yablans asked. "Very sick, 105, 106; something like that," answered the filmmaker. "God Peter, if it goes any higher you could die." Bogdanovich concurred, "Yeah, that's why I'm calling you. You have to get me a doctor." Yablans asked, "Are you going to do *Paper Moon* [1973]?" Bogdanovich became irate, "What! What kind of question is that to ask me now?" The studio head persisted, "Are you going to do *Paper Moon*? Because if you don't give it to me, I don't give a f*** if you live or die. You can find your own damn doctor."

⭐ On the set of the comedy *Trading Places* (1983), producer/director John Landis warned the women working on the production about its star, Eddie Murphy. "Don't go out with him," Landis ordered. "He's going to f*** you if you go out with him, and it will f*** the movie up. Stay away from him." On the set, the comic gave Landis a full Nelson, and Landis reportedly later grabbed Murphy by the balls. Eddie once choked Landis, until the moviemaker cried out, "Eddie!" Eddie let go and Landis ran out of the room.

⭐ When studio honcho Barry Diller barged into a meeting of vendors, a mid-level studio guy introduced him around the room. Diller was furious and chewed out the executive, "Never introduce me to someone I do not know."

⭐ Producer/director Robert Altman was adamant about getting Shelley Duvall to play Olive Oyl in *Popeye* (1980). So Altman put together a twelve-minute reel of Duvall's work and showed it to executives at Paramount Pictures. After the reel, Don Simpson, president of production at the studio, stood up and said, "Well, I don't want to f*** her. And if I don't want to f*** her, then she shouldn't be in the movie."

⭐ During the making of *King Solomon's Mines* (1950), the producers at MGM were upset when they found out that the African natives didn't really look, well, enough like African natives. So they imported two hundred Afro wigs from California and put them on the heads of the on-camera natives.

⭐ During the filming of *One Flew Over the Cuckoo's Nest* (1975) in Salem, Oregon, cast members bought marijuana from the locals. To avoid possible embarrassment, the producers arranged things so that the staff bought the pot in bulk and a production assistant put it into baggies for the crew.

⭐ Jack Cohn of Columbia Pictures suggested that he and his studio head brother Harry produce a big religious epic. "What do you know about the Bible?" Harry scoffed. "I'll bet you fifty dollars you don't even know the Lord's Prayer." Jack paused, then recited, "Now I lay me down to sleep. . . ." "Well, I'll be damned," Harry said, pulling fifty bucks out of his pocket. "I honestly didn't think you knew it."

⭐ Producer Harry Cohn claimed he had a foolproof method for figuring out whether a movie was destined to be a hit or a flop when he screened it. "If a picture is great," Cohn explained, "I sit still. If a picture is good, I move just a little. But if a picture stinks, my a** wiggles all over the place."

⭐ The mega-rich producer Howard Hughes bought the RKO studios sight unseen. After he finally took a look around the multi-million dollar facility, his only comment was "Paint it!"

⭐ Samuel Goldwyn was given a book entitled *The Making of Yesterday: The Diaries of Raoul de Roussy de Sales, 1938–1942*. "How do you like that?" Goldwyn said in amazement. "Four years old and the kid keeps a diary."

⭐ Goldwyn acquired the screen rights to a classic novel called *The Well of Loneliness*. One of his executives complained, "We can't make that as a picture, Mr. Goldwyn, the book deals with lesbians." Goldwyn snapped back, "So all right, where they got lesbians we'll use Austrians."

⭐ Producer Sam Zimbalist asked writer Graham Greene to help him with the movie epic *Ben-Hur* (1959). "You see," the producer confided, "we find a sort of anti-climax after the crucifixion."

⭐ MGM's top production executive Louis B. Mayer had the reputation as king of the casting couch at his studio. It was said that any woman who starred in one of his pictures had to screw him first. When actress Jean Harlow came to his office, Mayer supposedly offered her a mink coat and told her to undress and try it on. Harlow refused. She told Mayer that the only way she would sleep with him would be if she got the clap. Then she would gladly do it for free.

⭐ Harry M. and Jack L. Warner founded Warner Bros. studio together with their siblings Albert and Sam. However, Harry hated Jack so much that he once chased his brother around the lot, waving a lead pipe and threatening to kill him. Later, when Jack met Albert Einstein, the producer said to the genius, "You know I have a theory about relatives too—don't hire them."

⭐ Warner Bros. production chief Darryl F. Zanuck used to accompany his boss Jack L. Warner into the bathroom. When Warner was done, Zanuck would flush the toilet for him.

⭐ For the New York City premiere of *Pinocchio* (1940), producer Walt Disney hired eleven little people dressed in Pinocchio outfits to frolic on the roof of the theatre marquee. For lunch they ate and drank free beer. They consumed so much beer that they stripped naked and sat up on the Broadway marquee shooting craps. Disney summoned the police who climbed to the roof and carried the culprits away in pillowcases.

⭐ During the pre-production of *Flashdance* (1983), producer Michael Eisner, now the head of Disney, gathered together a group of laborers to view the screen tests of Jennifer Beals, Demi Moore, and Leslie Wing. Eisner reportedly asked the crowd, "Which one of these girls do you most want to f***?" Jennifer Beals got the most grunts.

⭐ Menahem Golan, one of the producers of *Fool for Love* (1985) supposedly said of his star Kim Basinger, "Just looking at her makes me want to screw her."

⭐ Producer Jon Peters got into a fight with a marketing executive and socked him. When the executive called the cops, Jon ran into a friend's office and hid under his desk. After the police left, Peters told one of his secretaries, "You have to tell them he hit me first."

⭐ Jon Peters' long time producing partner Peter Gruber had a curious habit. He liked to talk dirty to women at business lunches. "You know," Gruber said to one of his female business associates, "if you put Chloraseptic on your c*** you can stay hard all night."

⭐ On the set of *A Star is Born* (1976), producer Peters got jealous when his girlfriend Barbra Streisand was about to perform a nude bathtub scene with her ex-lover and costar Kris Kristofferson. "We're engaged," Peters pleaded. "Do it with a bathing suit . . . I don't want your d*** floating around in the tub with her leg right there." Kris jumped into the tub buck naked.

✪ Later on, Barbra and Kris got into a shouting match on the set. "Listen to me when I talk to you, goddamnit!" Barbra screeched. "F*** off," Kirstofferson yelled back. At that point, Jon Peters butted in and said, "You owe my lady an apology." Kristofferson snarled, "If I need any s*** from you, I'll squeeze your head."

✪ Robert Evans produced *The Cotton Club* in 1984. When one of the other producers of the movie was murdered by a woman who had been Evans's girlfriend and cocaine supplier, Evans tried to escape the emotional turmoil of the ensuing drug scandal by doing lots of drugs.

 Evans, who produced *Love Story* (1970), reportedly invited two hookers to his home for a party one evening. The trio chomped down a bunch of Quaaludes, snorted a bunch of coke, and then hit the bedroom. According to one of the hookers, "Bob seemed so horny at the moment that I believe a lampshade would have looked good to him." Evans was horny, but so out of it that he couldn't perform.

✪ Robert Evans later married Catherine Oxenberg. The marriage, his fifth, lasted twelve days. Oxenberg claimed she married Evans after being brainwashed into helping people on a spiritual retreat. Evans said the marriage was "irrational behavior caused by my stroke."

✪ In the summer of 1995, producer Don Simpson (*Flashdance* [1983], *Beverly Hills Cop* [1984], *Top Gun* [1986]) consumed the following drugs daily: injections of Toradol, Librium, Ativan, Valium, Depakote, Thorazine, Cogentin, Vistaril, and Lorazepan. That list did not include the vast quantities of alcohol and cocaine he consumed daily. Simpson's bill for all this medication? $60,000 per month.

✪ Don Simpson yelled at one of his secretaries because there were too many clouds on one of his plane trips. When he couldn't open the window in his hotel room, he threw a chair through it, then made his secretary pay for the damage. He required another of his secretaries to read porno and referred to her as "stupid bitch," "garbage brain," and "dumb s***."

✪ Simpson once declared, "Anybody who thinks they can f*** their way into this business is an idiot." However, when one actress came to audition for a part, Simpson interrupted her reading and said, "Okay, do you want to do some coke, or would you like to f*** me?" He explained later, "We could either discuss this nicely and you could probably get a part, or you could go through the charade of reading for it."

★ Simpson kept his secretary as busy as an aspiring actress. She had to clean up piles of cocaine he left in his office, read porno, watch porno, and schedule his call girls. He told another would-be secretary that one of her jobs would be "staying up with me all night, just to make sure I'm not dead."

★ Between 1988 and 1994, Don Simpson went through at least ten feature-altering surgeries, including collagen injections into his cheeks, chin, and lips; a forehead lift, liposuction on his belly, a buttock lift, testosterone implants in his butt, and injections of fat into his penis to make it chunkier. After the penile injections got infected, a friend commented, "You can't believe how p***ed Don was."

★ Producer Jeffrey Katzenberg opened his film *Dick Tracy* (1990) on the same day that Don Simpson opened his film *Days of Thunder*. Simpson faxed Katzenberg claiming, "You can't escape the Thunder!" Katzenberg sent back a fax claiming, "You won't believe how big my d*** is!"

★ Actor Alec Baldwin described Jeffrey Katzenberg as "the eighth dwarf—Greedy." For a time, Katzenberg worked with equally high-powered and astute Michael Eisner at Disney. After Katzenberg left Disney, he filed a lawsuit claiming some $250 million in lost compensation. The case went to trail in 1999, but was settled out of court. What did Eisner think about the man who helped him rule the Magic Kingdom for a while? Reportedly, he said, "I think I hate the little midget."

BIBLIOGRAPHY

Following is a list of the main sources used in compiling all of this dumb stuff.

PERIODICALS

A&E Biography Magazine
Current Biography
Details
Entertainment Weekly
Esquire
Hollywood Reporter
Globe
Los Angeles Daily News
Los Angeles Times
Movieline
National Enquirer
New Orleans Times-Picayune

New York Daily News
New York Times
People
Playboy
Premiere
Rolling Stone
Spy
Star
Us
Vanity Fair
Variety

WEB REFERENCE SITES

ABC's Oscar Site www.oscar.com

Academy of Motion Picture Arts & Sciences www.oscars.org

All-Media Guide allmovie.com

Clark Gable Foundation Website
www.geocities.com/Hollywood/Bungalow/2739/

Club Love www.clublove.com

CyberSleaze www.cybersleaze.com

E! Online www.eonline.com

Golden Years Website
www.geocities.com/Hollywood/9766/gable.html

International Movie Database www.us.imdb.com

John Belushi www.geocities.com/~jolietjake

Mr. Showbiz.com www.mrshowbiz.com

Official James Dean Website www.jamesdean.com/

People Online www.people.com

TV Guide Database www.tvgen.com

Whitney Houston Home Page
www.aristarec.com/aristaweb/WhitneyHousto/index.html

REFERENCE BOOKS

Brooks, Tim, and Earle Marsh. *Complete Directory to Prime Time Network Cable TV Shows*. New York: Ballantine, 1995.

Bystedt, Karen Hardy. *Before They Were Famous: In Their Own Words*. Santa Monica, CA: General Publishing Group, 1996.

Connors, Martin, and Jim Craddock. *VideoHound's Golden Movie Retriever Annual*. Detroit, MI: Visible Ink, 1998.

Halliwell, Leslie, edited by John Walker. *Halliwell's Filmgoer's Companion & Video Viewer's Companion 1997 (Twelfth Edition)*. New York: HarperCollins, 1997.

Hollywords: From Marlon Brando to Mae West: Gems of Wisdom and Outrageous Wit. Glendale Heights, IL: Great Quotations Publishing Co., 1993.

Maltin, Leonard. *Leonard Maltin's Movie Encyclopedia*. New York: Plume, 1995.

————. *Leonard Maltin's 1999 Movie & Video Guide*. New York: Signet, 1998.

Medved, Harry and Michael. *The Golden Turkey Awards: Nominees and Winners—The Worst Achievements in Hollywood History*. New York: G. P. Putnam's Sons, 1980.

Quinlan, David. *Film Lovers Companion*. Secaucus, NJ: Carol Publishing, 1997.

Who's Who in Entertainment: 1998–1999. New Providence, NJ: Marquis Who's Who, 1997.

OTHER BOOKS

Agan, Patrick. *Decline and Fall of the Love Goddesses*. New York: Pinnacle Books, 1979.

Amende, Coral. *Hollywood Confidential*. New York: Plume/Penguin, 1997.

Ammons, Kevin, with Nancy Bacon. *Good Girl, Bad Girl: An Insider's Biography of Whitney Houston*. Secaucus, NJ: Carol Publishing, 1996.

Andersen, Christopher. *Citizen Jane: The Turbulent Life of Jane Fonda*. New York: Dell, 1990.

Andrews, Nigel. *True Myths: The Life and Times of Arnold Schwarzenegger*. New York: Birch Lane Press, 1996.

Anger, Kenneth. *Hollywood Babylon*. New York: Dell, 1975.

————. *Hollywood Babylon II*. New York: Dutton, 1984.

Barrymore, Drew, with Todd Gold. *Little Girl Lost*. New York: Pocket Books, 1989.

Bell, Simon, Richard Curtis, and Helen Fielding. *Who's Had Who*. New York: Warner Books, 1989.

Belushi, Judith Jacklin. *Samurai Widow*. New York: Carroll & Graf, 1990.

Berlin, Joey. *Toxic Fame: Celebrities Speak on Stardom*. Detroit, MI: Visible Ink, 1996.

Biskind, Peter. *Easy Riders, Raging Bulls: How the Sex—Drugs—and—Rock 'n' Roll Generation Saved Hollywood*. New York: Simon & Schuster, 1998.

Blackwell, Mr. *From Rags to Bitches*. Santa Monica, CA: General Publishing Group, 1995.

Bona, Damien. *Starring John Wayne as Genghis Khan: Hollywood's All-Time Worst Casting Blunders*. New York: Carol Publishing, 1996.

Brown, Peter H., and Jim Pinkston. *Oscar Dearest*. New York: Perennial, 1984.

Burkhart, Jeff, and Bruce Stuart. *Hollywood's First Choices*. New York: Crown, 1994.

Caddies, Kelvin. *Kevin Costner: Prince of Hollywood*. New York: Plexus Publishing Ltd, 1992.

Cader, Michael. *Famous Mugs: Arresting Photos and Felonious Facts for Hundreds of Stars Behind Bars*. Kansas City, MO: Andrews and McMeel, 1996.

Cameron-Wilson, James. *Young Hollywood*. Lanham, MD: Madison Books, 1994.

Cawthorne, Nigel. *Sex Lives of the Hollywood Goddesses*. London: Prion, 1997.

Chandler, Suzanne. *Children of Babylon*. New York: Longmeadow Press, 1993.

Chaplin, Sydney. *My Father, Charlie Chaplin*. New York: Popular Library, 1961.

Cher, with Jeff Coplon. *The First Time*. New York: Simon & Schuster, 1998.

Clarkson, Wensley. *Quentin Tarantino: Shooting from the Hip*. Woodstock, NY: Overlook, 1995.

Coffey, Frank. *The Complete Idiot's Guide to Elvis*. New York: Alpha Books, 1997.

Coleman, Emily R. *Complete Judy Garland*. New York: HarperCollins, 1990.

Collins, Joan. *Past Imperfect: An Autobiography*. New York: Simon & Schuster, 1984.

Considine, Shaun. *Bette and Joan: The Divine Feud*. New York: Dell, 1989.

Crane, Cheryl, with Cliff Jahr. *Detour: A Hollywood Story*. New York: William Morrow, 1988.

Crawford, Christina. *Mommie Dearest*. Moscow, ID: Seven Springs Press, 1978.

Crawley, Tony. *Bebe: The Films of Brigitte Bardot*. New York: Citadel Press, 1977.

Cunningham, Ernest W. *The Ultimate Barbra*. Los Angeles: Renaissance Books, 1998.

Davis, Bette, and Michael Herskowitz. *This 'n' That*. New York: G. P. Putnam's Sons, 1987.

Dunaway, Faye, with Betsy Sharkey. *Looking for Gatsby*. New York: Pocket Books, 1995.

Edwards, Anne. *Streisand: A Biography*. Boston: Little, Brown & Co., 1997.

Eells, George, and Stanley Musgrove. *Mae West: A Biography*. New York: William Morrow, 1982.

Ekland, Britt. *True Britt*. Englewood Cliffs, NJ: Prentice-Hall, 1980.

Epstein, Edward Z., and Joe Morella. *Mia: The Life of Mia Farrow*. New York: Delacorte Press, 1991.

Ferris, Paul. *Richard Burton*. New York: Geoghegan, 1981.

Fleming, Charles. *High Concept: Don Simpson and the Hollywood Culture of Excess*. New York: Doubleday & Co., 1998.

Flynn, Errol. *My Wicked, Wicked Ways*. London: Heinemann, 1960.

Gabler, Neal. *An Empire of Their Own: How the Jews Invented Hollywood*. New York: Crown, 1988.

Gabor, Zsa Zsa. *One Lifetime Is Not Enough*. New York: Delacorte Press, 1991.

Gaines, Steven. *Simply Halston: The Untold Story*. New York: G. P. Putnam's Sons, 1991.

Gilmore, John. *The Real James Dean*. New York: Pyramid, 1975.

Givens, Bill. *Film Flubs: Memorable Movie Mistakes*. New York: Citadel Press, 1998.

Glatt, John. *Lost in Hollywood: The Fast Times and Short Life of River Phoenix*. New York: St. Martin's Press, 1995.

Goldberg, Whoopi. *Book*. New York: Avon Books, 1997.

Golden, Eve. *Platinum Girl: The Life and Legends of Jean Harlow*. New York: Abbeville Press, 1991.

Grey, Rudolph. *Nightmare of Ecstasy: The Life and Art of Edward D. Wood,* Jr. Portland, OR: Feral House, 1992.

Griffin, Nancy and Kim Masters. *Hit & Run: How Jon Peters and Peter Guber Took Sony for a Ride in Hollywood.* New York: Simon & Schuster, 1996.

Grobel, Lawrence. *Conversation with Brando.* New York: Hyperion, 1991.

Groteke, Kristi. *Mia & Woody: Love and Betrayal.* New York: Carroll & Graf, 1994.

Guiles, Fred Lawrence. *Joan Crawford: The Last Word.* New York: Pavilion Books, 1995.

Guralnick, Peter. *Careless Love: The Unmaking of Elvis Presley.* Boston: Little, Brown & Co., 1999.

Hadleigh, Boze. *Hollywood Babble On.* New York: Carol Publishing, 1994.

Harris, Warren G. *Sophia Loren.* New York: Simon & Schuster, 1997.

Hay, Peter. *Movie Anecdotes.* Oxford, England: Oxford University Press, 1990.

Heymann, C. David. *Liz: An Intimate Biography of Elizabeth Taylor.* New York: Birch Lane Press, 1995.

Higham, Charles. *Errol Flynn: The Untold Story.* New York: Doubleday & Co., 1980.

Holden, Anthony. *Behind the Oscar: The Secret History of the Academy Awards.* New York: Simon & Schuster, 1993.

Hosoda, Craig. *Bare Facts Video Guide, 1996 Edition.* Los Angeles: Bare Facts, 1995.

Hyman, B. D. *My Mother's Keeper.* New York: William Morrow, 1985.

Israel, Lee. *Miss Tallulah Bankhead.* New York: G. P. Putnam's Sons, 1972.

Johnston, Sheila. *Keanu.* London: Sidgwick & Jackson, 1996.

Kelley, Kitty. *Elizabeth Taylor: The Last Star.* New York: Simon & Schuster, 1981.

———. *His Way: The Unauthorized Biography of Frank Sinatra.* New York: Bantam, 1986.

Lawford, Patricia Seaton. *The Peter Lawford Story: Life with the Kennedys, Monroe and the Rat Pack.* New York: Carroll & Graf, 1988.

Leigh, Wendy. *Liza: Born A Star.* New York: Dutton, 1993.

Levin, Martin. *Hollywood and the Great Fan Magazines.* New York: Arbor House, 1970.

Levy, Shawn. *King of Comedy: the Life and Art of Jerry Lewis*. New York: St. Martin's Press, 1996.

————. *Rat Pack Confidential: Frank, Dean, Sammy, Peter, Joey, & The Last Great Showbiz Party*. New York: Doubleday & Co., 1998.

Locke, Sondra. *The Good, The Bad & The Very Ugly: A Hollywood Journey*. New York: William Morrow, 1997.

Louvish, Simon. *The Man on the Flying Trapeze: The Life and Times of W. C. Fields*. New York: W. W. Norton & Co., 1997.

Madsen, Axel. *The Sewing Circle: Female Stars Who Loved Other Women*. New York: Birch Lane Press, 1995.

Malone, Andrew. *Hollyweird*. London: Michael O'Mara Books, 1995.

Manvel, Roger. *Chaplin*. Boston: Little, Brown & Co., 1974.

Martin, Mart. *Did She or Didn't She? Behind the Bedroom Doors of 201 Famous Women*. New York: Citadel Press, 1996.

Marx, Arthur. *The Nine Lives of Mickey Rooney*. New York: Stein and Day, 1986.

McClelland, Doug. *Hollywood Talks Turkey: The Screens Biggest Flops*. Boston and London: Faber and Faber, 1989.

McGilligan, Patrick. *Jack's Life: A Biography of Jack Nicholson*. New York: W. W. Norton & Co., 1994.

McKeon, Elizabeth, and Linda Everett. *The Quotable King*. Nashville, TN: Cumberland House, 1997.

McNeil, Alex. *Total Television*. New York: Penguin Books, 1984.

Medved, Harry and Michael. *The Golden Turkey Awards: Nominees and Winners—The Worst Achievements in Hollywood History*. New York: G. P. Putnam's Sons, 1980.

Milton, Joyce. *Tramp: The Life of Charlie Chaplin*. New York: HarperCollins, 1996.

Morella, Joe, and Edward Z. Epstein. *Lana: The Public and Private Lives of Miss Turner*. New York: Dell, 1971.

Munn, Michael. *Hollywood Rogues (a.k.a. Hollywood Bad)*. New York: Transaction, 1992.

Munshower, Suzanne. *Don Johnson: An Unauthorized Biography*. New York: New American Library, 1986.

————. *Warren Beatty: His Life, His Loves, His Work.* New York: St. Martin's Press, 1983.

Musso, Peter. *Brando: The Biography.* New York: Hyperion, 1994.

Nash, Bruce, and Allan Zullo. *Amazing But True Elvis Facts.* Kansas City, MO: Andrews and McMeel, 1995.

Nickson, Chris. *Keanu Reeves.* New York: St. Martin's Press, 1996.

Parish, James Robert. *Today's Black Hollywood.* New York: Pinnacle, 1995.

————. *Whoopi Goldberg: Her Journey from Poverty to Mega-Stardom.* Secaucus, NJ: Birch Lane Press, 1997.

Parish, James Robert, and Don Stanke. *Hollywood Baby Boomers.* New York: Garland Publishing Co., 1992.

Parker, John. *Bruce Willis: The Unauthorized Biography.* London: Virgin, 1997.

————. *Warren Beatty: The Last Great Lover of Hollywood.* New York: Carroll & Graf, 1993.

Paskin, Barbra. *The Authorized Biography of Dudley Moore.* London: Sidgwick & Jackson, 1997.

Patterson, Alex. *Spike Lee.* New York: Avon Books, 1992.

Peary, Gerald, ed. *Quentin Tarantino: Interviews.* Jackson, MI: University Press of Mississippi, 1998.

Petras, Ross and Kathryn. *Stupid Celebrities: Over 500 of the Most Idiotic Things Ever Said by Famous People.* Kansas City, MO: Andrews & McMeel, 1998.

Quirk, Lawrence J. *The Complete Films of Joan Crawford.* New York: Citadel Press, 1988.

Resnick, Sylvia Safran. *Burt Reynolds: An Unauthorized Biography.* New York: St. Martin's Press, 1983.

Reynolds, Burt. *My Life.* New York: Hyperion, 1994.

Riese, Randall. *Her Name Is Barbra.* Secaucus, NJ: Birch Lane Press, 1993.

Riley, Lee, and David Schumacher. *The Sheens: Martin, Charlie, and Emilio Estevez.* New York: St. Martin's Press, 1989.

Riordan, James. *Stone: The Controversies, Excesses, and Exploits of a Radical Filmmaker.* New York: Hyperion, 1995.

Riva, Maria. *Marlene Dietrich.* New York: Knopf, 1992.

Robb, Brian J. *Johnny Depp: A Modern Rebel*. London: Plexus, 1996.

Robin, Liza, Linda, and Tiffany, as told to Joanne Parrent. *You'll Never Make Love in This Town Again*. Los Angeles: Dove, 1995.

Robinson, Jeffrey. *Bardot: An Intimate Portrait*. New York: Primus/D. I. Fine Books, 1995.

Rodriguez, Elena. *Dennis Hopper: A Madness to His Method*. New York: St. Martin's Press, 1988.

Rooney, Mickey. *Life's Too Short*. New York: Ballantine, 1991.

Rovin, Jeff. *TV Babylon*. New York: New American Library, 1991.

———. *TV Babylon 2*. New York: New American Library, 1992.

Rubin, Sam, and Richard Taylor. *Mia Farrow: Flower Child, Madonna, Muse*. New York: St. Martin's Press, 1989.

Sanello, Frank. *Eddie Murphy: The Life and Times of a Comic on the Edge*. Secaucus, NJ: Birch Lane Press, 1997.

———. *Naked Instinct: The Unauthorized Biography of Sharon Stone*. Secaucus, NJ: Birch Lane Press, 1997.

Sarlot, Raymond, and Fred E. Basten. *Life at the Marmont*. Santa Monica, CA: Roundtable Press, 1987.

Shields, Brooke. *On Your Own*. New York: Villard Books, 1985.

Shipman, David. *Judy Garland: The Secret Life of an American Legend*. New York: Hyperion, 1992.

———. *Movie Talk: Who Said What About Whom in the Movies*. New York: St. Martin's Press, 1988.

Siegel, Barbara and Scott. *Jack Nicholson: The Unauthorized Biography*. New York: Avon Books, 1991.

———. *The Jim Carrey Scrapbook*. New York: Citadel Press, 1995.

Spada, James. *The Divine Bette Midler*. New York: Macmillan, 1984.

———. *Grace: The Secret Lives of a Princess*. New York: Dell, 1988.

———. *Judy & Liza*. New York: Doubleday & Co., 1990.

———. *More Than a Woman: The Intimate Biography of Bette Davis*. New York: Bantam, 1993.

———. *Shirley & Warren*. New York: Collier Books, 1985.

———. *Streisand: Her Life*. New York: Crown, 1995.

Spoto, Donald. *Blue Angel: The Life of Marlene Dietrich*. New York: Doubleday & Co., 1992.

———. *Marilyn Monroe: The Biography*. New York: HarperCollins, 1996.

———. *A Passion for Life: The Biography of Elizabeth Taylor*. New York: G. K. Hall, 1995.

———. *Rebel: The Life and Legend of James Dean*. New York: HarperCollins, 1996.

Sprinkle, Annie. *Annie Sprinkle: Post-Porn Modernist: My 25 Years as a Multimedia Whore*. San Francisco: Cleis Press, 1998.

Stenn, David. *Bombshell: The Life and Death of Jean Harlow*. New York: Doubleday & Co., 1993.

———. *Clara Bow: Runnin' Wild*. New York: Doubleday & Co., 1988.

Stephens, Autumn. *Drama Queen: Wild Women of the Silver Screen*. Berkeley: Conari Press, 1998.

Sullivan, Steve. *Va-Va-Voom: Bombshells, Pinups, Sexpots, and Glamour Girls*. Los Angeles: GPC/Rhino Books, 1995.

Swenson, Karen. *Greta Garbo: A Life Apart*. New York: Scribner, 1997.

Taylor, Robert Lewis. *W. C. Fields: His Follies and Fortunes*. New York: Doubleday & Co., 1949.

Thomas, Bob. *Joan Crawford: A Biography*. New York: Bantam, 1979.

Thompson, Douglas. *Clint Eastwood: Riding High*. Chicago: Contemporary Books, 1992.

Thompson, Peter. *Jack Nicholson: The Life and Times of an Actor on the Edge*. Secaucus, NJ: Birch Lane Press, 1997.

Tornabene, Lyn. *Long Live the King*. New York: G. P. Putnam's Sons, 1976.

Tosches, Nick. *Dino: Living High in the Dirty Business of Dreams*. New York: Dell, 1993.

Turner, Lana. *Lana Turner: The Lady, the Legend, the Truth*. New York: Dutton, 1982.

Vadim, Roger. *Bardot, Deneuve, Fonda: My Life with the Three Most Beautiful Women in the World*. New York: Simon & Schuster, 1986.

Vankin, Jonathan. *The Big Book of Scandal*. New York: Paradox Press, 1997.

Waldman, Allison J. *The Bette Midler Scrapbook*. Secaucus, NJ: Carol Publishing, 1997.

Waters, John. *Shock Value*. New York: Thunder's Mouth Press, 1981.

Wayne, Jane Ellen. *Crawford's Men*. New York: St. Martin's Press, 1990.

———. *Grace Kelly's Men*. New York: St. Martin's Press, 1991.

———. *Lana: The Life and Loves of Lana Turner*. New York: St. Martin's Press, 1995.

Winnert, Derek. *Barbra Streisand: Quote Unquote*. New York: Crescent, 1996.

Winters, Shelley. *Shelley Also Known As Shirley*. New York: Ballantine, 1980.

Woodward, Bob. *Wired: The Short Life and Fast Times of John Belushi*. New York: Simon & Schuster, 1984.

INDEX

ABOUT THE AUTHORS

Margaret Moser has been writing about rock 'n' roll for alternative newspapers since 1976. In addition to *Rock Stars Do the Dumbest Things*, she co-authored the hip travel guide *Edge Austin* (Longstreet Press, 1999). Moser has also edited tourist magazines in Hawaii, performed on MTV's *The Cutting Edge* with Dino Lee & His White Trash Revue, and directs the annual Austin Music Awards show for the South by Southwest Music & Media Conference. Moser has written for such publications as the *Austin Sun*, the *Austin American-Statesman*, *Performance Magazine*, *Pop Culture Press*, *Rocky Mountain Musical Express*, and is an annual contributor to the *Village Voice's* Jazz & Pop Critics' Poll.

Moser has been interviewed for, quoted in, contributed to, or been referenced in such books as *Stevie Ray Vaughan: Caught in the Crossfire* by Joe Nick Patoski and Bill Crawford; *Stevie Ray Vaughan: Soul to Soul* by Keri Leigh; *Rolling Stone's Rock of Ages* by Ed Ward, Ken Tucker, and Geoffrey Stokes; *Texas Rhythm Texas Rhyme* by Larry Willoughby; *Michael Bloomfield: The Rise and Fall of a Guitar Star* by Ed Ward; *Dissonant Identities: The Rock & Roll Scene in Austin, Texas* by Barry Shank; *Generation Eccch* by Jason Cohen and Michael Krugman; and *The Lunch Box Chronicles* by Marion Winik. Moser also regularly appears on panels at the South by Southwest Music & Media Conference, has written liner notes and band biographies for musicians like Candye Kane, the Johnny Depp/Gibby Haynes aggregation P, and Cowboy Mouth, and is a founding co-host of *Check This Action* for the Austin Music Network. She is currently a senior writer at the *Austin Chronicle*, where she writes about pop culture and rock 'n' roll.

Michael Bertin was born and raised in Austin, Texas. After high school, he wound up surrounded by Catholics and snow in South Bend, Indiana, where he picked up a couple of degrees in Philosophy and Economics. After college, he spent time underachieving with a vengeance before returning to central Texas and entering graduate school at the University of Texas at Austin. There he jumped on the fast track to unemployment by earning a master's degree in Philosophy. During graduate school, Bertin began writing about music at the *Daily Texas* (mainly for the schwag). He moved on to the *Austin Chronicle* and continued writing about music as well as other issues of less local importance, while also freelancing for a few other insignificant and quite possibly now-defunct publications. He currently lives in L.A. because the people there are so genuine. This is his first book.

Bill Crawford is a graduate of Phillips Academy, Andover, Harvard, and the University of Texas at Austin, where he earned an MBA. Crawford decided not to pursue a corporate career after he took LSD on the job one day and nobody noticed. He has written for the *Austin Chronicle, Texas Monthly, Runner's World, American Way*, and a number of other magazines. He is the co-author of four previous books, including *Stevie Ray Vaughan: Caught in the Crossfire* (Little, Brown, 1993) and *Rock Stars Do the Dumbest Things* (Renaissance, 1998). Crawford has two incredibly athletic kids and is married to a brilliant and successful lawyer, which is how he can afford to have so much fun.